GARDEN OF THE HESPERIDES

*"A word fitly spoken is like apples of gold."*

WINNING WORDS

# Winning Words

By HENRY I. CHRIST

D. C. HEATH AND COMPANY BOSTON

Cartoons by MARK E. KELLEY, JR.

# PREFACE

W<small>E AMERICANS</small> are in danger of being drowned in a flood of words. Thousands of radio stations constantly pour forth a torrent of information, news, entertainment, advice, pleas, and suggestions. Whole forests are destroyed daily to give us our morning newspapers. Magazines tower high on the newsstands. Books roll off the presses in ever-increasing numbers. Words rule our lives.

In a very real sense, all phases of human activity are dependent upon words. Even fighting involves knowing how to read and write, as the Army insisted in World War II. Army classification tests, civil service examinations, and one survey after another have emphasized that our rating on intelligence tests and the size of our vocabularies are very closely related. Studies have proved that the people who get to the top in all fields generally have superior vocabularies. Realizing the truth of this statement we Americans have bought tremendous quantities of wordbooks, vocabulary builders, and self-help texts in attempts to increase our word stock. Actually, though, raising the level in our word reservoir is only half the battle.

There are two dangers we must beware of: first, believing that merely acquiring "a word a day" from Dr. X's list will in time automatically bring fame, fortune, and the good life; second, thinking of words as separate, individual, self-contained units — something like cherries in a bowl.

If we look at the first danger closely, we wonder whether people are not going back to witch doctor days, when anyone could buy a charm to guarantee success in anything he attempted. Is not increased vocabulary really something that goes *along with* success? Is it not the wide-awake, vigorous, persistent person who reaches the top? Is it not just this sort of person who is likely to read and listen attentively and intelligently, absorbing and learning new words as he goes along?

If this is true, what should a wordbook try to do — set up a list of a thousand words to be memorized or stimulate an attitude of alertness and interest? The answer is obvious. Incidentally, few wordbooks agree on the particular words to teach. Compare word indexes; you

will find wide disagreement. An alert person, however, will be likely
to learn those words which are related to his interests. He will pick
them up and, what is more, he will keep them alive and working for
him. There is, then, no royal road to success by the word-a-day
method.

The second danger is more serious by far. Nothing in this world
exists in a vacuum. All things have meaning only in relation to their
surroundings. Unfortunately, there have been all too few attempts
to emphasize the part played by words *in action*, words doing things
in relation to living situations. Have we a right to teach anyone to
read and write unless we teach him also how to avoid being enslaved
by the word magicians in our civilization? Words can be tricky,
changeable bits of dynamite. Merely making up sample sentences of
words which are somewhat mechanically jotted down each day in a
notebook is not enough. We must wrestle with these words in living
contexts, learn to use them in action before we can truthfully say, "I
have a stock of winning words." The title, you see, has a double-
barreled meaning.

All these ideas I have had in mind in writing this book. I kept
before me two goals: to stimulate interest in word lore and to develop
an awareness of how words may confuse rather than communicate,
excite rather than inform. To achieve these goals, I have tried to do
the following:

1. Include as many useful words as I could within the limits of
these pages and show how our native tongue has developed so richly
and so variously.

2. Select words that suggest new possibilities of experiences, trying
never to imply that we have reached a limit.

3. Foster a desire to know more words and know more about
words — not for the sake of having a showy vocabulary, but rather
to increase the number of our new ideas and experiences. This is an
important part of living a more interesting and valuable life.

4. Emphasize actual ways of systematically accomplishing this
result.

5. Help readers learn to use the tools of research by appealing to
their curiosity and their desire to meet a challenge.

6. Get behind the scenes and show how words actually work —

not as museum pieces propped up for casual display, but as functional, powerful, ever-changing symbols of what is going on around us today.

7. Include all phases of word study, the dangers of word magic as well as the surprises of word derivation.

We learn best by doing things ourselves. I have tried to say as little as possible and get my readers to do as much as possible. Part One introduces a great number of words through matching, multiple choice, and completion questions, word games, cartoons, "detective puzzles," anecdotes, tests based upon illustrations, and so on. These are words that have been tested as being appropriate to high school students. I have used Thorndike's *The Teacher's Word Book of 20,000 Words* as my principal source, with Buckingham and Dolch's *A Combined Word List* to confirm Thorndike's selections.

The chapters vary in the maturity demanded; there is enough material so that the book may be adapted to many different class levels. Each class may select and rearrange the activities to fit its own needs.

While Part One stresses the use of colorful, exact words, varied and unrepetitious, Part Two attacks jargon, haziness of meaning, and the dishonest manipulation of words. In Part One we do a great deal of work with the dictionary, while in Part Two we go behind the dictionary and examine words in their varying surroundings. When he finishes this book, I am sure the reader of this preface will know what I mean when I say that Part One deals with denotations of words, principally; Part Two, with connotations.

Part Two is a pioneering attempt to show high school students certain ways of words in action, ways which have up to now been disregarded or minimized because this subject was considered entirely too difficult. Since this phase of word study is the most vital and permanently useful of all, I have given about as much attention to the problems of using words as to the problems of building up a mature vocabulary.

Chapter One in Part Two motivates the entire section by choosing entertaining illustrations of clever word use. The symbolic nature of words, a difficult but fundamental concept, is treated in Chapter Two by analogies and by many simple activities which I feel will lead the average pupil to a mature grasp of language as symbolism. Disguised drill and needed repetition are included to clinch points made earlier. This key chapter is followed by others growing out of it, chapters on connotation and denotation, the influence of tone and gesture, idiomatic expressions, levels of usage, subjective writing, and figurative language. I try to show metaphor not as poetic ornament, but as the basis of language. We need alert, literate, open-eyed citizens. This section aims at producing them.

Most of the activities in Part Two have been pretested in my own classes. Most of my students were fascinated by the unsuspected Jekyll-Hyde aspect of words and did the activities with relish. Sentences that were unduly puzzling were supplanted by others. No amount of explanation can make a difficult concept clear without numerous illustrations. The activities provide these.

For general background I am indebted to those original and creative language scholars who have blazed trails in modern language study, men like Jespersen, Weekley, Skeat, Kennedy, Trench, L. P. Smith, Murray, Mencken, Greenough, and Kittredge. I have received much assistance from the books, both popular and scholarly, written by Korzybski, Walpole, Chase, Hayakawa, and Ogden and Richards.

I am grateful to the Merriam-Webster Company, publishers of Webster's dictionaries, for consenting to my using selections from their publications, and to Harper and Brothers for allowing me to use a selection from the writings of Mark Twain.

To Dr. J. C. Tressler, former Head, English Department at Richmond Hill High School, New York City, I owe a special expression of thanks for encouraging me to undertake this project when I first considered writing it, for reading the original prospectus of this book, and for supplying helpful suggestions. Without the many years of wise guidance and valuable training gained while assisting in the *English in Action* series, I might never have undertaken the present text.

To Dr. Stewart W. Holmes, of the Editorial Department of D. C. Heath and Company, I am indebted for a helpful critical reading of the finished manuscript and many constructive suggestions based upon his own experience as a teacher in this particular field.

Mr. A. H. Lass, Head of the English Department at Fort Hamilton High School, New York City, provided a good portion of the impetus by interesting me many years ago in the application of semantics to high school vocabulary teaching. Miss Maud Randles, of Fort Hamilton High School, provided several colorful examples.

To my good friend and collaborator on many textbooks, Mr. Jerome Carlin, Reading Counselor at the George Westinghouse Vocational High School, I am indebted for reading sections of the manuscript and making valuable recommendations.

For the typing and preparation of the manuscript, for the reading of it in its entirety and for many concrete suggestions, for unswerving faith in the book and the need for it in these anxious times, I am deeply indebted to my wife, Marie.

HENRY I. CHRIST
*Head of the English Department*
*Andrew Jackson High School*
*New York City*

# TABLE OF CONTENTS

## PART ONE. Building a Vocabulary

Chapter | Pages
--- | ---
1. *Words That Win* | 3
2. *Pepper and Salt* | 23
3. *Five Avenues to a Full Life* | 32
4. *Buried Treasure* | 39
5. *The English Backbone* | 53
6. *Our Rich Relations* | 65
7. *The Greeks Had a Word for It* | 85
8. *Give and Take* | 96
9. *Language Evolution* | 102
10. *High Hat and Dungarees* | 110
11. *Birds of a Feather* | 118
12. *When Opposites Attract* | 134
13. *E Pluribus Unum* | 141
14. *What's in a Name?* | 148
15. *At Your Service* | 157
16. *When Guessing Helps* | 164

## PART TWO. Using Words

1. *The Magic of Words* | 181
2. *Words Are Symbols* | 190
3. *Specific and General Words* | 212
4. *Tone and Context* | 222
5. *Connotation vs. Denotation* | 242
6. *Unpleasant Connotations* | 255

Chapter                                                          Pages

7. *Pleasant Connotations*                               271
8. *Two-Value Judgments*                                 280
9. *Subjective vs. Objective Writing*                    286
10. *Metaphor*                                           298
11. *Figurative Language*                                308
12. *Idioms, Phrases, Allusions*                         319
13. *Levels of Usage*                                    325
14. *Jargon and Gobbledygook*                            332

PART ONE

# BUILDING A VOCABULARY

Civilization Rests Upon Words

# Words That Win

## INTRODUCTION

*Suppose for a moment that all the words of all languages sud-
denly became meaningless. Suppose that as you were reading this
page, it and all pages everywhere, all written and spoken language,
suddenly became so much nonsense. Communication with our
fellows would be almost out of the question. What then? Living
would become utterly confused and difficult, if not impossible.
Trains would stop running. Food would rot in warehouses. Govern-
ments would tumble. Civilization itself would totter and fall.
Overnight, man would be thrust into worse than savagery. Such a
catastrophe will not happen, but it does emphasize the tremendous
importance of the little printed and spoken symbols we call words.
Our lives do depend upon them. We are surrounded by them. We
hear them, read them at every turn. We are governed by words.
We think in words. To be sure, many people misuse words — some
through ignorance, others through a desire to mislead us, as we
shall see in later chapters. As citizens of a democracy we must
understand language, its uses and abuses.*

## WHY BUILD A VOCABULARY?

Knowing the correct meaning of a word may save your life!
Does this statement sound farfetched? Here's proof. Our
government's Bureau of Standards has been trying for years to
have all combustible material marked *Flammable*. Previously
common practice was to label *inflammable* those articles that

would burn easily. Unfortunately, however, many people think that *inflammable* means *not flammable*, whereas actually it means the same as *flammable*. Many fatal accidents have resulted from similar ignorance. One unfortunate individual thought that *inedible* mushrooms are good to eat. Another drank water from a spring marked *Polluted* in the belief that he was drinking a fine brand of mineral water.

Fortunately, fatal mistakes are rare, though serious ones are common. Many an employee has lost his chance for promotion because of an obviously meager vocabulary. Many a secretary has lost her job because her inadequate vocabulary caused her to ask her employer about every three-syllable word he dictated. A study made by the Human Engineering Laboratory under the direction of Johnson O'Connor proved that the best jobs were held by those with superior vocabularies. As Wilfred Funk and Norman Lewis have put it, "Your boss has a bigger vocabulary than you have. That's one good reason why he's your boss!"

## How We Acquire Our Vocabularies

Wide reading and intelligent listening are basic in the building of good vocabularies. Conversation, the radio, the motion picture, good books and magazines, the newspaper — all these are gold mines for finding new words to master. Most important is your attitude. If you are merely annoyed to find a word you don't know, if your curiosity doesn't send you to the dictionary, your vocabulary is probably quite small.

Small children begin to build their vocabularies at an early age. Though a very small child begins to speak with a few words like *Mama* or *Dada*, in a short time he has picked up a considerable number of words. According to one authority the average two-year-old, for example, already has a vocabulary of about 300 words. By the time the child has entered school, the total has jumped to about 2000. Throughout elementary school the average pupil picks up about 1000 new words each year, so that he knows about 10,000 by the time he gets his elementary school diploma.

High school opens up a new world to pupils. New words keep

popping up at a surprising rate. The wise student resolves early that he will not let a new word go unchallenged. He jots it down, looks it up, and perhaps keeps a notebook for thorough mastery. Soon he is leaving behind the lazy fellows who let these new words pass unchallenged. Do you try to learn new words as they appear or are you content to let them remain hazy blotches in your memory?

### ACTIVITY 1. Analyzing Your Vocabulary

The words in the following list should have been learned by the end of elementary school. If you cannot successfully define most of the words, your vocabulary needs first aid. Select the letter of the word or expression at the right that most nearly defines the word at the left.

1. servitude means (*a*) working for a living (*b*) freedom (*c*) condition of a slave (*d*) acting as housemaid (*e*) attitude toward work

2. sheath (*a*) piece of paper (*b*) meadow (*c*) empty space (*d*) sword case (*e*) shelf

3. reproach (*a*) blame (*b*) fear (*c*) surprise (*d*) terrify (*e*) approach

4. remnant (*a*) body (*b*) cloth (*c*) army corps (*d*) bargain (*e*) remainder

5. glean (*a*) scour (*b*) shine brightly (*c*) gather grain (*d*) cut (*e*) slender

6. requisite (*a*) necessary (*b*) questionable (*c*) doubtful (*d*) unhappy (*e*) beautiful

7. beneficial (*a*) unhelpful (*b*) warm (*c*) keen (*d*) gay (*e*) profitable

8. cleave (*a*) abandon (*b*) cut (*c*) clear (*d*) run away (*e*) stick

9. dusky (*a*) dark (*b*) sad (*c*) dirty (*d*) sunny (*e*) woody

10. edible (*a*) rough (*b*) unsoiled (*c*) not poisonous (*d*) believable (*e*) sweet

11. counselor (*a*) foreign agent (*b*) ambassador (*c*) lawyer (*d*) accountant (*e*) athlete

12. hearth (*a*) organ of the body (*b*) noise (*c*) fireside (*d*) radiator (*e*) poor hearing

13. dimension (*a*) wall (*b*) narrowing (*c*) relate (*d*) mention (*e*) measure

14. recount (*a*) subtract (*b*) relate (*c*) divide (*d*) question (*e*) gain a title

15. sprightly (*a*) nervous (*b*) lively (*c*) gloomy (*d*) lamely (*e*) weird

ACTIVITY 2. Checking High School Words

The following list of words is a bit more difficult. These should all be learned at some time during high school. Approximately the first half should be mastered before the end of the first year. Select the letter of the word or expression at the right that most nearly defines the word at the left.

1. remorse means (*a*) pity (*b*) contempt (*c*) kindness (*d*) repetition (*e*) regret

2. harmonious (*a*) tuneful (*b*) friendly (*c*) an instrument (*d*) unmusical (*e*) loud

3. anguish (*a*) loud cry (*b*) bad temper (*c*) wish (*d*) terror (*e*) extreme pain

4. affliction (*a*) joy (*b*) influenza (*c*) affection (*d*) dismay (*e*) illness

5. calico (*a*) a new dress (*b*) foreign (*c*) kind of cotton (*d*) woolly (*e*) linen

6. curtail (*a*) lengthen (*b*) shorten (*c*) tie at the end (*d*) speak briefly (*e*) reverse

7. apparition (*a*) two of a kind (*b*) mountain view (*c*) ghost (*d*) preparation (*e*) surgery

8. insinuate (*a*) hint (*b*) burn up (*c*) enter upon (*d*) move slyly (*e*) commit a crime

9. catarrh (*a*) instrument (*b*) animal (*c*) game (*d*) ailment (*e*) loud noise

10. capricious (*a*) fickle (*b*) vicious (*c*) careless (*d*) covered (*e*) pleasant

11. catastrophe  (*a*) small fire  (*b*) mountain lion  (*c*) great misfortune  (*d*) heavy rain  (*e*) grammatical error

12. reprimand  (*a*) reappear  (*b*) scold  (*c*) suggest  (*d*) discharge  (*e*) demand

13. granary  (*a*) style of hat  (*b*) dry goods store  (*c*) hospital  (*d*) grain storehouse  (*e*) bird

14. satellite  (*a*) master  (*b*) star  (*c*) moon  (*d*) mineral  (*e*) chair

15. detriment  (*a*) damage  (*b*) soil left after explosion  (*c*) avoidance  (*d*) terror  (*e*) nutriment

## CAN YOU READ THE NEWSPAPER?

A good way to test your vocabulary is to read a good newspaper. Note the words you don't know and can't with certainty guess from the use in the sentence. Papers vary in difficulty, but even the simplest dailies use words that will challenge you.

### ACTIVITY 3. Checking Newspaper Vocabulary

The following sentences were taken from the magazine section of one issue of the *New York Times*. How many do you know? Select the letter of the word or expression that most nearly defines the italicized word.

1. When America is shut off by *internal* developments, the rest of the world goes off balance.

(*a*) everlasting  (*b*) unexpected  (*c*) pertaining to the body  (*d*) domestic  (*e*) foreign

2. Mr. Vinson's first official act was to sell a bond to Mr. Morgenthau, his *predecessor*.

(*a*) man he succeeds  (*b*) man that succeeds him  (*c*) chief  (*d*) former enemy  (*e*) former employer

3. The *assent* of other nations can be obtained.

(*a*) decline  (*b*) expansion  (*c*) assistance  (*d*) agreement  (*e*) defeat

4. None of the *advocates* of cartels has ever undertaken to set forth standards of regulation.

(*a*) foes (*b*) guardians (*c*) originators (*d*) backers (*e*) victims

5. This will call for all the *fortitude* of which the government is capable.

(*a*) spending (*b*) firmness (*c*) leadership (*d*) foresight (*e*) economy

6. We have now arrived at the *crisis* of modern civilization.

(*a*) turning point (*b*) catastrophe (*c*) ailment (*d*) decline (*e*) inflation

7. It has power of a *magnitude* equaled as yet not even by Russia.

(*a*) kind (*b*) size (*c*) attraction (*d*) nature (*e*) fierceness

8. They sought *immunity* from competition at home.

(*a*) exemption (*b*) help (*c*) a fortune (*d*) profits (*e*) cure

9. For three years they have engaged in one great *relentless* battle with the enemy.

(*a*) lost (*b*) victorious (*c*) unceasing (*d*) forgotten (*e*) unfortunate

10. Even these arguments are *specious*.

(*a*) deceptive (*b*) excellent (*c*) all-inclusive (*d*) valuable (*e*) careless

11. Cartels themselves are *aggregates* of steadily expanding power.

(*a*) enemies (*b*) pictures (*c*) combinations (*d*) examples (*e*) business firms

12. America desires the establishment of *equilibrium* on the European continent.

(*a*) peace (*b*) struggle (*c*) balance (*d*) racial equality (*e*) democracy

13. Making a peace that will leave the world reasonably secure against the *recurrence* of war is not a simple process.

(*a*) havoc (*b*) reappearance (*c*) reaction (*d*) eruption (*e*) reality

14. Beside Laski sat *pugnacious*, diminutive Jock Corrigan.

   (*a*) cowardly   (*b*) small in size   (*c*) cruel   (*d*) quarrelsome
   (*e*) misshapen

15. The *antithesis* of our own Federal Union is found in the Balkan countries.

   (*a*) image   (*b*) model   (*c*) opposite   (*d*) constitution   (*e*) body of laws

16. It is *crucial* to the peace of the future.

   (*a*) trivial   (*b*) unimportant   (*c*) related   (*d*) opposed   (*e*) critical

17. Against a background of disorder and *recrimination*, they have defended their own past actions.

   (*a*) violence   (*b*) indifference   (*c*) disagreement   (*d*) counter-charges   (*e*) criminal action

18. The raw-material countries have been victims of cartel *exploitation*.

   (*a*) exploration   (*b*) forceful expulsion   (*c*) careless neglect
   (*d*) unfair treatment   (*e*) mutual assistance

19. Like many another *platitude* drawn from human experience, this one, too, is true.

   (*a*) commonplace statement   (*b*) unwise statement   (*c*) sermon
   (*d*) lesson   (*e*) literary work

20. We can do a great deal through *unilateral* action.

   (*a*) prompt   (*b*) decisive   (*c*) broad   (*d*) one-sided   (*e*) unceasing

WORD CURIOSITY

Try to build on the words you know. When you meet a word and learn it, try to find out whether it has relatives you might like to meet. Frequently a common word will have a first cousin worth knowing. For example, most people know that *autumnal* means *pertaining to autumn*. How many know the word which means *pertaining to spring?* The word is *vernal.* Add it to your word-stock now.

Build your vocabulary by becoming word-curious. With familiar words associate synonyms, antonyms, words with the same root, or words connected through their histories.

ACTIVITY 4. Guessing Meanings of Related Words

The following words are paired for one of the reasons mentioned above — having similar roots or connected histories, being antonyms or synonyms. Since you will probably recognize one member of each pair, try from that to guess the meaning of its relative. After you have written down what you think the words mean, check your definitions with those in a good dictionary.

atheist, deist
canine, equine
iris, iridescence
synonym, pseudonym
satisfy, rarefy

speed, celerity
benefactor, malefactor
prophet, Cassandra
habitation, habitat
juvenile, senile

ECONOMY IN WORDS

Often in the motion pictures a college professor is represented as a wordy old fellow with a tremendous vocabulary. When he opens his mouth to speak, he sends forth a mighty torrent of five-syllable words. This is inaccurate, of course. Those with good vocabularies actually have to talk *less* than those with poor vocabularies because they choose economical words. They make one word do the work of several. Instead of saying, "Thomas Jefferson lived about the same time as John Adams," they say, "Thomas Jefferson was John Adams' *contemporary.*" Instead of saying, "Mr. Parry is a specialist in that branch of physics dealing with the atmosphere and the weather," they say, "Mr. Parry is a *meteorologist.*" Sometimes one adjective can paint as vivid a picture as a long phrase; for example, "The loser hung his head sorrowfully and dejectedly" may be shortened to "The loser was *crestfallen.*"

Chip away unnecessary wordings.

ACTIVITY 5. Choosing Economical Words

From the word pool below select the word which can best be substituted for each of the italicized word groups in the following sentences.

*Word Pool*

| | |
|---|---|
| antiquated | ludicrous |
| avaricious | perennial |
| deciduous | querulous |
| immutable | sophisticated |
| lucid | unscrupulous |

1. Carver Doone was *without principles of any kind.*
2. Those trees are *of the type that loses its leaves every fall.*
3. Ethan Frome's wife was *perpetually finding fault and complaining.*
4. Bill expresses ideas *of a kind held by past generations.*
5. Certain physical laws seem to be *not subject to any change.*
6. The play was *of a kind to excite laughter.*
7. He considered himself *worldly-wise through experience.*
8. When we saw the ill patient, he was *characterized by a sane or normal state of the faculties.*
9. He was *interested in amassing money for its own sake.*
10. This plant is *of a kind that lives from year to year.*

What "economical" words do you find here?

### Keeping a Vocabulary Notebook

Since vocabulary improvement is a lifetime job, you will be wise to keep a vocabulary notebook. Begin now and you will notice a decided increase in your vocabulary long before you start to earn your own living. Some pupils prefer the small assignment note pads. Others prefer the larger notebooks. A combination of both is ideal, the smaller for jotting down the word when you find it and the larger for making a permanent record. By pasting small tabs for each letter of the alphabet you can readily thumb-index your book. Do it neatly and you will be proud to keep the notebook for your lifetime.

Leave more pages for A, B, C, and D than for K, X, Y, or Z. You can estimate the correct proportions by observing in a good dictionary the number of pages used by each letter. With this complete you are ready to begin. In your reading note unfamiliar words and copy them in your notebook. If possible, copy also the sentence in which the word appears, for this will help you to *use* the word properly. Merely knowing the *definition* will not guarantee that you can use the word.

The following sentence was taken from the *New York Times*: "The ratification of the Charter was not a final and *explicit* answer." A pupil who didn't know the word *explicit* would list the word and the sentence under E in his vocabulary notebook. Then he would add the dictionary definition: "Distinctly stated; plain in language; clear; as an *explicit* declaration; outspoken." Finally he would use the word in a sentence of his own. He might also include the word derivation — from the Latin *explicare*, meaning *to unfold*.

Whether you choose to do a complete job or merely list the word, its definition, and its use in the sentence, you will find the keeping of a vocabulary notebook one of the most profitable activities you can undertake. The Chinese say that the journey of a thousand miles begins with a single step. This book will help to guide you along that journey. Begin to increase your vocabulary systematically now.

## Sample Page of a Vocabulary Notebook

PERPETUAL "The inventor thought he had invented a perpetual motion machine."

*Definition:* continuing forever, everlasting, unceasing, endless, eternal, indefinitely long-continued in use

*Derivation:* from the Latin *perpes*, meaning *lasting throughout*

*My sentence:* "The people must keep perpetual watch over their freedoms."

*Usage checks:*

PROFUSELY "The book is profusely illustrated with line drawings."

*Definition:* liberally, generously, lavishly

*Derivation:* from the Latin *pro*, meaning *forth;* and *fundo*, meaning *pour.* Anything *profuse* is *poured forth.*

*My sentence:* "The visitor apologized profusely for his mistake in addressing the wrong person."

*Usage checks:*

ACTIVITY 6. Beginning a Vocabulary Notebook

Start a notebook for vocabulary only. Set aside pages for each letter of the alphabet. From the radio, the newspaper, a magazine, a book, or from conversation list three words that are unfamiliar to you. Enter the sentences in which the words appear. Record dictionary definitions. Write a sentence of your own for each word or, preferably, for each definition. Have your notebook ready for inspection tomorrow.

THE USE VOCABULARY
AND THE RECOGNITIONAL VOCABULARY

Everyone's vocabulary is divided into two sections: words actually used in speaking and writing, and words recognized though not actually used. For all of us, the second group is by far larger than the first. If we would increase our vocabularies, we must consciously try to move words over from group two into group one. Here is an example. According to one authority the word *dismal* should be learned by the fifth grade of elementary school. Most elementary school children know what it means — *gloomy*, *dreary*, *cheerless* — yet few actually use it in their writing and speaking. Do you use it?

If you would like to use more words intelligently, miss no opportunities to try out your discoveries. Try to use each new word at least three times in conversation. The first time it will seem strange, but by the third trial the word will be yours. In your next letter to a friend or in your next composition, try to put the new word in somewhere. Place a check next to it in your vocabulary notebook when you have used it successfully three times. Come back to it occasionally, so that it doesn't gather dust on your mental shelves. In general avoid specialized terms like *paramecium* or *phthisis*.

ACTIVITY 7. Fixing New Words by Use

How many of the following words can you recognize? How many of them do you use constantly? Select three that are not in your use vocabulary. Check their meanings and use each at least three times in writing or speaking during the next twenty-four hours. Tomorrow be ready to tell the class when you introduced each, and supply at least one sentence using each word.

| | |
|---|---|
| appall | jubilant |
| hostility | legendary |
| impair | rarity |
| imply | rebuff |
| impulsive | recollect |

ACTIVITY 8. Playing a Word Game

In each of the following select the letter of the word or expression that best completes the statement.

1. If Dad bought a *meerschaum* he would probably (*a*) ride in it (*b*) dance with it (*c*) eat it (*d*) smoke it (*e*) fly it

2. If you were offered the use of a *cabriolet*, you would (*a*) go for a ride (*b*) play it (*c*) put it in your closet (*d*) sing to it (*e*) saddle it

3. If you saw someone dressed as a *hobgoblin*, it would probably be (*a*) Christmas (*b*) Thanksgiving (*c*) Easter (*d*) Halloween (*e*) St. Valentine's Day

4. To buy *cymbals* you would go to (*a*) a hardware store (*b*) a dry goods store (*c*) a music store (*d*) a stationery store (*e*) a fruit store

5. A *tarpaulin* would be very useful for (*a*) covering a truck (*b*) papering a wall (*c*) mending a road (*d*) wading in the surf (*e*) typing a paper

6. If you were involved in an *imbroglio*, you'd probably be (*a*) excited and happy (*b*) tempted to overeat (*c*) confused and embarrassed (*d*) tired but cheerful (*e*) shaken by the ride

7. *Hypotenuse* is an important term to a teacher of (*a*) English (*b*) zoology (*c*) geography (*d*) mathematics (*e*) history

8. A *harpsichord* is a cousin to a (*a*) cavalry officer (*b*) French horn (*c*) heavy truck (*d*) piano (*e*) harvester

9. A *lampoon* will probably (*a*) hurt somebody's feelings (*b*) illuminate a courtyard (*c*) catch a whale (*d*) decorate a party (*e*) be trapped in a cage

10. Some people wear a *talisman* (*a*) to keep warm (*b*) to show off their wealth (*c*) to help their posture (*d*) to tell time (*e*) to keep bad luck away

## DIAGNOSTIC TEST

Our doctors tell us that we should come to them once a year for an examination. If we have anything wrong, they can diagnose our ailment, discover its cause, and prescribe a cure. Here is an examination which will lay bare any weaknesses you may have in your vocabulary. The rest of Part One is your cure. At the end of Part One we shall check up your vocabulary strength to see how much you have profited by the cure. Day by day, in every word way, you ought to get better and better.

Write the letter of the word or expression at the right that most nearly defines the italicized word at the left. The words are arranged in approximate order of difficulty.

1. a *conspiracy* against the king (*a*) speech (*b*) vote (*c*) fight (*d*) decision (*e*) plot

2. buy new *apparel* (*a*) furniture (*b*) clothing (*c*) upholstery (*d*) farm machinery (*e*) textbooks

3. *blighted* grain (*a*) tasty (*b*) fast-growing (*c*) planted (*d*) harvested (*e*) ruined

4. laughed in *derision* (*a*) silence (*b*) triumph (*c*) scorn (*d*) agreement (*e*) good fellowship

5. a brief *respite* (*a*) delay (*b*) report (*c*) speech (*d*) short story (*e*) revenge

6. a *wary* visitor (*a*) serious (*b*) midnight (*c*) disguised (*d*) carefree (*e*) cautious

7. to *scuttle* a vessel (*a*) paint (*b*) overhaul (*c*) put on a new keel (*d*) sink (*e*) race

8. *secular* affairs  (a) separate  (b) religious  (c) civil  (d) upset  (e) well-regulated

9. an *indispensable* officer  (a) high-ranking  (b) noncommissioned  (c) essential  (d) nonessential  (e) unpleasant

10. a state of *anarchy*  (a) democracy  (b) despair  (c) emotion  (d) monarchy  (e) lawlessness

11. trapped by the *deluge*  (a) strange beast  (b) fire  (c) flood  (d) plot  (e) earthquake

12. merited *approbation*  (a) sermon  (b) reward  (c) praise  (d) disdain  (e) victory

13. a clever *artifice*  (a) painting  (b) sculpture  (c) plan for skyscraper  (d) trick  (e) cartoon

14. intent to *defraud*  (a) expose  (b) sue in court  (c) cheat  (d) make a claim  (e) make adjustment

15. to *delude* one's friend  (a) deceive  (b) applaud  (c) understand fully  (d) scold  (e) support

16. an Egyptian *dynasty*  (a) kind of pottery  (b) mummy case  (c) succession of rulers  (d) power plant  (e) dam

17. *eluded* his foes  (a) slew  (b) took prisoner  (c) baffled  (d) surrendered to  (e) scorned

18. to *mitigate* grief  (a) enjoy  (b) make less severe  (c) anticipate  (d) fear greatly  (e) accept

19. a *voluble* applicant  (a) heavy  (b) talkative  (c) shy  (d) careless  (e) neatly dressed

20. the hunter's *decoy*  (a) repeating rifle  (b) sport jacket  (c) deceptive trap  (d) collapsible canoe  (e) camping equipment

21. a *mutinous* crew  (a) efficient  (b) rebellious  (c) nautical  (d) calm  (e) indifferent

22. to *efface* an inscription  (a) copy  (b) scrutinize  (c) erase  (d) underline  (e) repeat

23. *embossed* letters  (a) block  (b) script  (c) raised  (d) capital  (e) printed

24. *impoverished* land (*a*) undiscovered (*b*) wealthy (*c*) poor (*d*) agricultural (*e*) industrial

25. an *officious* fool (*a*) meddlesome (*b*) holding high office (*c*) obvious (*d*) employed (*e*) attendant upon a king

26. to *supplicate* earnestly (*a*) argue (*b*) disapprove of (*c*) beg (*d*) work (*e*) operate a machine

27. to *assess* property (*a*) value for taxation (*b*) redistribute (*c*) survey (*d*) mark into lots (*e*) foreclose

28. unhesitating *compliance* (*a*) counterattack (*b*) yielding (*c*) disloyalty (*d*) reply (*e*) reversal

29. to resort to *compulsion* (*a*) strategy (*b*) direct appeal (*c*) force (*d*) dishonesty (*e*) slander

30. a *diluted* solution (*a*) weakened (*b*) strengthened (*c*) pure (*d*) poisoned (*e*) milky-white

31. to *disintegrate* completely (*a*) disagree (*b*) despise (*c*) go to pieces (*d*) displease (*e*) misunderstand

32. to *endorse* a candidate (*a*) approve (*b*) check upon (*c*) revile in speech (*d*) write about unfavorably (*e*) elect

33. a government *edict* (*a*) official (*b*) public proclamation (*c*) plebiscite (*d*) election (*e*) repealed law

34. a *carnivorous* animal (*a*) savage (*b*) grain-eating (*c*) water-loving (*d*) meat-eating (*e*) domesticated

35. a roving *marauder* (*a*) news reporter (*b*) soldier (*c*) one who plunders (*d*) naturalist (*e*) one who looks for talent

36. a *pert* miss (*a*) lovely (*b*) complete (*c*) careful about dress (*d*) saucy (*e*) unfriendly

37. to *perpetuate* a memory (*a*) dishonor (*b*) lose temporarily (*c*) make permanent (*d*) stir up (*e*) weaken

38. to *demolish* a building (*a*) reinforce (*b*) tear down (*c*) construct rapidly (*d*) put a cellar under (*e*) cover with heavy shingles

39. to *elicit* information (*a*) ask for (*b*) draw out (*c*) reveal (*d*) conceal (*e*) repeat

40. an *inherent* quality  (a) undesirable  (b) likable  (c) valuable  (d) belonging by nature  (e) vigorous

41. a *venomous* remark  (a) uncalled for  (b) clever  (c) unexpected  (d) offhand  (e) spiteful

42. a *volatile* nature  (a) vicious  (b) untrained  (c) lighthearted  (d) dreamy  (e) quiet

43. a *vindictive* act  (a) vengeful  (b) unrehearsed  (c) sudden  (d) unexplained  (e) remarkable

44. to *sully* a reputation  (a) build up  (b) spread about  (c) dislike  (d) disregard  (e) soil

45. a model of *decorum*  (a) proper conduct  (b) decoration  (c) vigor  (d) indifference  (e) overelaborateness in clothes

46. a *droll* comment  (a) biting  (b) impersonal  (c) amusing  (d) serious  (e) gloomy

47. *morbid* curiosity  (a) feminine  (b) excessive  (c) slight  (d) unwholesome  (e) unaroused

48. to *remonstrate* vigorously  (a) put on a show  (b) repeat  (c) make comparisons  (d) invade  (e) protest

49. a *skeptical* critic  (a) severe  (b) agreeable  (c) doubting  (d) theater  (e) colorful

50. to *vindicate* oneself  (a) bathe  (b) accuse  (c) justify  (d) take care of  (e) thrust forward

51. a funny *caricature*  (a) inverted image  (b) distorted picture  (c) trick mirror  (d) work of art  (e) photograph

52. a *penal* code  (a) secret  (b) undecipherable  (c) pertaining to punishment  (d) telegraphic  (e) law

53. a charge of *perjury*  (a) judgment  (b) violation of an oath  (c) contempt of court  (d) disorderly conduct  (e) petty larceny

54. a *pliant* rod  (a) steel  (b) fishing  (c) bending  (d) broken  (e) stiff

55. a *propensity* for soccer  (a) complete equipment  (b) liking  (c) try-out  (d) lack of skill  (e) unconcern

56. to arouse one's *ire* (*a*) interest (*b*) curiosity (*c*) anger (*d*) emotions (*e*) feelings of happiness

57. of ancient *lineage* (*a*) family (*b*) appearance (*c*) furnishings (*d*) times (*e*) years

58. a serious *misdemeanor* (*a*) attitude (*b*) misunderstanding (*c*) criticism (*d*) crime (*e*) manner

59. to *lubricate* the gears (*a*) clean (*b*) recut (*c*) polish (*d*) oil (*e*) reset

60. constant *drudgery* (*a*) grudging respect (*b*) disagreeable toil (*c*) pleasant relaxation (*d*) clowning (*e*) cruelty

61. a *fictitious* story (*a*) imaginary (*b*) exciting (*c*) autobiographical (*d*) clever (*e*) serialized

62. an *untutored* lad (*a*) barefoot (*b*) ingenious (*c*) stupid (*d*) unschooled (*e*) stubborn

63. a *wry* smile (*a*) open (*b*) twisted (*c*) friendly (*d*) unpleasant (*e*) insincere

64. an *improbable* event (*a*) foreseeable (*b*) unpredictable (*c*) avoidable (*d*) undesirable (*e*) unlikely

65. an eager *aspirant* (*a*) victim (*b*) medical student (*c*) candidate (*d*) runner (*e*) learner

66. an *obsequious* attendant (*a*) unduly flattering (*b*) inefficient (*c*) constant (*d*) helpful (*e*) outstanding

67. a low *obeisance* (*a*) overhanging roof (*b*) official (*c*) bow (*d*) doorway (*e*) reclining position

68. a *tepid* bath (*a*) icy cold (*b*) steaming hot (*c*) lukewarm (*d*) regular (*e*) shower

69. a thin *veneer* (*a*) kind of cake (*b*) cracker (*c*) washable wallpaper (*d*) floor (*e*) surface layer

70. *devious* methods (*a*) wicked (*b*) indirect (*c*) direct (*d*) honest (*e*) various

71. an *inveterate* string-saver (*a*) old (*b*) habitual (*c*) economical (*d*) miserly (*e*) belonging to the army

72. a beautiful *vista* (*a*) guest (*b*) view (*c*) Mexican town (*d*) passport (*e*) Spanish plate

73. a *vivacious* girl (*a*) lively (*b*) delicate (*c*) serious (*d*) studious (*e*) uninteresting

74. unbecoming *levity* (*a*) behavior (*b*) dress (*c*) speech (*d*) lightness (*e*) gloom

75. a *lucrative* job (*a*) boring (*b*) factory (*c*) profitable (*d*) office (*e*) manual

76. a *nomadic* tribe (*a*) warlike (*b*) agricultural (*c*) primitive (*d*) wandering (*e*) poorly governed

77. a *precipitous* drop (*a*) sudden (*b*) gradual (*c*) frightening (*d*) steep (*e*) cushioned

78. a *truculent* reply (*a*) witty (*b*) savage (*c*) careless (*d*) pleasant (*e*) forgotten

79. to *expunge* remarks (*a*) analyze (*b*) erase (*c*) affirm (*d*) reassert (*e*) copy

80. a *terse* report (*a*) wordy (*b*) vague (*c*) pointed (*d*) daring (*e*) lengthy

81. to be in a *quandary* (*a*) rock pit (*b*) state of doubt (*c*) a kind of carriage (*d*) sports arena (*e*) state of great excitement

82. to *resuscitate* successfully (*a*) repair (*b*) renew (*c*) retaliate (*d*) revive (*e*) retrace

83. to *rescind* an order (*a*) issue (*b*) explain (*c*) make void (*d*) post (*e*) bellow forth

84. to *condone* an offense (*a*) prosecute (*b*) condemn (*c*) make more serious (*d*) reveal (*e*) pardon

85. to *countermand* an order (*a*) emphasize (*b*) issue (*c*) revoke (*d*) discuss (*e*) study carefully

86. a *denizen* of the jungle (*a*) monster (*b*) inhabitant (*c*) caged animal (*d*) kind of vegetation (*e*) species of tiger

87. *fortuitous* circumstances (*a*) unexpected (*b*) controlled (*c*) by chance (*d*) foreseen (*e*) happy

88. *innocuous* attempts  (*a*) persistent  (*b*) halfhearted  (*c*) harmless  (*d*) insane  (*e*) uncanny

89. a *lugubrious* expression  (*a*) mournful  (*b*) comical  (*c*) expectant  (*d*) set  (*e*) hopeful

90. a  *paradoxical* statement  (*a*) exaggerated  (*b*) contradictory  (*c*) philosophical  (*d*) satisfactory  (*e*) thoughtful

91. a *nonchalant* air  (*a*) healthful  (*b*) pure  (*c*) overheated  (*d*) indifferent  (*e*) excited

92. a *pusillanimous* act  (*a*) forthright  (*b*) considerate  (*c*) subtle  (*d*) violent  (*e*) cowardly

93. to *fabricate* a story  (*a*) retell  (*b*) typewrite  (*c*) make up  (*d*) improve  (*e*) forget

94. an attack of *vertigo*  (*a*) consumption  (*b*) measles  (*c*) dizziness  (*d*) indigestion  (*e*) smallpox

95. *urbane* manners  (*a*) pertaining to the slums  (*b*) polished  (*c*) incorrect  (*d*) hypocritical  (*e*) careless

96. *efficacious* remedies  (*a*) useless  (*b*) effective  (*c*) harmful  (*d*) prescribed  (*e*) old-fashioned

97. an *effervescent* liquid  (*a*) bubbling  (*b*) drinkable  (*c*) poisonous  (*d*) steaming hot  (*e*) iced

98. a  *pretentious* house  (*a*) well-planned  (*b*) corner  (*c*) showy  (*d*) solidly built  (*e*) unfurnished

99. a *depletion* of resources  (*a*) survey  (*b*) using up  (*c*) collection  (*d*) restocking  (*e*) discovery

100. an obvious *charlatan*  (*a*) pretender  (*b*) genius  (*c*) athlete  (*d*) circus manager  (*e*) convert

# 2

# Pepper and Salt

## VIGOROUS LANGUAGE

*"A tortoise-shell cat having a fit in a platter of tomatoes."
That was Mark Twain's description of a painting by Turner. The
description, unjust though it may be, holds attention for its colorfulness and vitality. Using words that command attention is an
art — an art that can be learned.*

## INGREDIENTS OF VIGOROUS WRITING

To write forcefully observe the following suggestions:

1. *Be direct.* Avoid roundabout ways of expressing yourself.
"Since it has come to my attention that you are desirous of
obtaining one of these booklets, I might say that you are welcome to one." How pretentious and flabby such a sentence is!
It is spineless, wordy, and shoddy, though sometimes admired
by those who think good English is merely the stringing together of quantities of words. A much better sentence is: "If
you'd like one of these booklets, take one." (See pages 332–340.)
In general, use the simpler word if it expresses your meaning
as well as a longer one.

2. *Use variety*, both in sentence structure and in word choice.
Don't repeat favorite words.

3. *Use concrete, specific words.* In a scathing denunciation
William Cowper Brann once described how a particular early
settler founded the family fortune. "By feeding himself but once

**Be direct!**

a day, half-soling his own pants with seaweed and going bare-foot in summer to save his shoes, he was able to hang onto his land until the industry and enterprise of others made it worth almost a dollar an acre, when he passed it on to his posterity simply because it wasn't portable."

4. *Use colorful phrases and expressions.* Ambrose Bierce defined *positive* as being "mistaken at the top of one's voice." Descriptions, occasional exaggerations, understatements, and comparisons add zest and variety to language. This book has included many colorful expressions. Look for them.

### Vigorous Verbs

At the heart of every sentence is the verb. Whether your language sparkles or droops depends largely upon the verbs you use. Weary, colorless, general verbs like *do*, *have*, and *get* occasionally need vacations. Instead of using an expression like *do well*, try the verb *excel*. Instead of *do poorly*, use *blunder*, *fail*, or *founder*. Instead of *have*, introduce *possess*, *maintain*, *occupy*, *enjoy*, or *control*.

English has many verb phrases, particularly verbs plus adverbs, like *talk explosively*, *agree to*, and *bounce back*. You will gain variety and vigor if you substitute single verbs occasionally, words like *splutter*, *acquiesce*, and *recoil*.

ACTIVITY 1. Matching Vigorous Verbs with Verb Phrases

For each verb phrase in column *A* find the single vigorous verb in column *B*.

| A | B |
|---|---|
| 1. stun with bewildered wonder | a. abscond |
| 2. dislike greatly | b. adhere |
| 3. steal off secretly | c. appraise |
| 4. jump in sprightly manner | d. astound |
| 5. separate from others | e. caper |
| 6. stick fast | f. capsize |
| 7. pass completely around | g. censure |
| 8. find fault with | h. corrugate |
| 9. get something by flattery | i. encircle |
| 10. set on fire | j. encumber |
| 11. place a burden upon | k. engulf |
| 12. feel one's way | l. enhance |
| 13. set a value on | m. extricate |
| 14. progress clumsily on all fours | n. grope |
| 15. make more important | o. kindle |
| 16. turn upside down | p. loathe |
| 17. dispute angrily | q. scramble |
| 18. swallow up completely | r. segregate |
| 19. form into wrinkles | s. wheedle |
| 20. free from difficulties | t. wrangle |

ACTIVITY 2. Selecting the Vigorous Verb

From the word pool below select a vigorous alternative for each italicized verb phrase in the sentences following.

| | |
|---|---|
| appeased | pilfered |
| corroded | premeditated |
| jabbered | reprieved |
| jangled | simpered |
| perturbed | speculated |

1. Elsa *smiled in a silly manner* as she greeted the newcomer.
2. The metal seemed thoroughly *eaten away*.
3. The crime was *considered in advance*.
4. He *theorized without evidence* as to the possibility of their coming.

5. The statesman *satisfied* the enemy *by yielding constantly*.
6. The governor *delayed the punishment of* the victim.
7. The bear *practiced petty theft on* the candy bars.
8. He was *very much disturbed* by the outcome.
9. The bells *sounded* noisily *out of tune*.
10. When the child became excited, he *talked rapidly and indistinctly*.

ACTIVITY 3.  Selecting Vigorous Synonyms for *Walk*

For each verb phrase in column *A*, find the single vigorous verb in column *B*.

| *A* | *B* |
|---|---|
| 1. walk aimlessly | a. drag |
| 2. walk rhythmically | b. glide |
| 3. walk unsteadily | c. hobble |
| 4. walk as if on parade | d. march |
| 5. walk unevenly | e. promenade |
| 6. walk stealthily | f. ramble |
| 7. walk noisily | g. stamp |
| 8. walk conceitedly | h. swagger |
| 9. walk wearily | i. tiptoe |
| 10. walk smoothly | j. toddle |

Select from column *B* the word that best completes each of the following sentences. You may use the past tense for some of these.

1. The child ——— across the room.
2. The young people ——— through the park, wandering from one place to another.
3. Everyone came out to ——— along the boardwalk.
4. After his exhausting toil, the weary peasant ——— himself home.
5. The platoon ——— along in perfect order.
6. The little old woman ——— across the street.
7. Greg ——— in, so that he might surprise his mother.
8. The boastful Zaroff ——— in front of Rainsford.
9. The dancers ——— along, unaware of everyone else.
10. Forsyte ——— out of the room in anger.

ACTIVITY 4. Supplying Colorful Verbs

Select five of the following verbs or verb phrases and for each supply as many colorful synonyms as you can.

EXAMPLE: *be angry*. Colorful synonyms include *rage, bluster, scowl, lower, pout, frown, snarl, growl, storm, gnash, boil,* and *foam*.

| | |
|---|---|
| amaze | frighten |
| be happy | ride |
| be hungry | sing |
| dislike | tear down |
| express doubt | tell |

## THE EXACT WORD

There is no place in forceful writing for fuzzy, vague, inexact words, nor for roundabout expressions. Many single words do the work of long-winded phrases. Adding these concise time-savers to your vocabulary will add power to your speaking and writing. Suppose, for example, you were to say of someone, "He thinks he's *incapable of making mistakes*." A single word, *infallible*, can do the job of the entire italicized phrase! Learn short cuts to forceful English.

ACTIVITY 5. Selecting the Exact Word

Match the phrases in column *B* with the appropriate words in column *A*.

| *A* | *B* |
|---|---|
| 1. auspicious | a. lying in wait to trap |
| 2. braggart | b. act of returning to a former condition |
| 3. culprit | c. part which remains |
| 4. estrange | d. one accused of a crime |
| 5. insidious | e. promising favorable results |
| 6. irretrievable | f. one who boasts immodestly |
| 7. residue | g. that which has been agreed upon |
| 8. reversion | h. quality of being stubborn |
| 9. stipulation | i. not able to be recovered |
| 10. willfulness | j. to cause to become separated |

Activity 6.  Checking Vocabulary Notebooks

Bring your vocabulary notebook to class tomorrow. Your teacher will grade it according to the following standards:

1. neatness and legibility
2. number of new words added
3. number of new words used three times (that is, starred)
4. appropriateness of new words added

Be ready to teach the class the most interesting new word you have learned.

## Obstacles to Vigorous Writing

Now that you've been reminded of some of the *do's*, you'll want to know the *don'ts*, too. If you fall into some of the pitfalls now to be mentioned, you will drain your language of strength and vigor.

### *Weak Superlatives*

A Hollywood producer asked a rival producer how a certain picture was faring.

"Excellent," replied the rival.

"Only excellent? That's too bad!" sympathized the other.

In Hollywood, land of enthusiastic adjectives, a word like *colossal* has come to be a synonym for *mediocre, average.* Copy writers use superlatives like *gigantic, terrific, tremendous,* and *thrilling* too often; when something comes along that really merits unusual praise, they have no words left to offer. Obviously not every motion picture produced can be called "the greatest."

America's temptation to overstate is illustrated by the story of the olive grower who had three grades of olives. He sorted them and bottled each separately. The smallest he called *Giant.* The intermediate size he labeled *Super-Giant.* For the largest, he had nothing better left in his word bag, so he labeled these merely *De Luxe!*

Traditionally, circuses have been users of bombastic language. "See this stupendous, thrilling, death-defying act," the barkers shout. Such extravagant language is permitted to circuses, but you'd do better to avoid it. Don't say, "I *adore* roller skating." Save the word for a more important occasion. Don't overwork *best*, *nicest*, and *finest*, or, like the boy who cried "Wolf!" too often, you'll find people unimpressed when you use a superlative.

## Counter Words

A college professor, weary of careless English, warned his class at the beginning of the semester, "There are two words that I forbid you ever to use in my class. One of them is *swell*, and the other is *awful*."

He paused for effect. Suddenly a timid freshman raised his hand and asked, "What are the two words, professor?"

Coins that are exchanged over the counter too often become worn with use. Words, too, lose their luster if they are overused. Words like *swell*, *awful*, *terrible*, *hectic*, *grim*, *sweet*, *lovely*, *nice*, and *fine* are called "counter words." They are shopworn and vague in meaning. Using them frequently in conversation may be a sign of carelessness. Using them in writing is an indication of poor vocabulary.

### ACTIVITY 7. Replacing Counter Words

In the following paragraph substitute vigorous adjectives for each of the italicized counter words.

All of us went on a *lovely* picnic Sunday to Sunset Park. We had a *fine* time, because the weather was *wonderful* and the food *swell*. We had a *fine* trip out in Tom's Ford. At the park a *lovely* surprise awaited us, for Marjorie played *pretty* songs on her guitar. During the day we had a *nice* time canoeing and hiking. The day was so *lovely* we hated to leave. At last, tired and happy, we set out for home, unanimous in the feeling we had enjoyed a *fine* day.

## Clichés

Springtime, it is said, brings forth young poets and their tributes to "ruby lips," "starry eyes," "teeth like pearls," "rosy cheeks," "flaxen hair," and "shell-like ears." These expressions were once fresh and striking, but long use has worn them out. Stale and flat, they weaken communication. We call such threadbare, trite expressions *clichés* (pronounced *klee shays'*). Avoid using them too frequently. Occasional use of clichés is inevitable in our speaking. Constant use is a confession of vocabulary bankruptcy.

Unaccustomed as I am . . . .

### ACTIVITY 8. Finding Clichés

There are more than twenty clichés in the following selection. How many can you find? This is a model of how *not* to write!

A prominent citizen, eminently successful in his line of work, rose to speak. "Gentlemen," he began, "unaccustomed as I am to public speaking, I must take this opportunity upon this festive occasion to say that I have taken a new lease on life. As luck would have it, though I once lay at death's door, I am now alive and kicking. It is my cherished belief that half the battle was won when I decided to join your happy throng. Rumor hath it that this club is better than medicine. I, at any rate, can safely say I gave the club the acid test and found it all to the good. I have had ample opportunity to see others, who are beneath contempt, come to grief through failure to realize one simple truth: that groups like this fill a long-felt want. Be that as it may, and to make a long story short, it does my heart good to be here, for this is the happiest moment of my life."

### ACTIVITY 9.  Replacing Clichés

What words or expressions can be substituted for each of the following clichés?

EXAMPLE: *down and out.* For this cliché we might substitute *destitute, poverty-stricken,* or *penniless.*

| | |
|---|---|
| as a matter of fact | give oneself airs |
| at wit's end | happy pair |
| back to the wall | heart-to-heart talk |
| bundle of nerves | no mean achievement |

### *Headline Clichés*

Newspapers help create clichés. Headline writers, particularly, who must fit news into a limited space, find themselves using certain small "headline words" over and over again. There is no room in the headline for *disagreement,* so *clash* is used. *Increase in production* is too bulky, so *speed-up* goes into the headline. *Claim* for *assert,* *accord* for *agreement,* and *ban* for *prohibition* are typical headline clichés. Many were once colorful and fresh, but overuse has tarnished them. Variety is essential. A diet of too many brief words is as indigestible as one overstuffed with long words and phrases.

### ACTIVITY 10.  Studying Headline Clichés

Match the more literary words under *B* with the typical headline clichés under *A*.

| | A | | | B | | |
|---|---|---|---|---|---|---|
| 1. | aid | 11. | key | a. revealed | k. | disapproves |
| 2. | back | 12. | lax | b. important | l. | investigation |
| 3. | bared | 13. | linked | c. careless | m. | support |
| 4. | curb | 14. | parley | d. assist | n. | conference |
| 5. | din | 15. | probe | e. connected | o. | reject |
| 6. | doomed | 16. | spurn | f. leader | p. | restrain |
| 7. | eye | 17. | spy | g. defeat | q. | uproar |
| 8. | head | 18. | top | h. highest | r. | espionage |
| 9. | hint | 19. | trim | i. forefront | s. | insinuate |
| 10. | hits | 20. | van | j. look at | t. | condemned |

# 3

# Five Avenues to a Full Life

## SENSE IMPRESSIONS

*"You who are reading this have only three days to see!"*

*Suppose such a statement were true! What would you do? What preparations would you make? How would you plan to use to the full your precious eyesight for those three days? This is the situation suggested by Helen Keller, blind writer, in a powerful essay,* Three Days to See. *Most of us, she points out, don't use our senses fully. We walk through life blind and deaf to beautiful sights and sounds. As children we probably were fascinated by clouds, bridges, locomotives, sunsets, and butterflies. As we approach adulthood too many of us close our eyes and lapse into easy boredom. A blind beggar once shocked passers-by into an awareness of their good fortune and his loss by writing on his placard, "It is May — and I am blind!" Are you, too, blind to the world about you?*

### ACTIVITY 1. Testing Powers of Observation

Play fair. Take this test without looking around you for the answers to some of the questions.

1. How many light fixtures are there in this room?
2. What color is the cover of this book?
3. What color dress (or suit) is the teacher wearing?
4. What are the colors in your living-room rug at home?
5. What is the design on the dishes you use every day?
6. Give the titles of three books in a bookcase at home.
7. What color dress did your mother wear this morning?

**Words give us new eyes.**

8. What is the exact color of your best friend's eyes?
9. Was last night clear or cloudy?
10. Was the moon up by eight o'clock?

## SENSE WORDS

We are often called upon to communicate our feelings and sense impressions to others. Some of us overwork stale or threadbare words like *nice* and *grand;* others introduce variety by using picture-making words. Chapter two suggested vigorous, colorful words and expressions. The present chapter will show how to use effectively words that appeal to the senses.

## SIGHT

"The cabin light *shone* through the woods. The moonlight *shone* on the water. A faint light *shone* in the distance. The gems *shone* in the sun."

Whoever constructed a series of sentences like these could rightly be accused of having an inadequate vocabulary. Many more vigorous and exact words than *shone* might have been introduced. Sentence one could have used *flickered;* two, *glistened;* three, *glimmered;* and four, *sparkled.* For the general word *shine* we have many substitutes: *glow, glitter, twinkle, blaze, dazzle, scintillate, shimmer, flare*, and *gleam*. Each of these presents a more exact picture than *shine*.

ACTIVITY 2. Describing a Scene in Picture Words

In a paragraph of five or six sentences describe one of the following scenes. Appeal chiefly to the sense of sight. Use specific, colorful picture words.

| | |
|---|---|
| a pine forest | a summer garden |
| a meadow at sunset | a cat crossing a muddy road |
| the first snowfall | the mountains in October |
| the ocean | a cypress swamp |
| a fire | an unfamiliar bird or animal |

ACTIVITY 3. Matching Colors with Objects

The color words in *B* are worth learning. With each of the items in column *A* associate a color word in *B*.

| *A* | *B* |
|---|---|
| 1. an overcast sky | a. cerulean |
| 2. a lion | b. crimson |
| 3. a cloudless sky | c. crystalline |
| 4. autumn oak leaves | d. emerald |
| 5. fresh spring grass | e. leaden |
| 6. a moonlit scene | f. pearly |
| 7. fresh spring water | g. piebald |
| 8. a horse | h. russet |
| 9. blood | i. silver |
| 10. a sea shell | j. tawny |

SOUND

"In the middle of the night Judson sat upright in bed. He had heard a noise."

Suppose you had read this sentence in a novel of suspense and found no further explanation; you might well be irritated. "What kind of noise?" you'd ask. "Was it loud or soft, high pitched or low? Was it a shout, a cry, a howl, a thump, a moan, a squeal, a rattle, a scratching, a shuffling, or a hissing?" Under the one general word *noise* are included all varieties of special words. It's the latter words that give sparkle and variety to language. A writer owes it to his readers to provide specific descriptions.

### ACTIVITY 4. Using Sound Words

From the word pool select words to fill each of the blanks in the sentences below.

| | |
|---|---|
| chirping | rustling |
| flapping | screeching |
| humming | snapping |
| muttering | splashing |
| murmuring | tinkling |

At first impression the forest glade seemed silent. Yet if you listened carefully you could distinguish various sounds. The ———— of the brook blended imperceptibly with the ———— of the tiny waterfall. Occasionally you could hear the ———— of birds, the ———— of twigs as a deer dashed away, and the ———— of bees that were enticed by the few wild flowers. Suddenly the ———— of a noisy jay broke the stillness. A startled crow rose with a loud ———— of wings. The ———— of thunder in the distance warned that a storm was coming. The rising wind started branches to ————. Then it came; the rain poured down, ———— noisily in the brook.

### ACTIVITY 5. Describing with Sound Words

In a paragraph of five or six sentences describe one of the following scenes. Appeal chiefly to the sense of hearing. Use specific, vivid sound words.

| | |
|---|---|
| a busy city street | a musical selection |
| a country meadow | a newspaper office |
| New Year's Eve | a museum |
| a surprise party | a baseball or football game |
| a fire engine | the surf |

## TASTE

"Have dinner on Thanksgiving with us at the Colonial Restaurant. A creamy soup, steaming hot and flavorsome, opens the meal. Then comes the side dish of crisp green salad, and tangy cranberry sauce. And then? Fluffy mashed potatoes buried in rich brown gravy, garden fresh vegetables, the turkey roasted to the peak of flavor — all seasoned as only our chef knows how. For dessert? Golden yellow pumpkin pie or rich apple pie made from the sweetest, juiciest McIntosh apples obtainable."

Did you find your mouth watering at that description? Look at the paragraph again. Notice how the advertiser cleverly inserted words rich in taste appeal. How much more effective these words are than general words like *tasty* or *swell*.

## ACTIVITY 6. Appealing to the Sense of Taste

Pretend that you are an advertiser attempting to sell one of the following products. By using words of strong appeal to taste, try to make your classmates' mouths water!

EXAMPLE: *a smoked ham*. Wouldn't you enjoy right now a slice of that mouth-watering, juicy ham, smoke cooked to golden brown perfection?

| | |
|---|---|
| an ice cream soda | a special stew |
| a roast beef | a breakfast cereal |
| a pastry | waffles and syrup |
| a salad | a malted milk |
| homemade bread | chow mein |

## ACTIVITY 7. Associating Taste Words and Food

Below are listed twenty vivid taste words. With each one associate a food or beverage. Most associations will be individual. You may find yourself disagreeing with the decisions of your classmates.

EXAMPLE: *sour*. With *sour* I associate *lemon* or *green apple*.

| | | | |
|---|---|---|---|
| acid | flat | pungent | sweet |
| biting | juicy | rancid | syrupy |
| bitter | mild | salty | tangy |
| briny | nauseating | sharp | thick |
| burnt | peppery | spicy | vinegary |

Touch

Suppose you were trying to describe the "feel" of velvet to one who had never seen or touched the material. Probably the best method would be by comparison — to compare it with a peach, and thus relate the unfamiliar material with a familiar object. Comparisons are excellent for communicating sense impressions. Rupert Brooke writes "The rough male kiss of blankets" and in six words creates a vivid sense impression.

English is rich in words expressing the sensations of touch. *Sharp*, *sandy*, *gritty*, *stifling*, *lukewarm*, *burning*, *tickling*, *satiny*, *freezing*, *silky*, *numbing*, and *cutting* are but a few. How many can you add?

Activity 8. Studying Words That Describe Feeling

Column *B* contains vivid words expressing sensations of feeling. Match column *B* with column *A*.

| A | B |
|---|---|
| 1. cactus | a. biting |
| 2. electric shock | b. icy |
| 3. feather | c. prickly |
| 4. hot, moist day | d. scalding |
| 5. January wind | e. smooth |
| 6. molasses | f. sticky |
| 7. mountain brook | g. sultry |
| 8. polished floor | h. tickling |
| 9. steaming water | i. tingling |
| 10. summer rain | j. warm |

Activity 9. Appealing to the Sense of Touch

What adjectives would you use to describe the sensations of touch or feeling for each of the following?

EXAMPLE: *sandpaper*. With *sandpaper* I associate the adjective *rough*.

| | | |
|---|---|---|
| barked shins | fur | silk |
| billiard ball | leather | soft mattress |
| coconut | massage | straw |
| cold cream | | |

SMELL

Who can ever forget the smell of a balsam forest, the fragrance of a garden after a shower, or the appetizing aromas that come from a kitchen where bread is being baked? To put these impressions into words is not so easy, perhaps, as with some of the other sense impressions. Yet English has an impressive number of words describing smells. Here are but a few of the more vivid examples: *earthy*, *grassy*, *fresh*, *foul*, *strong*, *smoky*, *burnt*, *perfumed*, *offensive*, and *suffocating*. Often we use comparisons; for example, "as clean smelling as newly laundered linen." Specific words and comparisons are likely to be good. Overworking words like *fragrant* produces a weak effect.

ACTIVITY 10. Appealing to the Sense of Smell

In a paragraph of five or six sentences describe one of the following. Appeal chiefly to the sense of smell. Use specific words or appropriate comparisons.

| | |
|---|---|
| bacon frying | the kitchen at Thanksgiving |
| a chemistry laboratory | a leaf fire |
| coffee boiling | a newly painted room |
| a freshly cut lawn | an old attic |
| a greenhouse | peanuts being roasted |

# 4

# Buried Treasure

## THE DICTIONARY

*You wouldn't try to drive a nail with your fingers, nor try to tear tin roofing with your hands alone. Rightly you recognize that there are tools for every purpose. Yet how often do you make blunders as serious by failing to use word tools available for you?*

## THE ABRIDGED DICTIONARY

The richest home is poor without a dictionary. Of all reference books the dictionary is most important; indeed, the dictionary is really several reference books in one, for word meanings are but part of a dictionary's treasure. Excellent abridged dictionaries may be obtained for little more than the cost of an ordinary novel. Unlike the novel, the dictionary will serve you as long as you live.

Most dictionaries in use are abridged, shortened versions of the large unabridged dictionaries found in public libraries, in schools, and in some homes. For most purposes you will find the abridged dictionary completely adequate. Become familiar with whatever dictionary you own, for dictionaries vary in their method of supplying information. Webster's dictionaries, for example, present the original word meaning first and the more recent meanings last. Funk and Wagnalls dictionaries, on the other hand, provide the most common meaning first. Some dictionaries supply biographical and geographical information in the body of the book; others have a separate section at the end for names and places. Study your own dictionary. Read the explanatory material in the introduction; it will help you to make full use of the book.

If you have not yet acquired the dictionary habit, become acquainted first with a dictionary aimed at high school students. The *Thorndike-Century Senior Dictionary* and the *Webster's Students Dictionary* are excellent for your purpose. After these you may wish to turn to a more advanced dictionary, like the *Webster's Collegiate* or the *Funk and Wagnalls New Desk*

**Yours for the looking**

*Standard.* Whatever dictionary you own, learn to use the guide words at the top of each page. By listing the first and the last word of each page, dictionaries enable you to locate your word quickly.

## USING AN ABRIDGED DICTIONARY

A selection from *Webster's Collegiate Dictionary* appears on page 41. Notice the definitions for *illusion.* Definition one provides the original historical meaning: "a deceptive appearance," as an optical *illusion.* Originally, then, *illusion* was something that *deceived the eye.* Definition two provides an extension of the original idea: "a false impression; misconception." *Illusion* thus can mean something that deceives the mind as well as the eye. Definition three goes one step further, linking *illusion* with *hallucination.* If *hallucination* is unfamiliar to you, look it up.

**il·lu′sion** (ĭ·lū′zhŭn), *n.* [OF., fr. L. *illusio*, fr. *illudere*, *illusum*, to illude.] **1.** An unreal or misleading image presented to the vision; a deceptive appearance. **2.** State or fact of being deceived; false impression; misconception. **3.** A perception which fails to give the true character of an object perceived. Psychologists recognize *normal* illusions, and *abnormal* or *pathological* illusions, which are often not distinguishable from hallucinations. **4.** A delicate net lace, for veils, scarfs, etc.; tulle. — **Syn.** See DELUSION. — **Ant.** Fact, actuality, reality.

**il·lu′sion·al** (-ăl; -'l), *adj.* Of the nature of illusion.

**il·lu′sion·ism** (-ĭz'm), *n.* Any doctrine which affirms that the phenomenal world is wholly illusory.

**il·lu′sion·ist** (-ĭst), *n.* **1.** One given to illusion; a visionary. **2.** An adherent of illusionism. **3.** A conjurer.

**il·lu′sive** (ĭ·lū′sĭv), *adj.* Deceiving by false show; illusory; unreal. — **il·lu′sive·ly**, *adv.* — **il·lu′sive·ness**, *n.*

**il·lu′so·ry** (-sô·rĭ), *adj.* Deceiving; fallacious; illusive.

**il·lus·trate** (ĭl′ŭs·trāt; ĭ·lŭs′trāt), *v. t.* [L. *illustratus*, past part. of *illustrare* to illuminate.] **1.** *Archaic.* To enlighten; illuminate. **2.** *Obs.* To make illustrious. **3.** *Obs.* To make luminous; to light up. **4.** To make clear; to explain, as by figures and examples. **5.** To provide with pictures or designs for elucidation or adornment; of pictures, etc., to elucidate or adorn.

**il·lus·tra′tion** (ĭl′ŭs·trā′shŭn), *n.* **1.** Act of illustrating, or state of being illustrated; specif.: **a** A making illustrious; distinction, or an instance or cause of it. **b** A making clear, evident, or distinct; elucidation. **c** Pictorial elucidation; adornment with pictures. **2.** That which illustrates; a comparison or example intended to make clear. **3.** A picture designed to elucidate or decorate a book, article, etc. Abbr. *illust.*

**il·lus′tra·tive** (ĭ·lŭs′trå·tĭv; ĭl′ŭs·trā′tĭv), *adj.* Tending or designed to illustrate. — **il·lus′tra·tive·ly**, *adv.*

**il·lus·tra·tor** (ĭl′ŭs·trā′tẽr; ĭ·lŭs′trā·tẽr), *n.* One who or that which illustrates.

**il·lus′tri·ous** (ĭ·lŭs′trĭ·ŭs), *adj.* [L. *illustris;* akin to L. *illustrare* to illuminate.] **1.** *Archaic.* Brilliant; lustrous. **2.** Characterized by greatness, nobleness, or the like; famous; renowned. — **Syn.** Noted, famed, glorious. See EMINENT. — **il·lus′tri·ous·ly**, *adv.* — **il·lus′tri·ous·ness**, *n.*

**ill will.** Inimical, esp. malevolent, feeling. — **ill′-willed′** (ĭl′wĭld′; 2), *adj.*

**ill′-wish′er**, *n.* One who wishes ill to another.

**il′ly** (ĭl′lĭ), *adv.* Badly; ill.

**Il·lyr′i·an** (ĭ·lĭr′ĭ·ăn), *adj. & n.* from ILLYRIA, *Gaz.*

**il′men·ite** (ĭl′mĕn·īt), *n.* [From *Ilmen*, a chain of the Ural Mountains.] *Mineral.* An iron-black mineral composed of iron, titanium, and oxygen, usually massive.

**I′lo·ka′no** (ē′lô·kä′nō), *n.; pl.* -NOS (-nōz; *Sp.* -nōs). [Sp. *Ilocano*, fr. *Iloko*, native name.] **1.** A member of one of the chief native peoples of the Philippines. They are Christian Malays. **2.** Their language, a Malayan tongue.

**im-** (ĭm-). An assimilated form: **a** Of *in-*, not, as in *immature.* **b** Of Latin or English *in-*, in, sometimes for earlier *em-*, as in *imbue, impeach.*

**I 'm** (īm). Colloq. contraction of *I am.*

**im′age** (ĭm′ĭj), *n.* [OF., fr. L. *imago, imaginis,* fr. the root of *imitari* to imitate.] **1. a** An imitation or likeness of any person or thing, sculptured, drawn, painted, or the like; esp., an imitation in solid form, as a sculptured figure; statue. **b** Hence, form; aspect; likeness; semblance. **2.** A copy or counterpart. **3.** A mental representation of anything not actually present to the senses; a picture drawn by the fancy; broadly, a conception; idea. **4.** *Archaic.* An illusory appearance; an apparition. **5.** A type; as, she is the *image* of devotion. **6.** A symbol; a representation. **7.** The optical counterpart of an object, produced by a lens, mirror, or other optical system.

**Syn.** Image, effigy. Image commonly suggests religious veneration; effigy is commonly limited to images as sculptured (esp. on sepulchral monuments) or engraved (esp. on coins), and to the phrase "to burn (or hang) in *effigy*." Except as here indicated, both words have been practically displaced by *statue.*

By permission. From Webster's Collegiate Dictionary

Fifth Edition

Copyright, 1936, 1941, by G. & C. Merriam Co.

A good dictionary does not lead you in circles, defining *illusion* as *hallucination*, and vice versa. Definition four is a rather specialized meaning: "a delicate net lace." Note that all four definitions are related, for all have something to do with deception.

## WHAT'S IN THE DICTIONARY?

Students use the dictionary for the answers to many questions. Let's examine the selection on page 41 to find what it contains.

1. Word definitions and correct spelling: see *illusion*
2. Capitalization of words: see *Illyrian*
3. Parts of speech: see *illusion, n.* (that is, *noun*)
4. Hyphenation: see *ill-willed*
5. Pronunciation: see the symbols in parentheses after each word
6. Placement of accent: see the accent mark over the second syllable of *illusion*
7. Synonyms and antonyms: see at the end of *image*
8. Etymology, or origin of word: see the information in brackets
9. Geography: see *Illyrian* and the reference to *Gaz.* (that is, *gazetteer*) at the end of the book
10. Proper plural forms: see *Ilokano*
11. Colloquial words: see *I'm* (Refer to pages 325–327 for a discussion of colloquial language.)
12. Cross references to other subjects: see *Syn.* (that is, *synonym*) under *illusion*

## SPECIAL TERMS

Each dictionary uses special words and abbreviations as key words throughout. Usually these are explained in the introduction. Page 41 includes the following terms.

1. *abbr.* abbreviation
2. *adj.* adjective
3. *adv.* adverb
4. *ant.* antonym
5. *archaic* archaic, no longer used except in special sense

6. *colloq.* colloquial; not used in formal English
7. *gaz.* see the gazetteer at the end of the book
8. *L.* from the Latin
9. *mineral.* used in the science of mineralogy
10. *n.* noun
11. *obs.* obsolete, no longer in use
12. *OF* from the Old French
13. *pl.* plural
14. *Sp.* from the Spanish
15. *syn.* synonym
16. *v.t.* transitive verb

PRONUNCIATION

Good dictionaries supply pronunciations for all words, but you must know the trick of interpreting the symbols. Usually at the bottom of each page you'll find a list of words like the following: āle, chåotic, câre, ădd, åccount, ärm, åsk, and sofá. These constitute the pronunciation key of your dictionary. Keys vary with each dictionary, but if you use one dictionary and one key consistently, you'll have no trouble unless you pronounce the key words incorrectly. The dictionary makers assume that all of us know how to pronounce the words in the key. Thus we find the *a* in *ale* with a long mark (–) over it. If we find, for example, the word *data* listed with the long *a* (dā'tà), we know that the correct pronunciation is "date'-uh." Some words have two or more pronunciations suggested, the first being preferred by the dictionary. Accent is indicated by a heavy slanting stroke (').

ACTIVITY 1.  Checking the Pronunciation of Key Words

To be sure you know how to pronounce the key words in your own dictionary, bring it to class and place on the board the key words listed. Your teacher will assign only one to write on the board if several have chosen the same dictionary. In class, pronounce each word in turn and compare your own pronunciation of key words with that of your classmates.

ACTIVITY 2.  Looking Up Words Often Mispronounced

In your own dictionary look up the correct pronunciation of each of the following words. Learn the definitions, too, for all unfamiliar words.

EXAMPLE: *harangue*. hà-răng′ a noisy speech

| | | |
|---|---|---|
| absurd | clique | preface |
| arctic | creek | probably |
| architect | derisive | quay |
| athletic | dirigible | radiator |
| attorney | dissect | recognize |
| bouquet | faucet | rinse |
| breadth | forehead | somersault |
| brooch | hiccough | status |
| champion | long-lived | surprise |
| chasm | often | worsted (cloth) |

ACTIVITY 3.  Studying the Dictionary

How many of the following questions can you answer? All are based upon page 41.

1. From what language did the word *image* originally come?

2. Why isn't the definition for *illustratively* provided? Can you supply it?

3. What single word has practically displaced, in one sense, the words *image* and *effigy*?

4. What are three synonyms for *illustrious*?

5. Where is the home of the *Ilokano* tribe?

6. May *illustrious* be used at present as a synonym for *brilliant*?

7. What is the preferred pronunciation for *illustrate*?

8. "Narcissus gazed fondly at his own *image* in the pond." What numbered definition of *image* does this use correspond to?

9. How should *illustration* be divided into syllables?

10. What is the plural for *Ilokano*? Why isn't a plural supplied for *illustrator*?

ACTIVITY 4.  Looking Up Word Origins

Word origins usually appear in brackets after a word. Look up the origin of the following and be ready to explain how each acquired its present meaning. Add any new words to your vocabulary notebook.

EXAMPLE: *achieve*. This came originally from the Latin and meant *to the end or head*. Thus, when we *achieve* something we bring it *to an end*, to a successful conclusion.

| | | | |
|---|---|---|---|
| aftermath | canary | hobby | rigmarole |
| blackmail | cancel | hobnob | senate |
| budget | crestfallen | hurricane | sherry |
| bunk | electricity | inkling | tycoon |
| campaign | galaxy | mountebank | ugly |

## ACTIVITY 5. Finding Definitions

Check your definitions of the following words. Use each word to complete one of the sentences below.

| | | | |
|---|---|---|---|
| acrid | defunct | infinitesimal | propitiate |
| alienate | deleterious | inscrutable | punctilious |
| antics | dilemma | laudable | tether |
| arraign | disparity | menial | ubiquitous |
| askew | inadvertently | nebulous | ulterior |

1. Carson's declared he's at the end of his ———.
2. The mosquitoes at camp seemed, unfortunately, to be ——— last season.
3. He wore his hat ———.
4. Some habits have a ——— effect.
5. He acted without ——— motives.
6. His ideas were still unformed and ———.
7. Odysseus offered a sacrifice to ——— the gods.
8. His unpleasant actions finally did ——— his friends.
9. He was ——— on matters of etiquette.
10. He slipped ——— and told the secret.
11. They dared not ——— him on the charge of manslaughter.
12. The ——— smoke choked them as they tried to enter.
13. The tiny stream supplies an ——— part of the Mississippi's waters.
14. After its latest failure, the committee became ———.
15. Alex found himself on the horns of a ———.
16. Despite the ——— in ages they enjoyed each other's company.
17. Your desire to help others is a ——— one.

18. The children enjoyed the ———— of the clown.
19. Though all sought to know his motives, he remained ————.
20. She considered such ———— tasks beneath her.

### ACTIVITY 6. Checking Biographical Information

By using the information in your dictionary, match column *B* with column *A*.

| *A* | *B* |
|---|---|
| 1. Seneca | a. American painter |
| 2. Charlotte Brontë | b. Dutch naturalist |
| 3. Montesquieu | c. Egyptian ruler |
| 4. Xenophon | d. English novelist |
| 5. Thomas Moore | e. French philosopher |
| 6. Francesco Petrarch | f. German writer |
| 7. Ivan Turgenev | g. Greek historian |
| 8. Flavius Josephus | h. Irish poet |
| 9. Johann Wolfgang von Goethe | i. Italian poet |
| 10. George Bellows | j. Jewish historian |
| 11. Anton van Leeuwenhoek | k. Norwegian dramatist |
| 12. Johann Pestalozzi | l. Roman philosopher |
| 13. Amenhotep | m. Russian novelist |
| 14. Coronado | n. Spanish explorer |
| 15. Henrik Ibsen | o. Swiss educator |

### ACTIVITY 7. Checking Geographical Information

By using the information in your dictionary, match column *B* with column *A*.

| *A* | *B* |
|---|---|
| 1. Yucatan | a. African mountain |
| 2. Sucre | b. American national park |
| 3. Kilimanjaro | c. Australian state |
| 4. Kashmir | d. Bolivian city |
| 5. Acadia | e. East Indian island |
| 6. Sumatra | f. European river |
| 7. New South Wales | g. Indian native state |
| 8. Elbe | h. Mexican state |
| 9. Lucerne | i. Russian mountain range |
| 10. Urals | j. Swiss lake |

ACTIVITY 8. Playing a Dictionary Game

This activity is planned for class work with dictionaries. The teacher will divide you into rows of four or five each. About each of the words listed below you are to supply certain information. For each word write down in your notebook the following:

1. most familiar definition
2. pronunciation
3. etymology (From what language is the word derived?)
4. a sentence of your own containing the word used correctly.

The row that finishes first receives three points; second place receives two points; and third place receives one point. Then the teacher will ask any of the four questions about the words in order. A pupil answering correctly earns one point for his team. The row securing the highest total score at the end wins the game. These are the words, but don't begin until your teacher gives the signal.

| | |
|---|---|
| aesthetic | indolence |
| connive | morass |
| culinary | nurture |
| culminate | obdurate |
| elixir | vanguard |

## THE UNABRIDGED DICTIONARY

For the answers to questions that your own dictionary doesn't answer, try one of the unabridged dictionaries. Two famous volumes, the *Webster's New International Dictionary* and the *Funk and Wagnalls New Standard Dictionary*, present rather complete information about all kinds of words. Page 48 reproduces from the *New International* a brief section corresponding in part to the selection on page 41 from the abridged dictionary. By comparing the two let's decide how the unabridged dictionary differs from the abridged. We find that

1. Definitions are more nearly complete;
2. More words are included; for example, the uncommon *illusionable*, *illusionary*, and *illusioned;*

3. Additional pictorial illustrations are introduced (see *optical illusions*);

4. More special terms are included; for example, the special use in *art* of the word *illusionism*.

**il·lu′sion** (ĭ·lū′zhŭn), *n.*   [OF., fr. L. *illusio*, fr. *illudere*, *illusum*, to illude.   See ILLUDE.]   **1.** *Obs.* **a** Deception, esp. by false appearances; delusion.   **b** Act or action of deriding or mocking.

**2.** An unreal or misleading image presented to the vision; a deceptive appearance; false show; apparition.

To cheat the eye with blear *illusions*.                    *Milton.*

**3.** State or fact of being deceived; false impression; misconception; as, the *illusions* of youth.

In doubt we come to see our *illusion;* the phantoms of the night of thought vanish; but the new light comes.          *Josiah Royce.*

**4.** A perception which fails to give the true character of an object perceived. Psychologists recognize *normal* illusions, or such as are contingent upon ordinary sense perception, and *abnormal* or *pathological* illusions, which are frequently characteristic of insanity and often not distinguishable from hallucinations.   Cf. HALLUCINATION.

Optical Illusions.   In Fig. 1, *a* is actually equal to *b* in length.   In Fig. 2, either the side *a* or *b* may appear nearer the observer, and in Fig. 3 *o* may be regarded as either the near or the far corner of the cube.

**5.** A plain, delicate net lace, usually of silk, used for veils, scarfs, dresses, etc.; tulle.

**Syn.** — Mockery, chimera, fallacy.   See DELUSION.

**Ant.** — Fact, actuality, reality.

**il·lu′sion·a·ble** (ĭ·lū′zhŭn·å·b′l), *adj.*   Liable to illusion.   *R.*

**il·lu′sion·al** (-ăl; -'l), *adj.*   Of the nature of illusion.

**il·lu′sion·ar′y** (-ĕr′ĭ *or, esp. Brit.,* -ẽr·ĭ), *adj.*   Of the nature of illusion; also, given to, or characterized by, illusions.

**il·lu′sioned** (ĭ·lū′zhŭnd), *adj.*   Under illusion.

**il·lu′sion·ism** (-zhŭn·ĭz′m), *n.*   **1.** Any doctrine which affirms that the phenomenal world is wholly illusory.

**2.** *Art.* The creation of illusion, as of vistas seen through painted windows, or of nonexistent architectural features.

**il·lu′sion·ist** (-ĭst), *n.*   **1.** One given to illusion; a visionary.

**2.** An adherent of illusionism (sense 1).

**3.** A producer of illusions, as a conjurer or prestidigitator. — **il·lu′sion·ist, il·lu′sion·is′tic** (-ĭs′tĭk), *adj.*

Unabridged dictionaries are surprising storehouses of all kinds of information. You can learn how a steam engine works, what the so-called "science" of phrenology attempts to do, or even how to quartersaw a log. The illustrations vary from a cross section of the pyramids to a diagram of a compound microscope. Special tables and charts present the chemical elements, the named stars, and coins of the world. How to identify our native trees, how to find a particular constellation in the sky, how to identify a particular color shade — answers to all these are found in the unabridged dictionary. Learn to search around in this richest of treasure houses. You'll find skipping about fascinating.

**Do you like unabridged luxury in your word travels?**

ACTIVITY 9. Exploring the Unabridged Dictionary

Each of the following has an interesting picture and an accompanying description or explanation. Select any ten, look up the explanations, and be ready to report to the class your discoveries.

*A. Webster's New International Dictionary*

| | | |
|---|---|---|
| alphabet | hive | pagoda |
| amoeba | Isis | percolator |
| beef | mask | pictograph |
| carburetor | moon | refrigerator |
| coin | oak | roof |
| fox terrier | order | Saturn |
| glacier | overshot wheel | willow pattern |

*B. Funk and Wagnalls New Standard Dictionary*

| | | |
|---|---|---|
| caisson | lighthouse | saw |
| calendar | Mithra | seal |
| Declaration of Independence | national airs | spectrum |
| diamond | ornament | thermostat |
| Dinosauria | patch | trap-door spider |
| facet | Reptilia | voice |

Are they just "birds" to you?

ACTIVITY 10. Examining the Resources of the Unabridged
Dictionary

Each of the following words is an important term in a subject
taught in high school. Select five, look up their definitions, and
be ready to explain each term in your own words.

annuity (business)                  emulsion (chemistry)
binomial theorem (mathematics)      epic (literature)
cathode ray (physics)               Gresham's law (economics)
chiaroscuro (art)                   Mendel's law (biology)
city-manager plan (government)      meridian (geography)
counterpoint (music)                miter box (shop)
electrotype (printing)              syntax (grammar)

ACTIVITY 11. Identifying Characters in Literature

Name the book and the author of the book in which these
characters may be found. Use the unabridged dictionary for
your answers.

Becky Sharp                Lochinvar
Desdemona                  Pudd'nhead Wilson
Hepzibah Pyncheon          Romola
Ichabod Crane              Rosinante
King Lear                  Uriah Heep

ACTIVITY 12. Studying Phrases in the Unabridged Dictionary

By examining definitions under *go*, find the precise meaning of the following phrases.

| | | |
|---|---|---|
| go about | go behind | go it |
| go all out | go better | go native |
| go along | go between | go snacks |
| go at | go beyond | go through |
| go back on | go Dutch | go under |
| go bad | go in for | go the whole hog |
| go begging | go into | go without saying |

## UNUSUAL EXPRESSIONS

The English language contains thousands of odd and interesting phrases whose meanings and origins are worth knowing. To be unaware of these is to be deficient in vocabulary. All of us should be familiar with important terms like *potential;* but

Codfish aristocracy viewing a mare's nest

we should also be able to explain word groups like *Trojan horse* and *Indian summer*.

Let's consider a typical example, the expression *weasel words*. What does it mean? Theodore Roosevelt made the phrase popular by explaining in a speech, "One of our defects as a nation is a tendency to use what have been called *weasel words*. When a weasel sucks eggs, the meat is sucked out of the egg. If you use a weasel word after another, there is nothing left of the other." He then proceeded to condemn use of the expression *universal voluntary training*, for he insisted that *universal* contradicts the meaning of *voluntary* and "sucks the meaning out of it," while leaving it, like the egg, apparently as good as ever. You will find the unabridged dictionary useful in explaining many similar unusual word groups.

ACTIVITY 13.  Studying Unusual Expressions

In an unabridged dictionary look up the meaning of the following expressions.

| | |
|---|---|
| Achilles' heel | Hobson's choice |
| Barmecide feast | mare's nest |
| codfish aristocracy | Parthian shot |
| first water | Robin Hood's barn |
| Frankenstein's monster | simon-pure |

# 5

# The English Backbone

## THE ANGLO-SAXON CONTRIBUTION

*If all the words of Anglo-Saxon origin were suddenly eliminated from our language, we'd scarcely be able to say a complete sentence. Most of our everyday words like* man, house, sun, moon, food, grass, good, high, child, sleep, ship, *and* stone *are of Anglo-Saxon derivation. The common personal pronouns —* I, we, you, he, she, it *— as well as the all-important verb* to be *are Anglo-Saxon. The constantly used conjunctions and prepositions are Anglo-Saxon; for example,* and, but, as, since, in, out, up, down, through. *The indispensable articles,* a, an, the, *trace their ancestry to the Anglo-Saxons. English has borrowed thousands of words from other languages, but the sinews of English are Anglo-Saxon. Though we find other borrowings extremely important, we could, in an emergency, make ourselves understood without them. Not so Anglo-Saxon. Though words of foreign derivation far outnumber Anglo-Saxon words in the dictionary, still an actual count of words used commonly would show a preponderance of Anglo-Saxon.*

Recall the brilliant opening lines of Oliver Wendell Holmes's *Old Ironsides:*

> Ay, tear her tattered ensign down!
> Long has it waved on high,
> And many an eye has danced to see
> That banner in the sky.

Except for *ensign*, *danced*, and *banner*, the words are all of Anglo-Saxon or Scandinavian origin. *Tattered* and *sky* are from closely related Scandinavian tongues.

Consider the opening lines of Hamlet's famous soliloquy:

> To be or not to be; that is the question.

All the words but the last are of Anglo-Saxon origin.

### Activity 1. Checking Anglo-Saxon Derivations

In a dictionary containing word derivations check the origin of each word in the following quotation (see page 42). (In most dictionaries the symbol for Anglo-Saxon is *AS*.) Why do Anglo-Saxon terms predominate?

Is life so dear, or peace so sweet, as to be purchased at the price of chains and slavery? Forbid it, Almighty God! I know not what course others may take; but as for me, give me liberty or give me death! (Patrick Henry)

### Activity 2. Checking Anglo-Saxon Terms in Conversation

Jot down three or four lines of a conversation held between your mother and you this morning. Look up the origin of each word in the dictionary. How many Anglo-Saxon words can you find? What conclusions can you draw as to the importance of Anglo-Saxon words in ordinary conversation?

## ANGLO-SAXON WORDS AND THE EMOTIONS

The first words we learn as children are mostly Anglo-Saxon words; for example, *mother*, *father*, *brother*, *dog*, *cat*, *horse*, *love*, *like*, *good*, *see*, *home*. Consequently, because they are associated with things we knew as children, they tend to arouse emotional responses in us. Under the stress of great emotion, of happiness, grief, or anger, people tend to use simple Anglo-Saxon words.

In one of the exciting moments of the chase in *Moby Dick*, Captain Ahab shouts, "Sail on the whale! Drive him off!" But the whale eludes them for a while until another cry rings out, "There she blows — she blows! — she blows! Right ahead!" Note the words uttered by the whalers under great stress. All those quoted are Anglo-Saxon. Foreign words are essential, of course, but Anglo-Saxon words remain the backbone of English.

### ACTIVITY 3.  Investigating Words Expressing Emotions

Select one of the following expressions of emotion. Look up each word in the dictionary. How many are of Anglo-Saxon origin?

1. I was deeply grieved to learn of the death of your brother.
2. Stay away from the stove; it's hot!
3. I just made a hundred on my spelling test!
4. Don't ever ask me to go there again!
5. Where did you leave the tickets for tonight's meeting? We'll be late!

## ANGLO-SAXON AND THE BIBLE

Most English versions of the Bible draw heavily upon Anglo-Saxon words. Consider the opening of *Genesis* in the King James Version:

In the beginning God created the heaven and the earth. And the darkness was without form, and void; and darkness was upon the face of the deep. And the Spirit of God moved upon the face of the waters. And God said, Let there be light; and there was light.

Beautiful, isn't it? All but a few words are of Anglo-Saxon origin. Simplicity, power, poetry, and stateliness are all here. Some of our greatest writers have molded their own styles after long contact with the Bible, for they have realized the power of simple words. Among modern books Pearl S. Buck's works in particular have a Biblical quality.

### ACTIVITY 4. Studying Word Beauty in the Bible

In a Bible approved by your own parents read Chapter 1 of *Genesis*, or any other chapter you choose. Note the majority of small, simple words. What effect does this simplicity have upon the reader? Why would long, difficult words in a translation mar the power and the beauty?

## A BRIEF HISTORY

Who were these Anglo-Saxons? They were Germanic tribes who lived in northern Europe in the middle of the fifth century. About five hundred years after the Romans first invaded Britain, these freebooters landed on the shores of "Britannia." Whereas the Romans had lived on fairly good terms with the natives of the island (who were called Celts), the barbarous Germans put the Romans and Romanized Celts to the sword, sacked the country, and settled down in the ruins of the once-luxurious cities of this Roman colony. Those Celts who could, escaped to the wilds of Wales, Ireland, and Scotland where their descendants live to this day and still speak Celtic tongues (Welsh, Erse, Gaelic) as well as English, the language of their conquerors. (*English* comes from *Anglish*, the language of the Angles.)

So thoroughly did the Angles and Saxons wipe out the civilization of "Britannia" that neither the Celtic nor the Roman language (Latin) made at this time any but the faintest trace on the language of these barbarians. A few place names like *Thames*, *Usk*, and *Avon*, a few picturesque words like *crag* and *brock* mark the extent of old Celtic influence upon English. Thus Anglo-Saxon, a Germanic language, became the basic tongue of the English people.

ACTIVITY 5.  Analyzing Anglo-Saxon Words

The words in the following list are all basic Anglo-Saxon words. What conclusions can you draw about one of the principal occupations of the early invaders? If any of the words are unfamiliar, look them up and add them to your vocabulary notebook.

| | | |
|---|---|---|
| cliff | oar | steer |
| east | sail | storm |
| flood | sea | strand |
| mast | ship | west |
| north | south | whale |

## THE SCANDINAVIAN INFLUENCE

The Anglo-Saxons were to have their troubles after a time, too. Vikings from Scandinavia began to send raiding parties to the English coasts. Finally raiders came in great numbers and put themselves ashore — permanently. King Alfred, hero-king of the Anglo-Saxons, defeated the Danes in the ninth century, but after his death they kept coming back. More than a century later, Canute, a Danish king, ascended the English throne, ruling for about twenty-five years.

Since the Anglo-Saxons had come from northern Europe originally, they found the invaders from Scandinavia a great deal like themselves in appearance and language. Certain language differences were apparent, though, and the differences are felt today. The *sk* sound is typically Scandinavian. Words like *sky*, *skin*, *skill*, *whisk*, and *scrape* are of Scandinavian origin. The Anglo-Saxons tended to use *sh* in place of *sk*. As a result we have two words, *skirt* and *shirt*, both originally from the same older word.

ACTIVITY 6.  Checking Meanings of Scandinavian Words

The italicized words are all of Scandinavian origin. How many do you know? In each sentence on page 58 select the alternative that is closest in meaning to the italicized word.

1. Suddenly there was a *rift* in the clouds.

    (*a*) crack  (*b*) trap  (*c*) storm  (*d*) bright spot  (*e*) drift

2. He found the *snare* where he'd left it.

    (*a*) tuba  (*b*) game  (*c*) rope  (*d*) trap  (*e*) bite of food

3. Imitation *down* is made from milkweed.

    (*a*) seed  (*b*) feathers  (*c*) mats  (*d*) flour  (*e*) milky beverage

4. He was large in *girth*.

    (*a*) stature  (*b*) heart  (*c*) circumference  (*d*) size of hand  (*e*) head

5. Aran builds a race of *rugged* people.

    (*a*) sea-going  (*b*) sickly  (*c*) curious  (*d*) hardy  (*e*) unusual

6. Fascist followers were recruited from the *dregs* of society.

    (*a*) worthless section  (*b*) escaped convicts  (*c*) pillars  (*d*) businessmen  (*e*) farmers

7. The day was *muggy*.

    (*a*) hot and dry  (*b*) cold and dry  (*c*) cold and moist  (*d*) warm and moist  (*e*) warm and dry

8. Hasn't he an unusual *gait*?

    (*a*) way of walking  (*b*) door  (*c*) manner of speaking  (*d*) half-door  (*e*) reading ability

9. Ichabod despised the *swains* who sought the hand of Katrina Van Tassel.

    (*a*) old men  (*b*) young farmers  (*c*) wealthy landowners  (*d*) members of the nobility  (*e*) rivals

10. They *ransacked* the house.

    (*a*) burnt  (*b*) searched  (*c*) destroyed  (*d*) bought at a sale  (*e*) painted

## STRONG VERBS

Let us return to our discussion of the Anglo-Saxon background of English. Anglo-Saxon was similar, in many respects, to old Latin, or modern German, its first cousin. Less importance was placed upon word order than upon inflections and case endings. Nouns, instead of having one form, had about eight. We have eliminated this troubling problem with nouns, but not with our personal pronouns. Thus we still have *he*, *his*, and *him; she*, *her*, and *hers*.

One of the most persistent of all Anglo-Saxon traits is the retention of the so-called *strong verbs*. Nowadays whenever we invent a new verb like *to telephone*, we make the past tense *telephoned*. In Anglo-Saxon days the past tense of verbs often was formed by changing the middle vowel. Thus, *begin* became *began* in the past tense, not *beginned*. Often little children, who haven't mastered the verb forms of the English language, will say, "I beginned" for "I began," or "I swimmed" for "I swam." Strong, or irregular, verbs are interesting fossils in our language, but they cause heartache to the American schoolboy who has to learn their principal parts (for example, *drink*, *drank*, *drunk*; *sling*, *slung*, *slung*).

### ACTIVITY 7. Studying Strong Verbs

In the dictionary find the principal parts (not including the *ing* form) for each of the following strong verbs.

EXAMPLE: *sing*. The principal parts are *sing* (present), *sang* (past), and *sung* (past participle).

| | | | | |
|---|---|---|---|---|
| arise | draw | grind | shine | sting |
| beat | drink | grow | sink | stride |
| behold | eat | hold | sit | strike |
| bind | fall | know | slay | swing |
| bite | fight | lie | slide | take |
| blow | find | ring | speak | tear |
| break | fly | rise | spin | throw |
| choose | freeze | run | spring | weave |
| cling | get | see | stand | win |
| come | give | shake | steal | write |

### COMPOUNDS

Our language is very much alive and growing. New words are constantly appearing to fill the needs of our complex civilization. Among the most useful are compounds of two or more words, like *classroom*, *schoolboy*, and *bookkeeping*. When a boat was equipped with new motive power, what better name for it could have been supplied than *steamboat?* The principal

The ancestry of windshield

difficulty with compound words is deciding whether to write them as two words (like *post office*), a single hyphenated word (like *make-believe*), or one word (like *football*). Most compounds eventually become single, solid words. Despite the writing headaches they provide for all of us, compound words perform a useful function in helping language to grow. Without them our language would be poorer.

The Anglo-Saxons had the fortunate skill of combining words, too. We merely follow their leadership when we invent useful compounds. A lamp was a *light-vessel*. A boat was called a *sea-wood*. Geometry was *earthcraft;* rhetoric, *wordcraft;* and a jeweler, a *gemworker*. Some of the compounds were poetic, indeed, like *whale-road* for the sea, and *day-red* for the dawn. Ingenuity and a feeling for words were characteristic of our linguistic ancestors.

## ACTIVITY 8. Forming Compounds

Match column *A* and column *B* to form present-day compound words. Explain the meaning of each compound to show that it is a true combination of both parts.

EXAMPLE: *basket ball. Basket* plus *ball* equals *basketball*, a game in which the scores are made by tossing an inflated ball through a hoop or basket.

*Note:* Each of the resulting compounds will be written solid, as one word.

| A | | B | |
|------|-------|--------|----------|
| black | rail | ache | mill |
| dress | saw | band | note |
| eye | sea | beam | road |
| foot | sky | board | rocket |
| gate | snow | boat | sickness |
| gold | sun | book | sight |
| hand | tooth | fish | storm |
| life | water | maker | stroke |
| moon | work | man | way |
| post | wrist | master | works |

## PREFIXES AND SUFFIXES

Let's examine the word *unmanly*. There are three obvious divisions within the word: *un, man,* and *ly. Man* is obviously the most important syllable. We call it the *root* or *stem* of the word. *Un,* meaning *not,* was placed *before* the stem. We call this the *prefix* — *pre* in Latin means *before. Ly,* meaning *like,* was placed *after* the stem. We call this the *suffix* — *suf* from *sub,* Latin for *under.* Prefixes and suffixes are helpful word fragments that enable us to form many words economically from one root. Thus the word *unmanly* means "not like a man." How much less waste there is in the single word! If we wish to emphasize that a friend of ours is not getting from his employer a sum of money corresponding to his abilities, we say merely that he is *underpaid.* How much more direct the single word is! A useful prefix *under* has provided us the shortcut.

Anglo-Saxon prefixes and suffixes are thoroughly embedded in our language. Note the following list of the most important:

| Prefix | Meaning | Example | Definition of Word |
|---|---|---|---|
| be- | completely | bedraggled | completely soiled |
| by- | near | bystander | one who stands near |
| for- | very strongly | forbid | command strongly |
| fore- | before front | forehead | the front of the head |
| mis- | wrong or wrongly | misdeed | wrong act |
| off- | from | offshore | away from the shore |
| out- | beyond surpassing | outstanding | standing beyond all others |
| over- | in excess of too much | overdo | do too much |
| un- | not | unhappy | not happy |
| under- | below | underbrush | bushes under trees |
| with- | against | withstand | stand against |

| Suffix | Meaning | Example | Definition of Word |
|---|---|---|---|
| -dom | state of | freedom | state of being free |
| -en | to make | lengthen | to make long |
| -ful | full of | hopeful | full of hope |
| -hood | state of | parenthood | state of being a parent |
| -ish | rather somewhat | brownish | somewhat brown |
| -less | without | childless | without a child |
| -ly | like in a like manner | weakly | in a weak manner |
| -ness | quality of condition of | happiness | quality of being happy |
| -ship | state of office of | hardship | state of being hard state of being difficult |
| -some | all in all together | foursome | a group of four |
| -ster | one who | trickster | one who plays tricks |
| -ward | course toward direction | homeward | toward home |
| -y | full of characterized by | stony | full of stones |

Your dictionary will give you many other meanings of these prefixes.

### ACTIVITY 9. Studying Prefixes and Suffixes

By analyzing the prefixes and suffixes show how each of the following words took on its present meaning.

EXAMPLE: *tighten.* The suffix *en* means *to make. Tighten* means *to make tight.*

| | |
|---|---|
| calmness | reddish |
| foretell | shorten |
| knighthood | sickness |
| merciless | unkind |
| misshapen | wisdom |

### ACTIVITY 10. Forming Words

Add to each of the following roots a prefix or a suffix or both to make an entirely new word. State the meaning of your new word.

EXAMPLE: *friend.* To this stem we may add the following suffixes and prefixes:

| -ly | friendly | like a friend |
|---|---|---|
| -ness | friendliness | the quality of being friendly |

Friend + li + ness = friendliness.

| -ship | friendship | the state of being friends |
| -less | friendless | without a friend |
| be- | befriend | to act as a friend to |
| un- | unfriendly | not friendly |

### Roots

| | |
|---|---|
| care | like |
| come | pass |
| go | sheep |
| ill | tell |
| king | young |

# 6

# Our Rich Relations

## THE LATIN CONTRIBUTION

*If Anglo-Saxon is the backbone of English, then Latin provides a goodly portion of the flesh. If English is a brother language to German, Dutch, and Scandinavian, then it must be at least a first cousin to Latin; for, like a wealthy generous relative, Latin has indulgently lent more and more words to English. Many Latin words, like* animal, vacuum, superior, alibi, *and* minimum, *have entered our language without change. Others, like* exquisite, establish, *and* despair, *are clearly of Latin origin, though changed somewhat in form. Some words have been borrowed directly; others have come to us through the French (like* rule), *the Italian (like* alto), *or some other Romance tongue. Some authorities have estimated that about fifty per cent of the words listed in the dictionary are of Latin origin!*

### ACTIVITY 1. Studying Latin Words in English

Each of the italicized words below entered English from Latin without change. How many can you define? Select that word from the list which best defines it. Check the meaning of each.

1. a sly *innuendo*   (a) invitation   (b) insinuation   (c) statement   (d) repetition   (e) expression of opinion

2. for the *interim*   (a) meantime   (b) entrance fee   (c) future   (d) inside   (e) eternity

3. to make an *affidavit*   (a) application   (b) lease   (c) explanation   (d) sworn statement   (e) denial

4. a favorite *nostrum* (*a*) pet (*b*) speaker (*c*) nose guard (*d*) platform (*e*) remedy

5. the prince and the *pauper* (*a*) nobleman (*b*) knight (*c*) poor person (*d*) coward (*e*) brave rider

6. the magnificent *rotunda* (*a*) round building (*b*) amusement ride (*c*) rotating wheel (*d*) circular stair (*e*) kind of bicycle

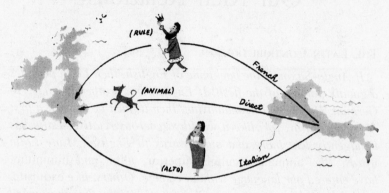

(RULE)

French

(ANIMAL)

Direct

(ALTO)

Italian

**Many word roads lead from Rome.**

7. a useful *memorandum* (*a*) good memory (*b*) recollection (*c*) name (*d*) record (*e*) memorization

8. the *terminus* of the line (*a*) conditions (*b*) portion (*c*) construction (*d*) planning (*e*) end

9. a valiant *gladiator* (*a*) happy person (*b*) fighter (*c*) statesman (*d*) aviator (*e*) acrobat

10. important *data* (*a*) dates (*b*) engagements (*c*) facts (*d*) words (*e*) speeches

ACTIVITY 2. Studying Latin Words in English

Each of the italicized words is of Latin origin. Select the alternative at the right that best defines each. Check the meaning of each.

1. an *accessible* spot (*a*) wholesome (*b*) easily reached (*c*) desirable (*d*) important (*e*) unclean

2. moved with *alacrity*  (a) care  (b) leisurely pace  (c) speed  (d) cowardly hesitation  (e) humor

3. a serious *altercation*  (a) change  (b) repainting  (c) dispute  (d) problem  (e) changed name

4. an *astute* leader  (a) elected  (b) appointed  (c) cowardly  (d) clever  (e) new

5. a *belligerent* attitude  (a) gentle  (b) indifferent  (c) warlike  (d) excited  (e) friendly

6. a *benign* countenance  (a) kindly  (b) coarse  (c) dark  (d) fierce  (e) expressionless

7. a victim of *calumny*  (a) assassination  (b) disappointment  (c) mistreatment  (d) persecution  (e) slander

8. Scrooge's *cupidity*  (a) love of children  (b) love of animals  (c) stupidity  (d) wealth  (e) greed

9. a *disconsolate* expression  (a) wicked  (b) weak  (c) sad  (d) horrible  (e) dreamy

10. to *emulate* an action  (a) imitate  (b) prepare  (c) undo  (d) arouse  (e) regard

11. a *flagrant* error  (a) unnoticed  (b) slight  (c) glaring  (d) comical  (e) unintentional

12. *frugal* habits  (a) fixed  (b) wholesome  (c) careless  (d) economical  (e) easily broken

13. a *garrulous* person  (a) understanding  (b) firm  (c) talkative  (d) happy  (e) stubborn

14. an annoying *impediment*  (a) interruption  (b) obstacle  (c) reversal  (d) lack of practice  (e) fear of the unknown

15. to speak *impromptu*  (a) without preparation  (b) rapidly  (c) with great emphasis  (d) carelessly  (e) loudly

16. *incessant* hammering  (a) noisy  (b) uninterrupted  (c) quiet  (d) skillful  (e) occasional

17. a *mediocre* performance  (a) thrilling  (b) tardy  (c) ordinary  (d) magnificent  (e) hilarious

18. to *mollify* a mob  (*a*) arouse  (*b*) lead  (*c*) calm  (*d*) scatter  (*e*) address

19. a *negligent* engineer  (*a*) courageous  (*b*) brilliant  (*c*) poorly dressed  (*d*) careless  (*e*) weary

20. a *nocturnal* insect  (*a*) biting  (*b*) unusual  (*c*) swiftly moving  (*d*) by night  (*e*) injurious

21. a *novice* in golf  (*a*) beginner  (*b*) expert  (*c*) determined player  (*d*) consistent performer  (*e*) braggart

22. a *pensive* mood  (*a*) angry  (*b*) thoughtful  (*c*) happy  (*d*) gloomy  (*e*) excited

23. a *pernicious* disease  (*a*) curable  (*b*) destructive  (*c*) beneficial  (*d*) mild  (*e*) pertaining to children

24. in a *precarious* situation  (*a*) humorous  (*b*) unexpected  (*c*) pleasant  (*d*) unusual  (*e*) insecure

25. *stringent* regulations  (*a*) strict  (*b*) unwise  (*c*) relaxed  (*d*) set forth in advance  (*e*) unusual

## Early Latin Influences

Oddly enough the first Latin words entered Anglo-Saxon before Caesar's legions invaded Britain. Extensive Roman conquests, campaigns into central and northern Europe, these brought the Germanic tribes into contact with Roman culture and Roman words. Typical borrowings of this period are *street*, *mile*, *wine*, and *pound*. The first two tell us that the Germanic tribes were impressed by Roman military organization and road building. The second two tell us that barter between Roman and Teuton was common.

The second period during which Latin contributed to our language was during the Roman occupation of the British Isles. Many British place names of today trace their origins to the Roman invasion. Those ending in *cester*, *caster*, or *chester* (like *Worcester*, *Lancaster*, and *Winchester*) were probably Roman camps two thousand years ago, since the Latin word for *camp* is *castra*. The *wich* in words like *Greenwich* comes from the Latin *vicus* or *village*. Thus a *bailiwick* is the bailiff's *vicus* or *village.* The *coln* in words like *Lincoln* comes from the Latin *colonia* or *colony.* By the time the Romans abandoned Britain in the fifth century they had left their mark, not only on the roads they had built, but also on the words they had introduced.

The third period of Latin influence was brought about by the introduction of Christianity into Britain at the end of the sixth century. Church words, like *temple* and *candle,* domestic words, like *cap* and *mat,* food words, like *lobster* and *lentil,* and general words, like *spend* and *consul,* entered our language at that time.

## THE NORMAN INVASION

The previous chapter described the situation in England after the many Danish invasions. A tremendously important invasion was yet to come, for soon after the Anglo-Saxon kings had re-established their control, William the Conqueror landed on English soil with his stalwart warriors from Normandy across the English Channel. A bloody, decisive battle at Hastings in 1066 ended Anglo-Saxon rule and placed William on the throne of England. The Norman invaders stayed on in their new home until through intermarriage they became part of the English people. The Norman language, like the Norman rulers, was absorbed into English.

Anglo-Saxon was a Germanic language. Norman was a French, or Romance, language; that is, its basic composition was Roman, or Latin. The joining of the two great tongues has resulted in modern English. Thus, though English is fundamentally Anglo-Saxon, or Germanic, it has a tremendously important Latin element. It has the benefit of two great languages, instead of one. This intermixture of two tongues has given us a wealth of synonyms, since both Anglo-Saxon and Latin words often refer to the same ideas or objects. *Hue* is Anglo-Saxon; *color* is Latin. *Mirth* is Anglo-Saxon; *hilarity* is Latin.

### ACTIVITY 3. Studying Pairs of Words

In the following pairs of words, the Anglo-Saxon word is at the left; the Latin word is at the right. With the assistance of the dictionary distinguish between the two. Why is it useful to have *both* in our language?

EXAMPLE: *storm, tempest. Storm* is a more general word and may refer to a brief thunderstorm as well as to a prolonged and violent hurricane. *Tempest* is a furious storm, usually accompanied by much rain. One might say, "We had a storm that lasted but a few minutes," but one could not use *tempest* in the same sentence.

| | |
|---|---|
| stir, commotion | fall, collapse |
| strike, collide | scare, terrify |
| tarnish, stain | learner, student |
| eat, devour | illness, disease |
| small, diminutive | wise, intelligent |

## ACTIVITY 4. Studying Anglo-Saxon and Norman Words

In *Ivanhoe* Sir Walter Scott tells of the Norman invasion through the eyes of embittered Anglo-Saxons. He points out that the very words used give a clue to the relationship between Anglo-Saxons and Normans. Column *A* below lists Anglo-Saxon words for commonplace objects. Column *B* lists Norman words for the same objects. Study the two columns and answer the questions at the end.

| *A* (Anglo-Saxon) | *B* (Norman) |
|---|---|
| ask | demand |
| calf | veal |
| chicken | poultry |
| deer | venison |
| house | mansion |
| sheep | mutton |
| swine | pork |

How good a detective are you?

1. Who were the masters, Normans or Anglo-Saxons? Prove your point.

2. Which group tended the animals when they were alive? Which gave their words to the flesh of the animals prepared for eating? What does that tell us about the relative position of Norman and Anglo-Saxon?

3. Which were probably able to live in better quarters? Prove.

### FIFTH PERIOD OF LATIN INFLUENCE

The influence of Latin upon our language was not to stop with the Norman invasion, for at the time of William Shakespeare and Queen Elizabeth — the period we call the Renaissance — thousands of Latin words were added. In an attempt to express themselves more forcefully and accurately, writers

Tribute to King's English from Roman merchant (50 B.C.), Roman soldier (A.D. 300), Roman monk (A.D. 700), Norman knight (A.D. 1200), English writer (A.D. 1600)

introduced new words, many of which have been forgotten, but some of which remain in use at present. Some were borrowed without change, words like *appendix*, *delirium*, and *exterior*. Others were made to conform with English counterparts, words like *adapt*, *alienate*, *dexterity*, and *exist*. Shakespeare and others contributed to this tremendous enrichment of our vocabulary. Many writers objected to these "inkhorn terms," as they called them. Now we find it hard to believe that a common word like *strenuous* or *audacious* was once condemned as "too learned."

The torrent of Latin additions to our language has not abated. English is still borrowing Latin words, some through other Romance tongues, but others directly from the Latin. Even so commonplace a word as *scientist* is scarcely more than a century old.

## Doublets

English, in its eagerness to borrow foreign words, has upon occasion borrowed the same word twice! *Poison* and *potion*, for example, both come from the same Latin word meaning *a drink*. *Poison*, however, came to English through the French. In time, it came to mean a special kind of drink, a *deadly potion*. Thus the same Latin word has given us a pair of words that differ in meaning. Similarly, *loyal* and *legal* both come from the Latin *lex* meaning *law*. *Loyal*, which came through the French, has acquired a different meaning from *legal*. English is rich in these double borrowings we call *doublets*.

### Activity 5.  Studying Doublets

The following pairs of words are doublets. Each member of the pair came to English from the same Latin original. However, the words have become differentiated in meaning. Explain what each means and show how the present meanings differ. Use the dictionary to check your answers. Add new words to your vocabulary notebook.

| | |
|---|---|
| abridge, abbreviate | frail, fragile |
| amiable, amicable | genteel, gentle |
| appraise, appreciate | human, humane |
| aptitude, attitude | hotel, hospital |
| cattle, capital | influenza, influence |
| channel, canal | pale, pallid |
| chieftain, captain | pity, piety |
| costume, custom | poor, pauper |
| coy, quiet | reason, ration |
| estate, state | strait, strict |

## Latin Families

Do you know families in which each individual is different from all the others, yet like all the others, too? Word families have the same characteristics. Let's look at the *press* family, for example. There are *repress, compress, suppress, impress, de-*

*press*, *express*, and *oppress*. They're all different, yet they all have something in common, too. The meaning of *press* — whether it be *press together*, as in *compress*, or *press down*, as in *depress* — is common to all words in the family. We call *press* the "root." Sometimes knowledge of a few of the most common roots is worth its weight in gold — if we know how to use this knowledge in analyzing words.

## ANALYZING WORDS

Suppose you saw the word *somnambulist* for the first time. As a word-detective you might get the meaning in one of three ways: first, by the way in which it is used. Sometimes, though, there is no clue in its use; for example, in the sentence, "Paul is, unfortunately, a somnambulist." Secondly, you might check the word in a dictionary. But, a dictionary is not always available. Finally, you might derive its meaning by analysis. It's fun and helps you to retain a word after you have checked its dictionary definition.

Let's analyze *somnambulist*. *Somn* suggests another word we know, *insomnia*. *Insomnia*, we recall, means *sleeplessness*. Evidently *somn* has something to do with *sleep*. The second part of the word is familiar, too. We have *amble*, *perambulator*, and *ambulance* — all similar to *ambulist*. Evidently it has something to do with *move* or *walk*, since *amble* means *to walk*, a *perambulator* is used for *walking* the baby, and an ambulance is a *moving* hospital. *Somnambulist*, then, must be *one who walks in his sleep*. We check with the dictionary and find our guess correct. We notice, too, that *ambulo* meant originally *to walk*. *Amble*, then, is closest to its original meaning. We are not likely to forget the meaning of a word if we remember the meanings of its parts.

## WORD BUILDING

Just as members of the Jones family have first names, like Tommy, Betty, and Ted, so word roots tend to have "first names." We call them prefixes. Thus the "first names" of the *press* family as listed were *re, com, sup, im, de, ex*, and *op*. These were prefixes. Knowing the meanings of the prefixes helps us to analyze the words. *Circum* is a prefix meaning *around. Navigate* means *to sail. Circumnavigate*, then, means *to sail around.*

CAUTION. Use your dictionary, too. Don't rely only upon analysis of the parts of a word. Look up the word first, if possible. Then note how the meanings fit. This procedure will help you to remember meanings. Latin words have been pouring into English for many, many years. They have changed in some respects. Sometimes the meanings provided by analysis do not seem quite to fit. The reason is that words grow and take on new meanings. Often it is possible to trace the original meaning, though; for example, *extravagant* comes from *extra*, meaning *beyond*, and the root *vag*, meaning *to wander. Extravagant* purchases *wander beyond* normal purchases. This is an example of buried metaphor. (See pages 305–306.) Knowing the common prefixes and roots will provide you with effective tools for mastering new words. However, *it is always wise to consult the dictionary* to discover whether the words have taken on new, enlarged meanings.

## USEFUL LATIN PREFIXES

These prefixes occur over and over again. Learn them now and save yourself trouble in mastering new words. Look up the meaning of all unfamiliar examples so that the way each word is put together is clear to you.

| Prefix | Meaning | Example |
|--------|---------|---------|
| a-, ab- | away, from | abnormal |
| ad- | to, toward | admit |
| ambi- | both | ambidextrous |
| ante- | before | antecedent |
| circum- | around | circumference |
| com- | with | compare |
| contra- | against | contradict |
| de- | down from, away | depose |
| dis-, di- | apart from, not | digress, differ |

| e-, ex- | out of | exit |
| extra- | beyond, additional | extraordinary |
| in- | into | insert |
| in- | not | inimical |
| inter- | between, among | intervene |
| intra-, intro- | within | intramural |
| non- | not | nonproductive |
| ob- | against, toward | obstruct |
| per- | through, thoroughly | pernicious, permit |
| post- | after | postpone |
| pre- | before | prearrange |
| pro- | forward, in place of | proclamation |
| re- | back, again | remit, reread |
| retro- | backward | retrograde |
| se- | aside, apart | secede |
| sub- | under | submarine |
| super-, supra- | above | superhuman |
| trans- | across | transmigrate |
| ultra- | beyond, extremely | ultramodern |
| vice- | in place of | vice-president |

## Prefixes Denoting Number

| Prefix | Meaning | Example |
| --- | --- | --- |
| semi- | half | semicircle |
| uni- | one | unanimous |
| bi- | two | biennial |
| tri- | three | triple |
| quadr- | four | quadrilateral |
| quinque-, quint- | five | quinquennial |
| | | quintuplets |
| sex- | six | sextet, sextant |
| sept- | seven | September |
| oct- | eight | October, octant |
| nona- | nine | nonagenarian |
| novem- | nine | November |
| dec- | ten | decimal |
| duodec- | twelve | duodecimal |
| cent- | hundred | centimeter |
| mill- | thousand | millennium |
| multi- | many | multitude |

### ACTIVITY 6. Studying Number Prefixes

Study the list of number prefixes. Then, without looking back, answer each of the following questions.

1. Of course it's an exaggeration, but according to the word meaning how many legs should a millipede have?
2. How many centimes are there in a franc?
3. About how old would an octogenarian be?
4. How many singers constitute a septet?
5. Into how many parts do you cut an object if you bisect it?
6. How many times a year does a semimonthly club meet?
7. How many decimeters are there in a meter?
8. How many musical notes are there in an octave?
9. Is a person engaged in multifarious activities interested in one, two, or more?
10. How many quadrants make up a circle?

### HELPFUL LATIN ROOTS

Look up the meaning of all unfamiliar examples.

| Root | Meaning | Example |
|------|---------|---------|
| ag, act, ig | do, act, drive | agile, action, exigency |
| ali | other | alien |
| anim | life, mind | animated, unanimous |
| ann | year | annual |
| aqu, aqua | water | aqueduct |
| aud | hear | audience |
| ben, bon | well, good | benefit, bonus |
| brev | short | brevity |
| cad, cas | fall | casualty, cadence |
| caed, cis, cid | kill, cut | homicide, incision |
| can, cant, chant | sing | incantation |
| cap, capt, cip | take | capture, incipient |
| ced, cess, cede, ceed | go | procedure, recede, excess, succeed |
| clud, claus, clus | shut | include, clause, conclusive |
| cogn | know | recognize |

| cor | heart | cordial |
| corp | body | corporal |
| cred | believe | credit |
| curr, curs | run | current, cursory |
| da, dat, don | give | donate, data |
| dic, dict | say | dictate, diction |
| dign | worthy | dignify |
| doc | teach | doctrine |
| dom | house | domicile |
| domin | master | dominate |
| dorm | sleep | dormant |
| duc, duct | lead | deduct, reduce |
| fac, fec, fic, fy | do, make | manufacture, infect, sufficient, satisfy |
| fer, lat | carry | refer, translate |
| fin | end | final |
| flect, flex | bend | reflect, flexible |
| flu, flux | flow | influx, influence |
| fort | strong | fortify |
| frang, fract, frag, fring | break | infraction, fragile, infringement |
| fug | flee | fugitive |
| fund, fus | pour | refund, confuse |
| ger, gest | carry | belligerent, digest |
| grad, gress | walk | gradual, progress |
| greg | flock | congregation |
| hab | hold | habit |
| jac, ject | throw | reject, projectile |
| jung, junct, jug | join | junction, conjugate |
| labor | work | laboratory |
| leg, lect | gather, read, law | collect, legible, legal |
| loqu, locut | speak | loquacious, elocution |
| luc, lum | light | translucent, illuminate |
| magn | great | magnify |
| mal | evil | malice |
| man | hand | manual |
| ment | mind | mental |
| mit, miss | send | transmit, commission |
| mort | death | immortal |
| mov, mot | move | movable, motor |

| Root | Meaning | Example |
|------|---------|---------|
| mut | change | mutable |
| nov | new | novel |
| pat, pass | suffer | patient, passive |
| ped | foot | pedal |
| pell, puls | drive | propeller, propulsion |
| pend, pens | hang | suspense, impending |
| pet | seek | centripetal |
| plaud, plaus, plod, plos | clap | applaud, explode |
| port | carry | import |
| prehend, prehens, prens, pris | seize | comprehend, apprehensive, comprise |
| prob | prove | probate |
| pugn | fight | pugnacity |
| quir, ques, quis | seek | inquire, question, inquisitive |
| rid, ris | laugh | ridiculous, derision |
| rog | ask | abrogate |
| rump, rupt | break | corruption |
| sal, salt, sult | leap | salient, insult |
| sci | know | science |
| scrib, script | write | describe, scripture |
| sec, sect | cut | section |
| sed, sess | sit | session |
| sequ, secu | follow | sequence, consecutive |
| sol | alone | solitary |
| solv, solut | loosen | solvent, solution |
| son | sound | resonance |
| spec, spect | see | inspect |
| sta, sist, stit | stand | consistent, distant |
| string, strict | bind | stringent, restrict |
| stru, struct | build | construct |
| sum, sumpt | use up, spend | consume |
| tang, tact | touch | tangent, intact |
| temp | time | temporary |
| ten, tent, tain | hold | tenant, retain |
| torqu, tort | twist | contortion |
| trah, tract | draw | attract |
| vad, vas | go | invade |
| ven, vent | come | convenient, adventure |

| vert, vers | turn | convert, reverse |
|------------|------|-------------------|
| via | way | trivial |
| vid, vis | see | provide, vision |
| vinc, vict | conquer | invincible, victory |
| viv, vict | live | revive, victuals |
| voc, voke | call | vocation, provoke |
| vol | wish, will | volunteer |
| volv, volut | turn | revolve, revolution |

### ACTIVITY 7. Supplying Latin Roots

Complete each blank by supplying the missing letters. Use the list of roots. The number of dashes is the clue to the number of letters needed.

EXAMPLE: *The color of sea water is often called ----marine.* We need four letters here. Since water is *aqua*, the complete word is *aquamarine.*

1. That which cannot be *heard* is in---ible.
2. To *say* in advance is to pre----.
3. To *shorten* is to ab----iate.
4. One who is *evil* is called ---ignant.
5. One not in his right *mind* is de----ed.
6. That which is *sent* back is a re----ance.
7. If we *believe* a report, we put ----ence in it.
8. That which has no *life* is called in----ate.
9. A name *other* than your own is called an ---as.
10. Those who *work* together are said to col-----ate.
11. That which *flees* the center is called centri---al.
12. People who like to *flock* together are called ----arious.
13. When things are *poured* together, ---ion takes place.
14. A man of *great* spirit and generosity is called ----animous.
15. That which shines with *light* is said to be ---inous.
16. A *new* idea or plan is called an in---ation.
17. To prevent someone from *knowing* you, you might travel in----ito.
18. People *come* together at a con----ion.
19. To *drive* back is to re---.
20. A group that *goes* away from another group se-----.
21. A snake that *binds* and crushes its foe is called a con------or.
22. If we *write* our names in a book, we in-----e it.

23. Actions which *follow* as the result of other actions are con----ent upon them.

24. A congressman *stands* in the legislature for his con----uents.

25. Those who *see* a game are called -----ators. Those who *hear* a concert constitute the ---ience.

### ACTIVITY 8. Studying Word Derivations

In an unabridged dictionary look up the meaning and origin of each of the following words. Show how the word took on its present meaning.

EXAMPLE: *proceed. Proceed* means *to go forth*, from *pro*, meaning *forward*, and *ceed*, meaning *go*.

| | | | |
|---|---|---|---|
| accord | credulous | indict | recur |
| advocate | deference | invincible | repugnant |
| amity | deride | missile | retract |
| aquatics | disruption | mobilize | sedentary |
| avert | dissect | perceptible | tenable |
| avocation | divert | pervasive | tenacious |
| compose | docility | precursor | transaction |
| conduction | emancipate | profuse | transfusion |
| convivial | flux | provident | transmute |
| corpulent | incur | recipient | transport |

### ACTIVITY 9. Studying Word Derivations

The following words contain certain roots that have not been listed in this book. By using a dictionary, unabridged if possible, (1) look up the meaning of each word, (2) point out the meaning of the root, and (3) show how the word took on its present meaning.

EXAMPLE: *coherent. Coherent* means *that which sticks together*, is *consistent*. The prefix *co* means *together;* the root *her* means *to stick*.

| | | | |
|---|---|---|---|
| accelerate | candid | confederate | eccentric |
| admonition | caprice | copious | equitable |
| alleviate | circuitous | deprecate | exasperate |
| atrocious | clarity | dexterity | exhilaration |
| augment | complacent | dubious | exonerate |

| | | | |
|---|---|---|---|
| fiscal | implacable | potentate | sinister |
| fraternize | irascible | proximity | strident |
| fruition | mercenary | rectify | vagary |
| hibernate | nullify | recumbent | vehement |
| impervious | occult | retard | veracity |

## INTERESTING WORD ORIGINS

Many words have really picturesque histories. The word *tawdry*, for example, came to us from the English fair of St. Audrey. During the celebration many objects were bought and sold, some of them cheap and gaudy. From this the word *tawdry* came to be applied to anything showy and shoddy, but lacking in good taste. *Bedlam*, our word for noise and confusion, was originally applied to the hospital of St. Mary of Bethlehem in London, where the insane were kept under unpleasant conditions. *Bedlam* was the common pronunciation for *Bethlehem;* now the term is applied to any place of loud disorder.

### ACTIVITY 10. Studying Interesting Word Origins

The following words have unusual histories. In an unabridged dictionary, in *Picturesque Word Origins* (a Merriam-Webster publication), or in *Dictionary of Word Origins* by Shipley, look up the history of twenty of the following words. Your teacher may wish to divide the class into five groups with twenty words each. Be ready to tell the story of each word. Not all are of Latin origin. Add new words to your vocabulary notebook.

| | | | |
|---|---|---|---|
| abominable | ambiguous | biscuit | diamond |
| abracadabra | ambition | bombast | disaster |
| abundant | ampersand | bonfire | dismal |
| accumulate | amuse | calculate | eliminate |
| acumen | anniversary | canary | enthusiasm |
| affluent | April | caper | equinox |
| aggravate | astonish | chrysanthemum | fiancee |
| alarm | atone | colossal | flamingo |
| alert | auction | companion | gamut |
| alimony | bacteria | consider | gerrymander |
| alligator | ballot | curfew | glamor |
| alphabet | bank | debonair | gossamer |

| | | | |
|---|---|---|---|
| hector | marshal | planet | shibboleth |
| husband | meander | plover | sideburns |
| idiot | nausea | profane | sincere |
| inaugurate | obituary | pseudonym | sorcerer |
| inspiration | orient | quarantine | spinster |
| intoxicate | ostracize | recalcitrant | strategy |
| jot | pandemonium | recipe | subjugate |
| journey | parasite | rival | supercilious |
| lady | pavilion | rubber | taxi |
| legerdemain | pecuniary | salary | vaccinate |
| lieutenant | pedigree | sandwich | villain |
| lilliputian | philippic | sarcophagus | volume |
| marathon | pinafore | sesame | wife |

## LATIN SUFFIXES

A knowledge of suffixes enables a writer or speaker to create two or more words where only one existed before. Consider the verb *act*. By adding suffixes we can create the nouns, *action* and *actor*, and the adjective, *active*. All are related. If we know one, we find it easier to remember the others. Notice the use of suffixes in the following list.

| *Noun* | *Verb* | *Adjective* |
|---|---|---|
| permission | permit | permissible |
| expansion | expand | expansive |
| infection | infect | infectious |
| orator | orate | oratorical |
| explanation | explain | explanatory |

When you acquire a new word, notice the suffix, if it has one. Try to form new words by adding other suffixes. After a while you will find that your vocabulary has been enormously increased by these related words. Of course, not every word can be so changed. Check compounds you make up by referring to your dictionary.

### ACTIVITY 11. Using Suffixes to Form Words

Using the chart above as a model, complete the following list. If the adjective form is given, supply the verb and the noun; if the verb form is given, supply the adjective and the noun; and if the noun form is given, supply the adjective and the verb.

| | Noun | Verb | Adjective |
|---|---|---|---|
| 1. | — | familiarize | — |
| 2. | acquisition | — | — |
| 3. | — | — | altered |
| 4. | — | — | preferable |
| 5. | — | submit | — |
| 6. | oppression | — | — |
| 7. | — | favor | — |
| 8. | — | — | informative |
| 9. | — | — | identifiable |
| 10. | injury | — | — |

### ACTIVITY 12. Using Suffixes to Form New Words

By adding or dropping suffixes form new words from each of the following. Give the definition of the newly formed word and show how it is related to the original. Check all words in the dictionary.

EXAMPLE: *ample*. From this word we can form *amplify*, *amplifier*, and *amplitude*. All have something to do with *size*. *Amplify* means *to make large*. *Amplifier* is a device in radio *to magnify* electric impulses. *Amplitude* is *largeness*.

| | | | |
|---|---|---|---|
| abhor | assail | deficient | fallacy |
| adapt | austere | effect | ferocious |
| agile | complement | errant | fraud |
| alien | conciliate | exult | gratify |

| | | | |
|---|---|---|---|
| hostile | inferior | pacify | reconcile |
| humid | intimidate | petulant | remedy |
| ignore | mature | piety | reputable |
| impose | meditate | precise | testimony |
| incongruous | naive | prostrate | tyrannous |
| inert | optimistic | rapture | valor |

# 7

# The Greeks Had a Word for It

## THE GREEK CONTRIBUTION

*When the atomic bomb burst upon the world in August, 1945, people gasped at this newest destructive weapon. The possibility of splitting the uranium atom may have been a new idea to our present-day world, but the idea of the atom and the word itself go back several thousand years to ancient Greek philosophers. Supposedly, they thought, if one kept cutting matter in half, eventually he would reach a portion so small that he could cut no further. This portion they called the atom, "that which could not be cut." Now that the atom has been split the name no longer quite fits, but as with most other words derived from ancient tongues, we continue to use it even as before. It's still true that the Greeks had a word for it!*

So far we have considered Anglo-Saxon and Latin as principal elements in our native tongue. Now we come to a third, the Greek. If it weren't for the Greeks, we'd have to invent other names for what we call the *telephone, micrometer, phonograph,* and *microscope.* If we took out all words of Greek origin, the language of science would be impoverished. Doctors would have to rewrite medical dictionaries, for *diphtheria, bronchitis, astigmatism* and other Greek words would have to be replaced. All the "ologies" would be gone, *biology, geology, meteorology,* and *philology.* Gardeners would have to replace words for the *aster,* the *hyacinth,* and the *iris.* Names like *Philip, George,* and *Sibyl* would be missed. Everyday words like *baritone, diameter, politics,* and *melancholy* would disappear. Even our most beloved word, *democracy*, would vanish. What a word-debt we owe to the ancient Greeks!

### ACTIVITY 1. Choosing the Right Word

The italicized words below are all of Greek origin. How many do you know? Select the alternative that is closest in meaning to the italicized word.

1. a *labyrinth* of corridors  (a) group  (b) picture  (c) destruction  (d) maze  (e) discovery

2. an *amphibious* operation  (a) dangerous  (b) on land and sea  (c) aquatic  (d) surgical  (e) careless

3. to suffer from *anemia*  (a) lung disease  (b) heart trouble  (c) lack of blood  (d) severe headaches  (e) homesickness

4. an excellent *anthology*  (a) melody  (b) kind of plant  (c) specimen  (d) collection  (e) exercise

5. the Greek *archipelago*  (a) strange animal  (b) collection of poetry  (c) group of islands  (d) builder of temples  (e) old prophet

6. an *authentic* painting  (a) oil  (b) landscape  (c) still-life  (d) imitation  (e) genuine

7. an amusing *anecdote*  (a) brief narrative  (b) performance  (c) clown  (d) long descriptive tale  (e) novel

8. a powerful *antagonist*  (a) fighter  (b) farmer  (c) foe  (d) nation  (e) leader

9. a feeling of *apathy*  (a) hunger  (b) sympathy  (c) indifference  (d) anger  (e) disgust

10. *celestial* navigation  (a) inexact  (b) exact  (c) aerial  (d) pertaining to the heavens  (e) pertaining to the sea

11. a state of *chaos*  (a) disorder  (b) great wealth  (c) suspended operations  (d) dictatorship  (e) gaiety

12. *diabolical* ingenuity  (a) devilish  (b) great  (c) clever  (d) inventive  (e) generous

13. a *dogmatic* statement  (*a*) canine  (*b*) indefinite  (*c*) opinionated  (*d*) misleading  (*e*) loud

14. an *enigmatic* remark  (*a*) puzzling  (*b*) contradictory  (*c*) repeated  (*d*) boisterous  (*e*) conceited

15. characterized by *lethargy*  (*a*) inactivity  (*b*) vigor  (*c*) great strength  (*d*) carelessness  (*e*) disease

16. a supposed *panacea*  (*a*) cure-all  (*b*) ailment  (*c*) invention  (*d*) sound proposition  (*e*) a kind of propaganda

17. a *paragon* of beauty  (*a*) woman  (*b*) model  (*c*) young girl  (*d*) building  (*e*) painting

18. *paramount* interests  (*a*) trivial  (*b*) varied  (*c*) supreme  (*d*) theatrical  (*e*) business

19. a *phlegmatic* temperament  (*a*) excitable  (*b*) active  (*c*) angry  (*d*) sluggish  (*e*) unpleasant

20. a *stentorian* voice  (*a*) pleasing  (*b*) rasping  (*c*) loud  (*d*) soft  (*e*) well modulated

21. temporary *amnesia*  (*a*) heart disease  (*b*) forgetfulness  (*c*) relief  (*d*) remedy  (*e*) vitality

22. a *chronic* ailment  (*a*) serious  (*b*) pertaining to the stomach  (*c*) continuing  (*d*) brief  (*e*) incurable

23. an *epitome* of the whole  (*a*) extract  (*b*) summary  (*c*) section  (*d*) major part  (*e*) picture

24. to *eulogize* another  (*a*) describe  (*b*) condemn  (*c*) discuss  (*d*) wish to see  (*e*) praise

25. a needed *antidote*  (*a*) story  (*b*) opposition  (*c*) remedy  (*d*) plan  (*e*) suggestion

## THE GREEK INFLUENCE

As we have seen, Latin had five great periods during which it influenced the English language tremendously: the period on the Continent before the Anglo-Saxons invaded Britain; the period of the Roman occupation of Britain; the period of the introduction of Christianity; the Norman period; the Renaissance.

Greek, too, influenced English at definite periods. Since Latin itself had been profoundly influenced by Greek, English gained many Greek words through the Latin. When Christianity took root in Britain, Greek words came with the Latin. This is the period when church words entered; for example, *angel, apostle, disciple, epistle, hymn, martyr, organ, psalm,* and *deacon.*

During the Renaissance, when Latin words entered English in a torrent, Greek words were added, too, by scholars and writers. Words like *academy* and *acme* can be traced to this period.

### THE POPULARITY OF GREEK TODAY

The borrowing still goes on. The popularity of Greek words in everyday use is traceable to a fortunate quality possessed by Greek roots, the ability to combine easily. *Geo* meaning *earth* combines readily with *logy* to mean *the study of the earth* (*geology*), and with *metry* to mean *the measure of the*

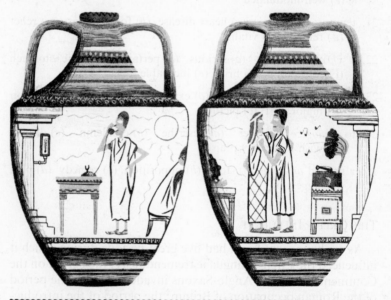

The Greeks had a word for it.

*earth* (*geometry*). *Thermo* meaning *heat* combines with *meter* to mean *a measure of heat* (*thermometer*) and with *iso* to mean lines *of equal heat* (*isotherms*) on a map. These easily formed compounds are a blessing to scientists, who must constantly invent new words to fit the new discoveries they are making.

ACTIVITY 2. Forming Compounds from Greek Roots

Join roots in group *A* with roots in group *B* to form English words. Look up the meaning of each word in the dictionary. Compare your list with your neighbors' lists. *You may use a root more than once.*

| *A* | | *B* | |
|------|------|------|------|
| auto | micro | algia | phone |
| chiro | neur | cracy | podist |
| cosmo | nost | graph | politan |
| demo | tele | logy | practor |
| metro | theo | nome | scope |

ACTIVITY 3. Guessing at the Meanings of Roots

In each of the following ten groups one root is common to all four words. At least three of the four words will be familiar to you in every group. Judging by the meanings of the words you know, what do you guess the meaning of the root to be? The answer will be found among the words following the root.

EXAMPLE: *phonograph, telephone, radiophone, euphony.* The root *phon* probably has something to do with *light, heat, sound,* or *water.*

Since the first three are familiar to you and have something to do with sound, you would answer *sound.* If the fourth word is unfamiliar to you, look up its meaning in a good dictionary. Does *euphony* have something to do with sound?

1. telegraph, autograph, biography, graphic
   *graph:* distance, writing, friends, or pictures

2. automatic, autograph, automobile, autocrat
   *auto:* ruler, self, only, or written

3. monotone, monopoly, monarchy, monogram
   *mono:* busy, loud, two, or one

4. democrat, aristocrat, autocrat, bureaucrat
   *crat:* person, rule, wealth, or nature

5. synonym, antonym, homonym, patronymic
   *onym:* name, opposite, father, or same

6. bicycle, cyclone, cycle, encyclopedia
   *cycl:* storm, circle, play, or two

7. centimeter, meter, metric, perimeter
   *meter:* coin, instrument, 100, or measure

8. biology, biography, autobiography, amphibian
   *bio:* book, life, science, or water

9. antislavery, antitoxin, antidote, antipathy
   *anti:* related, before, against, or afterward

10. microscope, microphotograph, microbe, microcosm
    *micro:* small, picture, germ, or telescope

### ACTIVITY 4. Playing a Word Game

Play this game in class. One student suggests a word with a Greek root to be placed on the blackboard; for example, *telegraph*. The next student suggests another word, with either one of the two halves of the preceding word. He might suggest *telephone* or *autograph*, let's say. Let's suppose he chose *telephone*. The next student would suggest a word with *phone*, for example, *phonograph*. Continue as long as you can. Try to list as many descendants of the original word as possible.

### ACTIVITY 5. Guessing at the Meanings of Roots

Each word in the following pairs has one root (italicized) in common with the other. From the word pool below select the word that you feel best expresses the root meaning. Look up each unfamiliar word in the dictionary.

EXAMPLE: tele*scope*, micro*scope*. *Scope.* which is common to both, probably means *to look* or *to see*, since a telescope is used to look at the stars, and a microscope is used to look at very small things.

| | |
|---|---|
| book | nature |
| breath | power |
| city | sight |
| concealed | skin |
| false | star |

1. *Bib*le, *bibl*iography
2. *crypt*ic, *crypt*ogram
3. *dynam*ite, *dynam*ic
4. epi*derm*is, taxi*derm*ist
5. *astro*nomy, *astro*logy
6. *opt*ometrist, *opt*ician
7. *poli*ce, *poli*tics
8. *pneu*matic, *pneu*monia
9. *pseudo*nym, *pseudo*pod
10. *physi*cs, *physi*ology

## GREEK PREFIXES

Knowledge of Greek prefixes often enables us to guess intelligently at word meanings. The list that follows includes the most important. Look up the meaning of examples that are unfamiliar to you and enter them in your vocabulary notebook.

| *Prefix* | *Meaning* | *Example* |
|---|---|---|
| a-, an- | no, not | atypical, anarchy |
| amphi- | around, both | amphitheater |
| ana- | up, again | analysis |
| anti- | against | anticlimax |
| apo- | off, away from | apology |
| cata- | down | catastrophe |
| dia- | across, through | diagonal |
| ec-, ex- | out of | exodus |
| en- | in | energy |
| epi- | upon | epigram |
| eu- | well | eulogy |
| hyper- | above | hyperbole |
| hypo- | under | hypocrite |
| meta- | after | metamorphosis |
| miso- | hatred of | misanthropic |
| para- | beside | paraphrase |
| peri- | around | periphery |
| poly- | many | polysyllable |
| pro- | before | program |
| syn- | with | synopsis, symphony |

## Important Greek Prefixes of Number

Look up the meaning of all unfamiliar examples and enter them in your vocabulary notebook.

| Prefix | Meaning | Example |
|--------|---------|---------|
| hemi- | half | hemisphere |
| mono- | one | monotonous |
| di- | two | diphthong |
| tri- | three | tricycle |
| tetra- | four | tetrameter |
| penta- | five | pentagon |
| hexa- | six | hexagonal |
| hepta- | seven | heptameter |
| octa- | eight | octagon |
| deca- | ten | decade |
| kilo- | thousand | kilowatt |

### Activity 6.  Using Greek Prefixes

Complete each blank by supplying the missing prefix. Use the list of prefixes as your guide. The number of dashes is the clue to the number of letters needed.

EXAMPLE: *The line across a circle is called the ---meter.* We need three letters here. Since *dia* means *across,* the complete word is *diameter.*

1. The *Ten* Commandments are often called the ---alogue.
2. A support with *three* feet is a ---pod.
3. A *thousand* meters is called a ----meter.
4. A professed woman-*hater* is called a ----gynist.
5. A guardian *against* infection is an ----septic.
6. A figure with *many* sides is called a ----gon.
7. A flood which washes *down* all before it is called a ----clysm.
8. A needle for piercing *under* the skin is a ----dermic.
9. That which goes *before* the rest of the story is the ---logue.
10. When we suffer *with* someone we extend him our ---pathy.

## Other Greek Roots

In addition to those already discussed in this chapter, the following Greek roots are worth knowing. Look up the meaning

Demagogue: "My people! Follow me to victory!"

of all unfamiliar examples and enter them in your vocabulary notebook.

| Root | Meaning | Example |
|------|---------|---------|
| andro, anthrop | man | anthropoid |
| arch, archi | chief, first | archbishop, architect |
| baro | heavy | barometer |
| chiro | hand | chiropodist |
| chrom | color | chromatic |
| chron | time | synchronize |
| demo | people | demagogue |
| dos | give | dose |
| erg | work | energy |
| gam | marriage | bigamist |
| gen | birth | eugenics |
| helio | sun | helium, heliotrope |
| hetero | different, other | heterogeneous |
| homo | same | homogeneous |
| hydr | water | hydraulics |
| lith, litho | stone | lithograph |
| morph | form | metamorphic |
| neo | new | neolithic |
| nom, nomy | law | economics |
| ortho | straight, correct | orthodox |
| pan | all | pan-American |
| phan, phen | show | phenomenon |

| Root | Meaning | Example |
|------|---------|---------|
| phil | loving | Philadelphia |
| phos, phot | light | photograph |
| pod | foot | podiatrist |
| proto | first | protoplasm |
| psych | mind | psychology |
| pyr | fire | pyre |
| soph | wise | sophomore |
| techn | art | technical |
| tele | far, far off | teletype |
| tom | cut | anatomy |
| trop | turn | tropic |
| typ | print | typography |
| zo | animal | protozoa |

### ACTIVITY 7. Using Greek Roots

Complete each blank by supplying the missing root. Use the list of roots as your guide. The number of dashes is the clue to the number of letters needed.

EXAMPLE: *A flower which turns toward the sun is called the -----trope.*
We need five letters here. Since *helio* means sun, the complete word is *heliotrope*.

1. An opinion that *differs* from other opinions is labeled ------dox.
2. One who *loves* wisdom is called a -----sopher.
3. That which is without *form* is a-----ous.
4. A *chief* angel is an ----angel.
5. One who makes many *marriages* is a poly---ist.
6. One who loves *mankind* enough to give money away is a phil-------ist.
7. A single block of *stone* is a mono----.
8. Something that appears out of its proper *time* is an ana-----ism.
9. The *art* of making woodcuts is a special -----ique.
10. The *first* animals are called -----zoa.
11. A speech of praise, formerly given before *all* the people of a town, is called a ---egyric.
12. An airplane made to land on *water* is called a -----plane.
13. A substance which glows with *light* in the dark is called ----phorus.

14. A disease that is visited upon the *people* is called an epi---ic.

15. One who *straightens* teeth is called an -----dontist.

16. A word that has the *same* pronunciation as another word is called a ----nym.

17. A wrapping that *shows* us the article through it is called cello-----.

18. *Fire*works are often called ----technics.

19. A person who seems to have unusual powers of *mind* is called -----ic.

20. The study of *animals* is called --ology.

# 8

# Give and Take

## WORD EXCHANGE WITH OTHER LANGUAGES

Lacquer, cravat, horde, cashmere, giraffe, shampoo, bamboo, coyote, chocolate, *and* turban — *what a gathering of words is here! What a story they could tell of their origins! Like the native costumes of the lands they came from, they give color and vigor to English — and a touch of strangeness, too. Here are words from every quarter of the globe. Here are words picked up by travel, conquest, and barter, words that pay tribute to the far-flung influence of the English language and to its capacity for absorbing what it needs. Tracking down words to their sources is as fascinating as a detective story. The words just mentioned are but a few drops in the great stream of borrowings from nearly every tongue and dialect the world over.*

Latin, Greek, and Anglo-Saxon have contributed the bulk of our present vocabulary, but other languages have contributed much of the flavor. Some words, like *tea*, *tulip*, and *moccasin*, entered the language when the objects were introduced. Strange foods brought strange new words: *rice*, *ginger*, and *cinnamon* from Asia; *banana* and *yam* from Africa; *tapioca*, *cocoa*, *potato*, and *tomato* from America. Other words remind us of our indebtedness to other lands for our entertainment; for example, *chess* and *checkers* came from Persia. Borrowing is always going on. If a new product is introduced from a foreign land, English-speaking people gladly accept both the product and its name.

Activity 1. Studying Borrowings from Other Languages

The italicized words below have come to us from languages other than Latin, Greek, or Anglo-Saxon. How many do you know? Select the alternative at the right that most nearly defines the italicized word. For extra credit find the country of origin of each word. Don't forget to record interesting strangers in your vocabulary notebook.

**English is a world traveler.**

1. A *shibboleth* is (*a*) a monster (*b*) a password (*c*) a proclamation (*d*) a flower (*e*) a game

2. A *seraph* is (*a*) a kind of printing (*b*) an old woman (*c*) a medicine (*d*) an angel (*e*) a mounted soldier

3. A *fez* is a kind of (*a*) fish (*b*) mythical animal (*c*) cap (*d*) coat (*e*) worship

4. A *taboo* is (*a*) a mark (*b*) a prince (*c*) a restriction (*d*) a narrative (*e*) a permit

5. An *argosy* is (*a*) a merchant vessel (*b*) a magazine (*c*) a story (*d*) a kind of cloth (*e*) a kind of food

6. A *bizarre* story is (*a*) fictional (*b*) true (*c*) scientific (*d*) unusual (*e*) sad

7. *Fanfare* involves (*a*) display (*b*) the use of a fan (*c*) charging admission (*d*) baseball (*e*) jealousy

8. *Turquoise* is a kind of (*a*) fowl (*b*) plant (*c*) color (*d*) powder (*e*) French dish

9. *Azimuth* is a term used in (*a*) painting (*b*) music (*c*) navigation (*d*) handicraft (*e*) the study of minerals

10. A *mazurka* is a kind of (*a*) broiled chicken (*b*) dance (*c*) vehicle (*d*) herb (*e*) building

11. A *freebooter* is (*a*) a football player (*b*) a member of a soccer team (*c*) a fighter for freedom (*d*) a pirate (*e*) a weaver

12. A *juggernaut* is something that (*a*) plays a tune (*b*) crushes (*c*) works automatically (*d*) takes care of gardens (*e*) can perform acrobatic stunts

13. *Wainscot* is (*a*) a ceremonial car (*b*) a kind of celluloid (*c*) a formal dinner (*d*) a roofing material (*e*) woodwork

14. *Quinine* is (*a*) a tropical disease (*b*) a medicine (*c*) a kind of dance (*d*) a paint ingredient (*e*) a beef tea

15. A *catamaran* is (*a*) a tiger-like animal (*b*) an insect (*c*) a Malayan hut (*d*) a kind of boat (*e*) a cure for malaria

16. A *bazaar* is (*a*) a cloak (*b*) a strange tale (*c*) a protest (*d*) a musical instrument (*e*) a fair

17. The *zenith* is (*a*) on the horizon (*b*) below one's feet (*c*) at a 45 degree angle (*d*) above one's head (*e*) at the equator

18. A *pariah* is (*a*) a staunch friend (*b*) an outcast (*c*) a religious fanatic (*d*) an oriental singer (*e*) a weak-willed person

19. A *mogul* is (*a*) weak (*b*) angry (*c*) tired (*d*) powerful (*e*) alien

20. A *jaguar* is (*a*) a medicinal root (*b*) an animal (*c*) a bird (*d*) a savage (*e*) a knife

21. *Azure* is the color of (*a*) a stormy sea (*b*) the earth (*c*) the sky (*d*) maple leaves (*e*) slate

22. *Buccaneers* are associated with (*a*) the Roman legions (*b*) Irish farmers (*c*) the Spanish Main (*d*) primitive man (*e*) astronomy

Signor Cantaloupe entertains a cosmopolitan audience.

23. The word *cherub* is often applied to  (*a*) an old man  (*b*) a hero  (*c*) an elderly lady  (*d*) a child  (*e*) a faithful pet

24. *Sable* is  (*a*) a fur  (*b*) the color green  (*c*) an arctic bird  (*d*) a low building  (*e*) an unusual invention

25. A *tattoo* is  (*a*) an African mammal  (*b*) a sturdy table  (*c*) a mark  (*d*) a hurricane  (*e*) a medal

## WORDS FROM PLACE NAMES

Among the ancient Greeks, citizens of Laconia, or Sparta, had the reputation of speaking directly, wasting no words. This characteristic has given us the word *laconic*. *Laconic* means *brief, to the point*. Many qualities or products of various places have given us new words. The American favorite, *hamburger*, is named after the city of Hamburg. *Italic* type originated in Italy. *Copper* took its name from Cyprus, as did *spaniel* from Spain. *China*, *turkey*, *cologne*, and *morocco* (leather) are self-explanatory. English has many such words.

ACTIVITY 2.  Checking Foreign Place Names in English

The words in column *A* have all been based upon the names of places in other lands. By looking up the origin and the meaning of each word in column *A*, match it with the country of origin in column *B*. Use an unabridged dictionary, if possible.

| *A* | *B* |
|---|---|
| 1. astrachan | a. China |
| 2. bayonet | b. England |
| 3. calico | c. England and Scotland |
| 4. cantaloupe | d. France |
| 5. cheviot | e. Germany |
| 6. coach | f. Hungary |
| 7. damask | g. India |
| 8. frankfurter | h. Italy |
| 9. muslin | i. Mesopotamia |
| 10. oolong | j. Mexico |
| 11. peach | k. Morocco |
| 12. polka | l. Persia |
| 13. tabasco | m. Poland |
| 14. tangerine | n. Russia |
| 15. worsted | o. Syria |

## CULTURAL CONTRIBUTIONS OF OTHER LANDS

All of us owe a great deal to the rest of the people on this earth. Our own priceless heritage is a combination, not only of our own contributions, but of the contributions of people from every corner of the world. If every nation kept entirely to itself, it would not benefit by the scientific progress and the artistic progress of other nations. The contributions are revealed in the words we now use. Thus the Hebrew words *amen, hallelujah, sabbath,* and *Pharisee* show our indebtedness to the ancient Hebrews for many of our religious terms.

### ACTIVITY 3. Studying Groups of Words from Other Languages

Below are listed groups of words from various other languages. Find out from what language each group of words came and match each group with the proper language in the word pool. What conclusions can you draw as to the cultural contributions of each nation listed? Be ready to define any of the words listed.

EXAMPLE: *arcade, balcony, colonnade, corridor, portico*. These are all of Italian origin. Since all have something to do with parts of buildings, we can safely assume that Italian contributions to architecture have been considerable.

| | |
|---|---|
| African | French |
| American | German |
| American Indian | Italian |
| Arabic | Persian |
| Dutch | Spanish |

1. hominy, maize, pecan, succotash, squash, persimmon
2. beret, cambric, chapeau, cretonne, trousseau
3. deck, dock, hoist, jib, skipper, sloop, yacht
4. bismuth, cobalt, Fahrenheit, gneiss, quartz, shale, zinc
5. alchemy, algebra, chemistry, cipher, zenith, zero
6. adobe, broncho, canyon, corral, lariat, sombrero
7. jasmine, lemon, lilac, orange, peach, tulip
8. andante, aria, opera, piano, soprano, violin
9. chimpanzee, gnu, gorilla, zebra
10. carborundum, cellophane, kodak, listerine, thermos, victrola

## GIVE AND TAKE

The borrowing has not been one-sided, by any means. All over the globe, in hundreds of tongues and dialects, English words have become securely lodged — changed perhaps in spelling and pronunciation, but recognizable, nevertheless. Someone has estimated that Japan, for example, has borrowed over 9000 words from English in recent years, including *boto* (for *boat*), *naifu* (for *knife*), *awri* (for *all right*), and *bese boru* (for *baseball*). France, to mention another borrower, has *biftek* (for *beef steak*), *poudingue* (for *pudding*), *snobbisme* (for *snobbery*), and *boulingrin* (for *bowling green*). An interesting example of give-and-take is the French word *redingote*, borrowed from the English *riding coat*. English proceeded promptly to reborrow the word as *redingote*, to mean a special kind of woman's coat. Constant interchange of words supplies new blood to languages, and contributes to better understanding among peoples.

# 9

# Language Evolution

## How Words Change

*At college alumni reunions, when school friends come together after being many years apart, witty remarks fly thick and fast. Good-natured jokes about putting on weight, losing hair, and becoming prosperous are likely to take up a good portion of the evening. We are always amazed at the changes in others.*

## Processes of Change

Men and women do not remain the same; neither do words. Like human beings words are born and die, become prosperous or go downhill. Some people take on weight; some words take on additional meanings. Some people lose weight; some words become narrower in meaning. The years that alter the appearance and fortunes of all of us are likely to do the same for words, though the word's life is likely to extend far beyond a mortal's span.

Students of language emphasize four processes constantly at work to change words: *elevation*, *degeneration*, *generalization*, and *specialization*. The words sound forbiddingly difficult, but the processes they name are easily understood.

## Elevation

Abraham Lincoln rose from log cabin to White House. Some words have followed a somewhat similar path. The word *queen*, for example, at first meant *wife* or *woman*. Then it came to be applied to the *chief* wife, the wife of a king. Similarly *regal*

Old    New        Old        New
  Queen              Chamberlain

originally meant *pertaining to a king*. Now it has the additional
meaning of *stately, splendid, magnificent*. *Chamberlain*, a word
sometimes applied to extremely important officials in European
countries, once meant nothing more than the attendant upon
the royal bedchamber. These words illustrate the tendency of
some words to prosper.

### ACTIVITY 1. Studying Elevation in Words

Each of the following words has gone up the social scale,
meaning now something more important or more favorable
than it did originally. Look up each in the dictionary. For each
tell its present meaning and its original meaning as indicated in
brackets after the word. Add new words to your vocabulary
notebook.

EXAMPLE: *fame*. *Fame* comes from a Latin word meaning *to speak*.
Fame, then, meant originally something *spoken* about one; now
it means something *spoken well* about a person. Thus it has risen
in meaning from mere *report* to *good report*.

| | |
|---|---|
| ambition | fond |
| chivalrous | knight |
| civilization | marshal |
| constable | precious |
| costly | splendid |

## Degeneration

Not all words, alas, go up the scale. Many have traveled the opposite path. *Boor*, now meaning a *rude, ill-bred person*, once meant merely a *farmer*. *Knave* once meant a *boy;* now it means a *wicked person*. The human tendency to put off doing something is nowhere better illustrated than in the history of words. The

Old    New          Old    New
Boor               Knave

terms *soon, by and by, presently, directly* once meant *instantly* or *immediately;* now they mean *in a little while*. When Mrs. Anderson calls Billy for supper and he answers, "Right away," we can reasonably suspect that he'll take a little longer. All of these words have gone down the scale slightly. Some words have degenerated, while closely related words have risen; *childish* is an unfavorable word, but *boyish* is favorable.

ACTIVITY 2. Studying Degeneration in Words

Each of the following words has gone down the social scale. Look up each in the dictionary. For each tell its present meaning and its original meaning as indicated in brackets after the word.

| cheap | enormity | hussy | sullen | vulgar |
| common | homely | servile | villain | wretch |

## SPECIALIZATION

The expression *meat and drink* is a clue to another tendency of language, *specialization*, for it shows us the word *meat* in its original sense. Once *meat* meant *food*, any solid food. After a time the meaning became narrower, so that the word included only the *flesh of animals used for food*. We have traces of the older, broader meaning in expressions like *sweetmeat*, or the *meat* of a peanut. Similarly the word *tyrant* was once applied to any absolute *ruler;* now it is applied only to *cruel rulers.* Its meaning has become narrower, more specialized.

### ACTIVITY 3. Studying Specialization in Words

Each of the following words has become narrower in meaning. Look up each in the dictionary. For each tell its present meaning and its original meaning as indicated in brackets after the word, or as explained in the definition. Remember your vocabulary notebook.

| | |
|---|---|
| apparition | engine |
| ballad | execute |
| concert | fowl |
| convert | ghost |
| corn | minister |

## GENERALIZATION

When we talk about *sailing* in a steamboat, we are illustrating the fourth tendency of words, to become more general in meaning. Originally *sailing* meant journeying in a *boat with sails*. Now it refers to any kind of boat. The word *journey*, just mentioned, is another example of generalization, for a *journey* was originally a trip of *one day's duration*, from the Latin *diurnus*, meaning *daily*. Many words become much broader in meaning with time.

### ACTIVITY 4. Studying Generalization in Words

Each of the following words has become broader in meaning. Look up each in the dictionary. For each tell both its present meaning and its original meaning as indicated in brackets after the word or as explained in the definition.

| | |
|---|---|
| arrive | hazard |
| brilliant | injury |
| course | miniature |
| dismantle | paper |
| front | scene |

## FOLK ETYMOLOGY

Small children trying to say *asparagus* frequently end up with *sparrowgrass* or something similar. The unfamiliar word *asparagus* tends to be made into something better known. What more natural than *sparrow* plus *grass*, both familiar terms. Some folk still refer to *cucumbers* as *cowcumbers* and *bronchitis* as *brownkitis*. The process of changing an unfamiliar word to one more familiar is called *folk etymology*. Tracing many of the popular changes to their source is a fascinating sport.

### ACTIVITY 5. Tracing Folk Etymologies

Use the dictionary to complete each of the following statements. Explain how each folk etymology might have arisen.

EXAMPLE: *A belfry originally had nothing to do with a bell, but instead* ———. To complete this statement we check with the dictionary and find that *belfry* comes from two words meaning to *guard peace*. It should be spelled *berfry*, but because of the association with *bell*, the word came to the spelling *belfry*. So we complete the statement by writing *with guarding the peace*.

1. The dish *Welsh rabbit* has nothing to do with a *rabbit*, but instead ———.
2. The word *pantry* is not related to our word *pan*, but instead ———.
3. A *hiccough* is not related to *cough*, but instead ———.
4. A *ravenous* appetite has nothing to do with a *raven*, but instead ———.
5. A *primrose* has nothing to do with a *rose*, for ———.
6. The word *pickax* is not related to the word *ax*, but ———.

7. A *barberry* hedge is not at all a *berry* hedge, for ———.

8. The word *buzzard*, for a bird of prey, has nothing to do with *buzz*, for ———.

9. The word *cutlet* is not related to *cut*, but instead ———.

10. The *buttery*, a room in a large mansion, has nothing to do with *butter*, but instead ———.

## How Language Is Enriched

Previous chapters have pointed out how English borrows from other tongues to add new words. This chapter has indicated how words change and take on new meanings, thus fulfilling needs as they arise. Language is enriched in other ways, too, for even as you read this, somewhere a familiar word is being used in an unfamiliar way. Some of the unfamiliar uses remain. Let's examine two or three of the processes that constantly add to the stock of English words.

## Changing Parts of Speech

A common tendency in English is to make a noun from a verb, or vice versa. Thus we may hear of a community *sing* or a fair *try*. Often people try to halt the process; for example, many people objected to the verb *contact* from the noun *contact*. The verb has been accepted, however. The process has helped to streamline English, for instead of having a noun *lecture* and an awkward verb phrase *to give a lecture*, we have both noun and verb *lecture*.

Another tendency is to take an adjective and make a noun out of it. Thus we have a *private* (soldier) and a *general* (officer) in the army. We hear of the *lame*, the *halt*, and the *blind*, the *good* and the *evil*. The *strong* protect the *weak*, and the *listless* envy the *energetic*. The italicized words are all used as nouns and therefore may be called nouns.

## Shortening Words

Long words are often clipped, forming new words of fewer syllables. *Bus* was formed from *omnibus*, *taxi* and *cab* from *taximetercabriolet.* Other shorter forms, some of them not yet acceptable literary English, are words like *phone* for *telephone, gas* for *gasoline, photo* for *photograph, rattler* for *rattlesnake, auto* for *automobile, flu* for *influenza,* and *memo* for *memorandum.*

**What World War II terms are suggested here?**

## New Coinages

Silver is sent to the mint, shaped, and impressed with a design. Then it circulates as a coin. Words, like money, are being coined all the time. New words appear, circulate for a time, and then either secure a lasting place in the language or slip unnoticed into oblivion. Sometimes a trade name is invented and absorbed as an ordinary word; for example, *vaseline* and *frigidaire.* Sometimes a writer will combine an established word with an old suffix — for example, *gang* plus *ster* to produce *gangster,* or *film* plus *dom* to produce *filmdom.* Not all survive to become established English words, though occasionally a slang expression like *bus*, *cab*, *hoax*, and *mob* will be accepted. A word must be accepted by the people. No one can predict whether a new word will last. Charles Sumner invented the shorter word *annexion* for *annexation*, but it did not survive. The war added many new words and enlarged the meaning of some words already in use; for example, *paratrooper*, *fifth column*, *blackout*, and *bombardier*. A living language is constantly changing and growing. English is very much alive.

### Activity 6. Studying Recent Additions

How many of the following words can you define? All are recent additions to English. Have these words any synonyms?

| | |
|---|---|
| all clear | jeep |
| all-out | jet propulsion |
| bottleneck | microfilm |
| ersatz | radar |
| flak | walkie-talkie |

# 10

# High Hat and Dungarees

## LEARNED AND POPULAR WORDS

"*Many of the repugnant vicissitudes of life are ineluctable.*"

*Can you ever imagine yourself using a sentence like that in conversation? Certainly it sounds artificial and unnecessarily stiff, particularly since a similar message can be presented in more familiar words: "Many of life's unpleasant happenings are unavoidable." The best writers tell us to use the simplest words possible to say what we mean. Yet we'd find ourselves handicapped if we limited our recognition vocabulary only to those words we actually use in conversation. To be educated is to have a wide acquaintance with words, many of which we may never use in our own conversation, but which we meet in our reading or use occasionally in our writing.*

### ACTIVITY 1. Enlarging the Use Vocabulary

Below, in the numbered column at the left, are words that are probably found in your speaking vocabulary. In the column at the right are words that may not be found in your speaking vocabulary, but many of which you should be able to recognize. Match the popular words at the left with the less common words at the right. What is the special meaning of the synonym at the right? Use the dictionary to check your answers. Try to add the words at the right to your *use* vocabulary, for you will find them helpful in expressing yourself with variety.

1. agree        a. concur
2. aggressive    b. corroborate

| | |
|---|---|
| 3. applause | c. perfidy |
| 4. beg | d. virtuoso |
| 5. belittle | e. colleague |
| 6. boast | f. venturesome |
| 7. confirm | g. fidelity |
| 8. courage | h. supersede |
| 9. daring | i. simpleton |
| 10. disagreement | j. allude |
| 11. endless | k. militant |
| 12. expert | l. disparage |
| 13. faithlessness | m. dissent |
| 14. fool | n. interminable |
| 15. invincible | o. mettle |
| 16. loyalty | p. acclaim |
| 17. partner | q. vaunt |
| 18. refer | r. indomitable |
| 19. reject | s. repudiate |
| 20. replace | t. implore |

## LEARNED WORDS ARE USEFUL, TOO

English, with its wealth of synonyms, often gives us a choice of the learned word or the popular word. Ordinary speaking encourages the use of the popular word, but occasionally we call upon the learned word to present a shade of meaning different from that of the popular. Consider the words *speech* and *oration*. Both refer to a vocal transmission of a message, but the aristocratic *oration* suggests greater formality than the simpler *speech*. We can refer to anyone as a *speaker*, even the little kindergarten youngster who retells a fairy tale. We could hardly call him an *orator*, except in fun. Thus, frequently the more learned word is useful to give a slightly different meaning.

ACTIVITY 2. Studying Learned and Popular Words

In each of the following pairs of words the popular word is at the left. Discuss the difference in meaning between the words in each pair. When would you use the popular word? Why is it important to know both the popular and the learned word?

Should you add any of these words to your vocabulary note-book?

1. fire, conflagration
2. brave, valorous
3. secret, cryptic
4. destroy, devastate
5. decorate, embellish
6. play, drama
7. teacher, instructor
8. air, atmosphere
9. paint, pigment
10. stiff, rigid

### ACTIVITY 3. Using Popular and Learned Words

In each of the following pairs of words the popular word is at the left. Check the meaning of each in the pair and indicate how meanings differ. Use each in a sentence of your own to prove that you understand the distinctions.

EXAMPLE: *foolish, preposterous*. Though both words refer to something that offends good sense, *preposterous* is stronger. A statement is *foolish* if it shows poor judgment, but it is *preposterous* if it has absolutely no basis in fact.

*Sentences:* The attempt to cross the mountain ridge in the dead of winter proved *foolish*. His request received no consideration because his reasons were *preposterous*.

1. appearance, mien
2. cruel, barbarous
3. doubtful, skeptical
4. false, perfidious
5. fool, idiot
6. gloomy, morbid
7. hostile, inimical
8. irritable, querulous
9. join, unite
10. lazy, indolent
11. letter, epistle
12. noisy, obstreperous
13. oily, unctuous
14. quiet, taciturn
15. revive, resuscitate
16. speed, alacrity
17. surrender, capitulation
18. tasteless, insipid
19. urge, exhort
20. wind, zephyr

### AVOIDING ARTIFICIALITY

Suppose you had been appointed business manager of the high school newspaper and had been asked to streamline all business activities. In your promise of hard work and pledge of co-operation to your editor or faculty adviser, which of the following sentences might you use? (1) "I shall endeavor to extirpate ineffectual and negligent work." (2) "I shall try to eliminate inefficiency."

Probably you instinctively prefer sentence two. Sentence one, like the sentence quoted at the beginning of this chapter, says very little if anything more than sentence two. Besides, it takes a long time to say it. Let's compare the words used. The simpler *try* is preferable here to the more formal *endeavor*. *Try* comes to the point directly. It is simple and accurate. *Endeavor* is too grand for this situation. *Eliminate* means *get rid of. Extirpate* implies taking out by the roots. *Eliminate* seems to do the job well enough. *Extirpate* seems boastful, unduly emphatic. *Inefficiency* here means the same as the four words *ineffectual and negligent work.* For economy alone it is preferable. Merely using high-sounding words for the sake of their impressiveness is faulty. Young writers are often addicted to the habit of putting in the longest words possible, when often a short, simple, direct word will be better. Summing up, then, we note that sentence two comes straight to the point, while sentence one "puts on airs."

Use the popular word if:

*a.* Sentence economy calls for it;
*b.* No additional refinement of meaning is gained by the use of the learned word;
*c.* The only reason for the use of the learned word is to "show off."

Use the learned word if:

*a.* It adds more exact meanings;
*b.* It gives variety to the sentence or paragraph.


Activity 4. Using Popular Words Correctly

In each of the following sentences a learned word is used where a popular word would have done at least as well, or perhaps better. In none of the sentences does the learned word add anything that the appropriate popular word in the word pool doesn't suggest. From the word pool select that word which best replaces each italicized word. If the learned word is unfamiliar to you, look up its meaning in the dictionary. Add new words to your vocabulary notebook.

| | |
|---|---|
| beggar | poverty |
| face | remedy |
| fear | weak |
| home | wealthy |
| pay | winding |

1. He took a *sinuous* path to reach the hilltop.
2. The athlete felt *decrepit* after the mile run.
3. He carelessly flipped a coin to the *mendicant* at the gate.
4. Can you suggest a *medicament* for my cold?
5. Did the farmer *reimburse* you well for your work as a fruit-picker?
6. *Trepidation* made his hand shake as he opened the squeaking door.
7. Oliver Twist saw hunger and *indigence* at first hand.
8. An *opulent* manufacturer gave a check to the hospital.
9. I'd like to have you visit my *residence* at the first opportunity.
10. He was afraid to show his *countenance* after his unexpected defeat.

ACTIVITY 5. Using Learned Words Correctly

The learned words that were misused in the previous activity may be used correctly. Each of the following sentences omits a key word. From the list below fill each blank space with the

**Suit the words to the occasion.**

word that best completes the meaning. Note that now the learned word provides additional meaning not suggested by the popular synonym. Add new words to your recognition vocabulary as well as to your vocabulary notebook.

countenance  opulent
decrepit  reimburse
indigence  residence
medicament  sinuous
mendicant  trepidation

1. This fire insurance covers the ———— at 47 Wistful Vista.

2. Old Barker always kept a kindly ———— for the world to see.

3. Though the two brothers were both wealthy, one lived rather simply while the other lived in ———— style.

4. Edward joined an order of ———— friars, who depended upon alms for their maintenance.

5. The frightened native watched the ———— movements of the leopard as he padded through the trees.

6. The insurance company promised to ———— him for his loss.

7. It is with some ———— that I try to explain a subject I am a bit hazy about myself.

8. His slightly frayed coat revealed his ————, but the inconspicuous patch revealed his pride.

9. The doctor prescribed a nasal ———— for treating the head cold.

10. The old man, so obviously worn out and ————, could scarcely reach the exit.

ACTIVITY 6. Selecting the Right Word

In each of the following sentences the blank space should be filled by one of the words in parentheses. Choose the word that seems to fit the meaning best and explain the reasons for your choice. Look up the meanings of unfamiliar words in the dictionary.

1. The room was unusually ———— for a dining room, extending twenty-five feet along the length of the house. (*large, colossal*)

2. We hold these truths to be ————, that all men are created equal. (*self-evident, manifest*)

3. All the snow had ——— by Christmas morning. (*melted, dissolved*)

4. On Thanksgiving all the soldiers had ——— turkey to eat. (*sufficient, enough*)

5. The unfortunate family had been ——— from their home. (*cast out, evicted*)

6. Keep at least a one-inch ——— on the page you are using for the composition. (*margin, border*)

7. I have ——— in the same house for nearly ten years. (*lived, resided*)

8. He ——— his face behind a large geography textbook. (*hid, secreted*)

9. They made a fine ——— perfume from coal tar. (*artificial, synthetic*)

10. The local court will have ——— over your case. (*power, jurisdiction*)

### ACTIVITY 7.  Reviewing New Words

How well do you remember the words that were listed in Activity 1? Without referring to previous pages take the following vocabulary test. Choose the word that comes closest in meaning to the italicized word. After you have taken the test, check to see whether you have added new words to your vocabulary.

1. Peg and Lois liked to indulge in one of those *interminable* discussions.

    (*a*) exciting (*b*) ineluctable (*c*) endless (*d*) bitter (*e*) feeble

2. To which one were you *alluding?*

    (*a*) pointing (*b*) referring (*c*) looking (*d*) appealing (*e*) speaking

3. The *indomitable* spirit of mankind is depicted in this book.

    (*a*) cruel (*b*) invincible (*c*) lighthearted (*d*) grasping (*e*) fierce

4. It is unwise to *disparage* the ability of your opponent.

   (*a*) overestimate   (*b*) talk about   (*c*) belittle   (*d*) compare
   (*e*) fear

5. *Dissension* in the ranks of seamen brought on the crisis.

   (*a*) good leadership   (*b*) poor leadership   (*c*) disease   (*d*) intelligence   (*e*) conflict

6. Jerry *corroborated* Sylvia's report.

   (*a*) rejected   (*b*) marked up   (*c*) confirmed   (*d*) denied   (*e*) tore

7. His *fidelity* to the organization was apparent to all.

   (*a*) loyalty   (*b*) faithlessness   (*c*) connection   (*d*) reference
   (*e*) indifference

8. The judge and the jury *concurred*.

   (*a*) recessed   (*b*) agreed   (*c*) disagreed   (*d*) conversed   (*e*) spoke
   up

9. New England *repudiated* the new tariff.

   (*a*) upheld   (*b*) supported   (*c*) introduced   (*d*) disowned
   (*e*) publicized

10. You'll have to see my *colleague* on that matter.

    (*a*) employer   (*b*) employee   (*c*) associate   (*d*) attorney
    (*e*) brother

# 11

# Birds of a Feather

## SYNONYMS

*"Am I a fit man for the job? Why, sir, you are looking at a man of rare tact, discretion, foresight, erudition, enlightenment, sagacity, scholarship, wisdom, profundity, discernment, good judgment and plain common sense. I am one of the keenest, cleverest, shrewdest, quickest, smartest individuals in this town!"*

*Have you ever heard a radio comedian rattle off such a string of words, astounding his partners and delighting his audience? We listeners enjoy a flow of high-sounding language. Of course, we appreciate the use of so many synonyms in fun, for in real life we are not likely to be so fluent. How often would we be thankful for even one of the synonyms tossed about so carelessly by the comedian! A sailor overseas floundered through a letter to his sweetheart: "The watch you sent me is certainly a useful gift. Every time I glance at it I realize again how useful it is. It surely was a useful present to receive." How grateful he would have been for some good substitutes for* useful, *words like* serviceable, suitable, *or* practical!

A football coach wisely calls in his first team from time to time and sends in substitutes to play the game. He has two purposes: to give his first team a much-needed rest and to train the substitutes for the future. So with words. We should learn to employ substitutes occasionally. Synonyms, words that mean approximately the same as words we already know, are helpful substitutes. They add color, exactness, and variety to our writing and speaking. They give our basic word stock a necessary

EDIBLE CHEESE*
IT'S DELECTABLE, TOOTHSOME
APPETIZING, DELICIOUS
FULL-FLAVORED, LUSCIOUS
SCRUMPTIOUS and YUMMY
*IT EVEN TASTES GOOD

**Caution! Synonyms at work**

rest and enrich our vocabularies for the future. The unabridged dictionaries and the Merriam-Webster *Dictionary of Synonyms* are the best places to look for information on this subject.

### ACTIVITY 1. Using Synonyms for Variety

In each of the following sentences avoid repetition of the italicized words by supplying synonyms for all but one. You may select words from the word pool. How does the use of synonyms improve the sentences?

EXAMPLE: *George gave his bride a tiny, beautiful wrist watch. She gasped when she saw its beautiful workmanship. Everyone admired its beautiful appearance.* If we substitute *exquisite* and *delicate* for the second and third *beautiful*, we add variety and exactness to the sentence.

| | | |
|---|---|---|
| agree to | eminent | qualm |
| articles | happenings | recall |
| assent to | merchandise | recollect |
| authority | obstinate | renowned |
| commodities | occupancy | revenue |
| distinguished | occurrences | suspicion |
| docile | ownership | tame |
| earnings | power | unyielding |

1. At the time of Tiberius the Roman Empire wielded great *influence*. Its *influence* reached from northern forest to southern vineyard. Later emperors extended Roman *influence* even farther.

2. We regret that we cannot *comply with* your present request. We have already *complied with* requests that you have made in the past. May we ask you to *comply with* our plea for further experimentation.

3. The plantation owners in the novel at first proved too *stubborn* for the railroad. The agent declared that the owners were foolishly *stubborn*, and sought a way to break their *stubborn* attitude.

4. We took legal *possession* of the new house on the 15th. We were proud of our *possession* of something substantial. We were settled in our actual *possession* of the house by the first of the month.

5. Gentlemen, may I introduce to you the *famous* naturalist and explorer, Mr. John Nash. He is not only *famous* as a scientist, but he is *famous* as a writer as well. There is little doubt that, among Asiatics and Europeans, he is a *famous* American.

6. Mr. Wilson in *The Red-Headed League* at first had no *doubt* concerning the unusual position he held. The first time he had any *doubt* at all was after the sudden closing of the office. To clear up his *doubt* he consulted the famous Sherlock Holmes.

7. The writer had a comfortable *income*. Not only could he depend upon the *income* from his books, but he always had the *income* from his lecture tours to fall back upon.

8. David Copperfield could *remember* all too clearly his mistreatment at the hands of Mr. Murdstone. He could *remember*, too, the kindliness of Betsy Trotwood. When he tried to *remember* the *events* of his very early childhood, he found that certain *events* stood out among all other *events*.

9. The *goods* we advertise in our present sale cannot be duplicated anywhere. We were able to purchase the *goods* at a fortunate price. We have always been proud of the *goods* we offer, but these *goods* are an exceptional value.

10. Flicka at first was not a *gentle* horse, but after Ken's loving care she became more and more *gentle*, until she seemed to those on the ranch to be one of the most *gentle* mares in Wyoming.

## VOCABULARY BUILDING BY SYNONYMS

We are more likely to learn the names of new acquaintances if we can associate their names with the names of people we already know. Thus, without too much effort, we can remember that Sylvia is Marie's friend. Sylvia and Marie seem to go together. We learn Sylvia's name readily because we associate it with Marie, the name of a girl we already know. Just as we learn the names of friends more easily when we can group them, so we learn associated words more easily than isolated ones. For proof of this tendency note many of our commonplace expressions—phrases that group synonyms: *to love and to cherish, down and out, vim and vigor,* and *trial and tribulation.*

We recognize the soundness of building a vocabulary by learning synonyms whenever we look up the meaning of a word like *obsolete* and memorize its synonym, *out-of-date.* When we associate in our minds *obsolete* and *out-of-date,* we enrich the meaning of both words for us.

### Activity 2.  Matching Synonyms

Match each word in column *A* with its synonym in column *B*. Use the dictionary to check doubtful choices.

| *A* | *B* |
|-----|-----|
| 1. dangerous | a. instigate |
| 2. emissary | b. hazardous |
| 3. healthful | c. clemency |
| 4. inactive | d. ostentatious |
| 5. mercy | e. listless |
| 6. provoke | f. salutary |
| 7. showy | g. sagacious |
| 8. waver | h. exterminate |
| 9. wipe out | i. fluctuate |
| 10. wise | j. messenger |

### Activity 3.  Supplying Synonyms

Supply a synonym for each of the following words. If you cannot think of a synonym, use the dictionary to complete the list. Compare your synonym list with your neighbor's. Add new words to your vocabulary notebook.

| answer | honest | necessary | renounce | thaw |
| burn | impetuous | neglect | rise | thick |
| busy | juvenile | nimble | rival | throng |
| dreary | leave | noble | roam | triumph |
| dry | legal | penetrating | sailor | try |
| follow | light | plain | saucy | ugly |
| freedom | live | plausible | secret | ungainly |
| give | mark | please | shameful | vacant |
| growl | measure | prosperity | ship | warn |
| help | mistake | puzzle | suppose | zero |

ACTIVITY 4. Finding Synonyms in a Paragraph

The following paragraph has six pairs of synonyms included within it. One of the pairs is listed as the example. Find the other five pairs and match each with one of the words below.

EXAMPLE: *cavalier, rider.* Both *cavalier* and *rider* mean the same as *horseman.*

|  |  |  |
|---|---|---|
| apparition | horseman | sadness |
| happily | marriage | unusual |

*The Specter Bridegroom*, by Washington Irving, is one of my favorite ghost stories. The wedding feast is set, but no groom arrives to attend the nuptials. Suddenly a solitary rider appears, a tall, pale cavalier. The mysterious stranger's gloom and melancholy leave him as he sees the beautiful bride. The evening passes merrily, until suddenly the stranger shocks those who are gaily enjoying the feast by saying, "I must away to Wurtzburg Cathedral. The worms! the worms expect me! I am a dead man." Read the story to discover its striking, extraordinary conclusion.

## RICHNESS OF ENGLISH SYNONYMS

As a language English is unusually rich in synonyms. Previous chapters have indicated the great contributions of other languages to English. English borrowings have had the invigorating result of adding thousands of synonyms to the language, each of which contributes new shades of meaning. Thus *bright* is a native English word, but *brilliant* came to us from the Latin.

*Brilliant* is more emphatic than the native word and contributes something new. Sometimes the foreign word is less emphatic, though useful. *Murder* is a native word; *homicide* is Latin, and may suggest unintentional slaying. Our courts would be handicapped without the word. Sometimes the two words, though originally synonyms, are now far apart in meaning, like *sunny* and *solar*. Here the foreign word contributes a completely new idea. We couldn't talk about the *sunny system* — for *solar system* — nor could we talk about a beautiful *solar day*. Both *sunny* and *solar* have distinct jobs to do. Fine shades of meaning are possible in English because we have borrowed extensively and wisely.

### ACTIVITY 5.  Matching Synonyms

The columns under *A* include representative Anglo-Saxon words. The columns under *B* contain some later borrowings, synonyms of the words in *A*. Match synonyms and show how the meaning of the word in column *A* differs from that in *B*.

EXAMPLE: *A. deep; B. profound. Deep* is a more general term. We may speak of a *deep* thinker, a *deep* pool, or a *deep* color. *Profound* is usually applied only to thoughts or feelings.

|  | A |  | B |
|---|---|---|---|
| 1. bit | 6. hate | a. devour | f. particle |
| 2. book | 7. nightly | b. astonishment | g. detest |
| 3. child | 8. sail | c. infant | h. misery |
| 4. do | 9. sorrow | d. volume | i. accomplish |
| 5. eat | 10. wonder | e. nocturnal | j. navigate |

### ACTIVITY 6.  Studying Synonyms

In each pair of words on page 124 the native word is at the left, the foreign word at the right. Look up in the dictionary the distinctive meaning of each. Use each in a sentence to indicate that you know the difference in meaning.

EXAMPLE: *hungry, famished.* Though both refer to a yearning for food, *famished* is much stronger than *hungry*. Normally a person is *hungry* at mealtime. He might be *famished* if he were almost dead of hunger.

*Sentences:* The lost explorer was found at last, *famished* and haggard. Exercise made the athlete *hungry* long before dinner.

| | |
|---|---|
| dog, canine | hue, color |
| borough, city | old, venerable |
| fall, collapse | seethe, boil |
| flood, cataclysm | stir, agitate |
| frighten, terrify | stir, commotion |

## Pitfalls in Synonyms

Though synonyms are words that are *approximately* alike in meaning, no two words are ever *exactly* alike. As you add more synonyms to your vocabulary, learn how each word differs from the others. (See pages 242–244.) *Ability* and *capacity*, for example, are often considered synonymous; yet there is an important shade of difference between them. *Ability* is the power to *do* something; *capacity* is the power to *hold* something. We may talk of a person's *ability to do a job*, and his *capacity for learning a fact*. We should not talk about a stadium's *ability* to hold 10,000 persons, but its *capacity*.

## Activity 7. Discriminating Synonyms

By consulting the dictionary, if necessary, insert the proper word in parentheses into each of the blanks.

EXAMPLE: *Will has remarkable ——— for remembering facts plus outstanding ——— in putting them to work.* (*ability*, *capacity*) The first blank requires *capacity* and the second, *ability*.

1. The ——— of radioactivity led eventually to the ——— of the atomic bomb. (*discovery*, *invention*)

2. He swore to ——— the death of his brother, and thus gain ———. (*revenge*, *avenge*)

3. The governor emphasized that to ——— the criminal was not to ——— his crime. (*pardon*, *excuse*)

4. Although he found ——— in occasional breaks in routine, he found true ——— only in his life's work, writing. (*happiness*, *pleasure*)

**Painter: artist**             **Painter: artisan**

5. The theater's —— were recruited principally from the —— of the large department store. (*customers, patrons*)

6. Her physical —— was not responsible for her —— to answer the telephone. (*inability, disability*)

7. His —— for research plus his —— for manipulating small specimens made him one of the outstanding scientists of his day. (*talent, aptitude*)

8. The steady —— of the lighthouse contrasted with the —— of moonlight on the water. (*gleam, glitter*)

9. Fred felt —— for his sorrowing friend, and sent him a letter of ——. (*sympathy, pity*)

10. Parker's hand —— with the cold, and Parker —— as he thought of the narrow escape he had just had. (*shuddered, shook*)

ACTIVITY 8. Discriminating Synonyms

Check the meaning of each word in the pairs on page 126. Point out how each synonym differs from the other in some way or other. Use each properly in a sentence. Your teacher may wish to divide the class into groups for this activity.

EXAMPLE: *amateur, novice.* The amateur does something for the love of it. The novice is new at what he is doing. "*Novices* in photography had better not compete with experienced *amateurs.*"

amateur, novice
artist, artisan
assassinate, kill
blockade, siege
blueprint, sketch
bravery, bravado
champion, winner
chance, accident
choice, preference
citizen, subject
command, dictate
competent, qualified
concede, grant
cool, cold
defect, blemish
despondent, hopeless
despot, ruler
dinner, banquet
disgrace, ignominy
dissatisfied, discontented
earth, world
esteem, respect
exempt, immune
expect, hope

facsimile, copy
fragile, brittle
gather, congregate
intrepid, bold
insolent, haughty
libel, slander
listen, hear
madden, infuriate
melody, tune
mirth, hilarity
motion, momentum
peculiar, unusual
pictorial, picturesque
pride, vanity
proficient, expert
reveal, divulge
satisfy, cloy
see, witness
slender, slim
small, diminutive
sophisticated, disillusioned
soul, spirit
symptom, sign
wit, humor

## SYNONYMS IN GROUPS

English is so unbelievably rich in synonyms that words often have, instead of one or two synonyms, five, six, or a dozen. Mastery of these large groups of synonyms is essential in building a vocabulary. Speakers with large vocabularies can choose the right word from a group of a dozen or more. Suppose you wanted to tell someone how Terry made a certain statement. You could say, colorlessly, "Terry said . . ." But you'd be neglecting the great number of synonyms for *said*, words that would express more exactly *how* Terry gave his statement. Was Terry positive? Very well, then, he probably *affirmed, asserted, professed, emphasized, certified, avowed, insisted, assured,* or *averred.* Did he speak without undue emphasis? Then he probably *put forth, proposed, announced, maintained, set forth, stated, declared, expressed, remarked,* or *observed.* In what tone of voice did he speak? Did he *shout, whisper, murmur, lisp, laugh, cry, thunder, boom, groan, mumble, mutter,* or *snap?* Did he speak directly, or did he *insinuate, hint, suggest, imply,* or *intimate?* Though we have listed over thirty words, we haven't exhausted the possible substitutes for *said.* Those with a good command of English choose the word they feel most suitable for the occasion.

### ACTIVITY 9. Studying Substitutes for *Said*

In any novel or short story you are now reading list the substitutes used by the author for the word *said.* Why does the author avoid repetition? What do the synonyms add to the story?

### ACTIVITY 10. Supplying Substitutes for *Saw*

From the list of words below select a word to fill each of the blanks in the following sentences. Indicate why you have chosen each word. What does each word suggest?

| | |
|---|---|
| distinguished | recognized |
| gazed | scanned |
| glowered | scrutinized |
| observed | stared |
| peered | surveyed |

1. The visitors ———— at the famous painting for a long time in admiration.
2. Deep in thought he ———— unseeingly out of the window.
3. His eye ———— the magazine hurriedly.
4. The small boy ———— earnestly through the knothole in 'an effort to see the baseball game.
5. He ———— the changes in society without alarm.
6. At that distance his eye 'ust ———— the climbers on the ridge.
7. From his viewpoint on top of Mt. Washington he ———— the entire countryside around.
8. The travelers ———— in the distance the familiar towers of home.
9. The art dealer ———— the painting for any traces of retouching.
10. The angry knight ———— at his opponent in the lists.

**Enjoy a ride on the synonym ferris wheel.**

ACTIVITY 11. Studying Synonyms in Groups

Select from the words listed at the end of each sentence or group of sentences proper words to fill each of the blanks. Indicate a reason for each choice.

EXAMPLE: *The audience ——— and even gloomy Dave ——— silently as they saw how the young girls ——— in the motion picture.* (chuckled, giggled, roared)

*Roared* belongs in the first blank, *chuckled* in the second, and *giggled* in the third. To *roar* is to laugh loudly; to *chuckle* is to laugh low or gently, and to *giggle* is to laugh with slight provocation. *Giggling* is usually associated with young people.

1. Good, ——— food, prepared under ——— conditions, is influential in keeping us ———. (*healthy, sanitary, wholesome*)

2. Charles renounced the ——— of French nobility he hated, and adopted the ——— of Darnay to conceal his real ——— of Evremonde. (*name, pseudonym, title*)

3. In an ——— Ford, like the knights of ——— times, the ——— suitor for the hand of the town widow rode forth. (*antiquated, elderly, olden*)

4. The ——— hadn't done any real ——— to the body tissues, though the ——— was considerable. (*damage, pain, wound*)

5. She was ——— though perhaps not ———. Her every motion was ———. (*beautiful, graceful, pretty*)

6. He ——— his goal in life when he ——— the 440-yard race. The coaches all agreed that he had ——— the victory. (*attained, earned, won*)

7. The circus people considered it a great ——— for the aerialists to attempt their daring ——— at every ———. (*achievement, feat, performance*)

8. A petty ——— led to a long and bitter ——— that brought ——— to the little town. (*feud, quarrel, strife*)

9. The ——— whistles and the ——— crowd made for a ——— celebration. (*boisterous, loud, shrill*)

10. His costume was so ——— and his manner of speaking so ——— that all of us considered the sight extremely ———. (*comical, funny, grotesque*)

## BOOKS OF SYNONYMS

Where can I go for help in discriminating synonyms? How can I learn the difference between *mental* and *intellectual, cogent* and *forceful?* If this chapter has led you to ask yourself these questions, it will have succeeded. There are many books which help in synonym discrimination. First of all, unabridged dictionaries, as well as many of the abridged, include at the end of the definitions, synonyms, with some discussion of the varying connotations. For example, *Webster's New International Dictionary* includes at the end of the definitions of the word *dry* the following synonyms: *uninteresting, insipid, vapid, sterile, dull, pointless, tiresome, fruitless, unprofitable*. In addition it distinguishes between the synonyms *dry, arid,* and *barren* by discussing them and including representative quotations from literature. The abridged edition, *Webster's Collegiate Dictionary,* includes all the synonyms listed, but discriminates between *dry* and *arid* only, and in less detail.

More useful for the student who is really interested in sharpening his word use are the special books of synonyms.

Some are merely lists of words. Others actually show how the words differ in use. Five useful books are listed below.

### Word Lists

*A Dictionary of Synonyms and Antonyms* — Joseph Devlin (World Book Company)

*Roget's Thesaurus of the English Language* — *in Dictionary Form* (many inexpensive editions)

### Synonym Discrimination

*Webster's Dictionary of Synonyms* (G. & C. Merriam Company)

*English Synonyms, Antonyms, and Prepositions* — James C. Fernald (Funk and Wagnalls)

Crabb's *English Synonyms* (Grosset and Dunlap)

For a discussion of dictionaries, see Chapter 4.

## How to Use a Book of Synonyms

Suppose you came across the following sentence in your reading: "Marjorie was an *amiable* young girl, but it was her sister Ellen who was the more *lovable*." Suppose, too, that you had always considered *amiable* and *lovable* interchangeable. How would you check your erroneous impression? You might check the meanings in a dictionary, preferably an unabridged, or you might go directly to a book of synonyms for a fuller discussion. The following excerpt from *Webster's Dictionary of Synonyms* on the opposite page will clarify their meanings.

The following hints will help you to read the excerpt intelligently:

1. Names in parentheses are authors quoted.

2. Passages in quotation marks have been taken from literature to indicate how the words have been used by those who set the standards of correctness.

3. *Ana.* at the bottom lists *analogous words*, words that are closely associated with *lovable* and *amiable*, though not synonymous. The suggestion, "see under REGARD," encourages further study of related words.

**lovable.** **Lovable, amiable** come into comparison only when the latter means, as the former invariably means, capable of inspiring affection or liking. **Lovable** is the more positive term, and implies warmth and sincerity of feeling and a definitely personal reaction. "I have never been able to love what was not *lovable* or hate what was not hateful out of deference for some general principle" (*Conrad*). "The wide sympathy with all that is human which is so *loveable* in Chaucer and Shakspere" (*J. R. Green*). **Amiable** (here compared only as applied to persons or things in their effect on another) often, especially in modern use, connotes little more than a definitely pleasant or agreeable (as opposed to a *distasteful* or *forbidding*) impression. "The philosopher Herbert Spencer . . . had the *amiable* trait in his character of an intense dislike to coercion" (*Shaw*). "Our modern appreciativeness is often only the *amiable* aspect of a fault—an undue tolerance for indeterminate enthusiasms and vapid emotionalism" (*Babbitt*).

*Ana.* Admired, respected, esteemed (see under REGARD, *n.*): idolized, adored, worshiped (see ADORE): attractive, alluring, charming, enchanting (see under ATTRACT): responsive, sympathetic, warm, warmhearted, \*tender. *Ant.* Hateful. — *Con.* Detestable, odious, abominable, abhorrent (see HATEFUL):  \*repugnant, repellent, distasteful, obnoxious.

4.  *Ant.* suggests the antonym, *hateful*, a word opposed in meaning to *lovable* and *amiable*.

5.  *Cont.* lists *contrasted words*, those that are not antonyms though somewhat opposite in meaning.

6.  The asterisk (*) next to a word like *tender* or *repugnant* indicates that the reader will find further synonym discrimination under those words.

ACTIVITY 12.  Studying Synonym Discrimination

By referring to the quoted excerpt from *Webster's Dictionary of Synonyms* answer the following questions:

1.  Which of the two terms is the stronger?
2.  Which is, in general, more complimentary? Why?
3.  Which is less personal?
4.  Which would you apply to a young puppy? Why?
5.  Why is *idolized* listed here? Why is it not listed in the paragraph itself?
6.  Why is *hateful* listed?

7. What is a *contrasted word?*

8. What words listed are probably discriminated in the body of the book?

9. Why does the name *Babbitt* appear in the paragraph?

10. How would you distinguish between *regard* and *adore?*

ACTIVITY 13. Studying Synonyms in Groups

By consulting a dictionary or a book of synonyms discuss the difference in meaning between the words in each of the following groups. Use each in a sentence to indicate your mastery of the word. Your teacher may wish to divide the class into several groups for this activity.

1. actor, impersonator, performer, player
2. adversary, antagonist, opponent
3. afflict, try, torment, torture
4. age, eon, epoch, era, period
5. angel, archangel, cherub, seraph
6. arena, circus, court, diamond, field, gridiron, ring, rink
7. associate, buddy, companion, comrade, crony, pal
8. bake, barbecue, broil, grill, roast
9. burn, char, scorch, sear, singe
10. busy, assiduous, diligent, industrious
11. care, anxiety, concern, solicitude, worry
12. change, alter, modify, vary
13. common, general, universal
14. compliment, adulation, flattery
15. conscientious, honorable, upright
16. covetous, acquisitive, greedy
17. deception, fraud, trickery
18. delete, cancel, blot out, obliterate
19. dismay, alarm, consternation, dread, horror
20. exchange, barter, interchange
21. explain, elucidate, interpret
22. falter, hesitate, vacillate, waver
23. gift, boon, favor, present
24. graphic, picturesque, vivid
25. haste, hurry, speed
26. impartial, fair, unbiased
27. inform, advertise, notify

28. internal, inner, interior
29. lack, need, require, want
30. like, enjoy, love, relish
31. meddle, interfere, tamper
32. museum, archives, gallery, library
33. neglect, ignore, omit, overlook
34. perfect, entire, intact, whole
35. posture, bearing, pose
36. quip, joke, witticism
37. rebound, recoil, reverberate
38. recover, recoup, regain, retrieve
39. revere, adore, venerate, worship
40. secret, clandestine, furtive, stealthy
41. sentence, condemn, doom
42. shelter, asylum, refuge, retreat, sanctuary
43. shy, bashful, coy, modest
44. skin, bark, hide, pelt, rind
45. slow, deliberate (*adj.*), leisurely
46. solitude, isolation, seclusion
47. steep, abrupt, sheer
48. stir, awaken, rally, rouse
49. support, advocate, uphold
50. trade, art, craft, handicraft, profession, vocation

# When Opposites Attract

## ANTONYMS

Feast or famine, friend or foe, ups and downs, to blow hot and cold — *all these commonplace expressions and phrases illustrate a tendency in our language to group antonyms together. An antonym is a word of opposite meaning, as* friend *is the opposite of* foe *and* hot *of* cold. *A word like* feast *may have both a synonym* — banquet — *and an antonym* — famine.

Antonyms are extremely useful. They help us to define; for example, "*blunt* means *not sharp*." They enrich our speech by introducing contrasts; "India is a land of unbelievable *poverty* and *wealth*." They help us to build vocabularies; for example, we can remember easily what *humility* means if we recall that it is the opposite of *pride*.

### ACTIVITY 1. Recognizing Antonyms

The following paragraph contains six pairs of antonyms. List five and supply a synonym for each word. One of the pairs is used as the example.

EXAMPLE: *long, short. Long* and *short* are antonyms, since they are opposite in meaning. A synonym for *long* might be *lengthy;* for *short, brief.*

*War and Peace* is one of the great novels of all times. Not only are the characters, strong and weak alike, of absorbing interest, but the historical background is accurate and exciting. The book describes Napoleon's bitter failure where he had hoped for success — on the approaches to Moscow. The long cold Russian nights and short, equally cold days soon cooled the hot ambitions of the would-be conqueror. The early fast invasion was matched by the inglorious slow retreat from the Russian capital. Like most conquerors Napoleon had considerd the people weak and found them strong. The book is well worth reading; indeed, many people consider it the best novel ever written.

## Pitfalls

Antonyms are not so easy to provide as are synonyms. There are two important pitfalls, as well as many minor ones. First of all, one word may have many antonyms, depending upon the way in which it is used. *Clear*, for example, is a word of many meanings. We may talk about a *clear* day, a *clear* conscience, or a *clear* style of writing. Obviously one antonym will not do for all of these. The antonym of the first use might be *overcast* or *cloudy;* of the second, it might be *troubled;* of the third, it might be *unintelligible*. No one antonym will serve for all uses of *clear*.

### Activity 2. Selecting Correct Antonyms

At the end of each sentence are three possible antonyms for the italicized word. Select the meaning that is opposite to the word as used in the sentence. Do not select a word that might be opposite in another sense. Add new words to your vocabulary notebook.

EXAMPLE: *He always felt gloomy as he heard the bells ringing in the new year*. (bright, cheerful, sunny)

The proper antonym here is *cheerful*. If *gloomy* were applied to a day, then the other antonyms, *bright* and *sunny*, might be used. Applied to a person it calls for the antonym *cheerful*.

1. The lions used in the circus are *tame*. (*fierce, inhuman, barbarous*)

2. Nearly four million workers were *idle*. (*active, alert, employed*)

3. The wax *melted* as the candle burned. (*froze, solidified, stuck*)

**Antonymous lions**

4. The meaning of that sentence is *obscure*. (*absolute, evident, famous*)

5. Robert Browning was an *obscure* poet during the early part of his writing career. (*absolute, evident, famous*)

6. Great writers have always been concerned with the power of *evil* in the world. (*friendliness, good, honesty*)

7. Fulton's steamboat was hailed as nothing short of *marvelous*. (*commonplace, contemptible, miserable*)

8. The Roman legions kept *order* throughout the Roman Empire. (*appeal, confusion, implore*)

9. By a *happy* coincidence the letter arrived just as we were leaving. (*dreary, unfortunate, sad*)

10. Everyone agreed that the umpire's decision was *fair*. (*stormy, unjust, ugly*)

To avoid the second pitfall, we must note that not all words have antonyms. Try to think of an antonym for each of the following words: *identify, glance, flag, journey, volume, greeting,* or *English*. There are no antonyms because the ideas do not admit of opposites. Some words have antonyms in one sense, but no antonyms in another. *Port* meaning *harbor* has no antonym, but *port* meaning the *left side* of a ship has the antonym *starboard*.

## ACTIVITY 3. Matching Antonyms

All but five of the words in column *A* have corresponding antonyms in column *B*. Match antonyms and indicate which of the words in *A* have no antonym.

| *A* | *B* |
|---|---|
| 1. early | a. late |
| 2. erect | b. negative |
| 3. firm | c. prone |
| 4. frank | d. flabby |
| 5. gay | e. reticent |
| 6. large | f. small |
| 7. machine | g. wrong |
| 8. news | h. miser |
| 9. parade | i. grave |
| 10. perceive | j. worthless |
| 11. positive | |
| 12. program | |
| 13. right | |
| 14. spendthrift | |
| 15. valuable | |

## ACTIVITY 4. Supplying Antonyms Without Using a Dictionary

Without using a dictionary this time supply an antonym for each of the following common words. Compare your list with your neighbor's. Your teacher might wish to make a game out of this by giving extra credit to the boys and girls in the row that finishes first and has a perfect score. See if your classmates supply you with new words for your vocabulary notebook.

| | | |
|---|---|---|
| 1. active | 11. in | 21. praise |
| 2. alive | 12. interior | 22. real |
| 3. calm | 13. joy | 23. scarce |
| 4. clean | 14. keen | 24. sweet |
| 5. commonplace | 15. knowledge | 25. top |
| 6. credit | 16. laugh | 26. victory |
| 7. east | 17. love | 27. wholesale |
| 8. fat | 18. majority | 28. wise |
| 9. find | 19. native | 29. young |
| 10. friendly | 20. new | 30. truth |

Activity 5. Choosing a Synonym or an Unrelated Word

In each group of three words in column *B*, one word is *not* opposed in meaning to the word in column *A*. Choose the one word and indicate whether it is a synonym or unrelated. Use the dictionary to check your selections.

EXAMPLE: *stout*      *lean, slender, portly*
             *loyal*      *false, clumsy, unfaithful*
In the first group, *portly* is not an antonym of *stout*, but a synonym. In the second group, *clumsy* is not an antonym of *loyal;* it is unrelated.

| A | B |
|---|---|
| 1. persist | falter, flinch, persevere |
| 2. establish | eradicate, evade, extirpate |
| 3. sadden | cheer, enliven, qualify |
| 4. scarcity | abundance, deficiency, plenty |
| 5. diminish | abbreviate, enlarge, increase |
| 6. remain | embarrass, emigrate, migrate |
| 7. crude | polished, refined, uncouth |
| 8. boldness | efficiency, shyness, timidity |
| 9. deny | acknowledge, admit, advise |
| 10. discord | accord, agreement, disagreement |

Activity 6. Supplying Synonyms and Antonyms

For each of the words numbered 1–20 supply from the word pool both a synonym and an antonym.

|  | Synonym | Antonym |
|---|---|---|
| EXAMPLE: *discourteous* | *rude* | *polite* |

### Word Pool

| | | | |
|---|---|---|---|
| abandon | combine | ease | limited |
| anguish | costly | easygoing | loquacious |
| answer | credulity | enlarge | majestic |
| appetizing | deathless | flat | mettlesome |
| arouse | decrease | ignoble | mortal |
| avoidable | divide | inescapable | often |
| broad | doubt | interrogate | peevish |

| recover | restrain | silent | uneven |
| resist | seldom | spiritless | worthless |
| respect | shame | tasteless | yield |

| | | | |
|---|---|---|---|
| 1. belief | 6. incite | 11. narrow | 16. separate (*verb*) |
| 2. distress | 7. increase | 12. noble | 17. spirited |
| 3. frequently | 8. inevitable | 13. precious | 18. submit |
| 4. honor | 9. irritable | 14. question | 19. talkative |
| 5. immortal | 10. level | 15. reclaim | 20. tasty |

Analogies: Boy is to girl as peacock is to . . . .

ACTIVITY 7. Playing the Game of Analogies

From the word pool select a word to complete each of the blanks. Look up the meaning of unfamiliar words.

EXAMPLE: *Mortal is to deathless as optimism is to* ———.

*Prestige is to authority as merge is to* ———.

In the first sentence *mortal* is the opposite of *deathless*, so a word opposite to *optimism* is needed, a word like *pessimism*. In the second sentence *prestige* is a synonym for *authority*, so a synonym for *merge* is needed; for example, *blend*. Of course, it is essential to know the first pair before you can solve the puzzle.

| | |
|---|---|
| accede | castigate |
| altruistic | haphazard |
| appertain | inept |
| arbiter | lavish |
| avid | onerous |

1. *Assay* is to *attempt* as *agree* is to ———.
2. *Terrified* is to *aghast* as *relate* is to ———.
3. *Languid* is to *energetic* as *selfish* is to ———.
4. *Atone* is to *expiate* as *punish* is to ———.
5. *Fastidious* is to *squeamish* as *burdensome* is to ———.
6. *Malevolent* is to *benevolent* as *indifferent* is to ———.
7. *Sluggish* is to *torpid* as *clumsy* is to ———.
8. *Festoon* is to *decoration* as *judge* is to ———.
9. *Obtuse* is to *blunt* as *hit-or-miss* is to ———.
10. *Obstinate* is to *yielding* as *sparing* is to ———.

# 13

# E Pluribus Unum

## FOREIGN PHRASES IN ENGLISH

*If you are told that you show* savoir-faire, *should you be insulted or flattered? If you speak* sotto voce, *are you giving away secrets, speaking softly, or repeating yourself? Is a writ of* habeas corpus *used in law, stock transactions, or insurance? When you order from the bill of fare at a restaurant, do you know the difference between* table d'hôte *and* à la carte? *Check each of the foregoing in a dictionary. Get the dictionary habit so that when you come across a foreign word or expression in your reading or listening, you will look it up. Many of these phrases have become so deeply impressed into our language that people find themselves handicapped if they don't know at least the common ones.*

ACTIVITY 1.  Checking the Meaning of Foreign Phrases
and Words

How many of the following are familiar to you? Match with the correct alternative. In the dictionary look up the meaning and *pronunciation* of each italicized word. (Some dictionaries include a list of foreign phrases at the end of the alphabet.) Add new words or phrases to your vocabulary notebook.

1. The *allegro* movement in a symphony is (*a*) slow (*b*) moderate (*c*) fast (*d*) sad (*e*) sometimes slow, sometimes fast

2. The phrase *corpus delicti* appears in (*a*) ballet (*b*) circuses (*c*) crime detection (*d*) gardening (*e*) construction

3. A *coiffure* is a kind of (*a*) coach (*b*) railroad depot (*c*) coat (*d*) headdress (*e*) disease

4. A *coup d'état* is (*a*) a sudden decisive move (*b*) a kind of wound dressing (*c*) a low shed (*d*) a state law (*e*) a style of decoration

5. A *gauche* person is (*a*) happy (*b*) awkward (*c*) clever (*d*) unpleasant (*e*) a skilled horseman

6. One who is *hors de combat* is (*a*) a cavalryman (*b*) out of action (*c*) cowardly (*d*) a mighty fighter (*e*) an officer

7. A *connoisseur* prides himself upon good (*a*) ability in sports (*b*) luck in gardening (*c*) taste (*d*) friends (*e*) foresight

8. *Leitmotif* is an expression used in (*a*) archery (*b*) finance (*c*) trade (*d*) jet propulsion (*e*) music

9. *Alma mater* is usually applied to (*a*) an old woman (*b*) a sports arena (*c*) a college (*d*) banking practices (*e*) a mother-in-law

10. *Lèse majesté* (or *lese majesty*) is a crime against (*a*) a sovereign (*b*) a minor (*c*) a relative (*d*) a landlord (*e*) a public utility

11. A *papier-mâché* mountain is usually seen (*a*) in the Alps (*b*) in the Rockies (*c*) on postcards (*d*) on the stage (*e*) in the Antarctic

12. A *per capita* tax is computed (*a*) by experts (*b*) on the basis of capital gains and losses (*c*) on the basis of real estate (*d*) for each individual (*e*) semiannually

13. One who is *persona non grata* is (*a*) popular (*b*) thankless (*c*) unwanted (*d*) careless (*e*) the life of the party

14. The *pièce de résistance* is (*a*) the main dish (*b*) an obstacle (*c*) a portion of vegetable (*d*) stubbornness (*e*) easy good nature

15. A *nom de plume* is often used by (*a*) an architect (*b*) a chicken raiser (*c*) a hat manufacturer (*d*) an author (*e*) a tree surgeon

16. *Pro rata* means the same as (*a*) moderately (*b*) proportionately (*c*) immediately (*d*) carefully (*e*) expensively

17. A *potpourri* is (*a*) a pan for cooking (*b*) a cream pitcher (*c*) a mixture (*d*) a dish (*e*) a spoon

18. A *tête-à-tête* is (*a*) a private conversation (*b*) a public gathering (*c*) a tea for four people (*d*) a rumor (*e*) good taste

19. A *sobriquet* is (*a*) a two-wheeled carriage (*b*) a seat at the opera (*c*) a nickname (*d*) a card game (*e*) a peasant dance

20. *Bas-relief* is a kind of (*a*) musical composition (*b*) French sport (*c*) sculpture (*d*) refreshment (*e*) entertainment area

## FOREIGN WORDS

Just as naturalized American citizens often retain foreign accents or other clues to their countries of origin, so words and phrases often retain strange pronunciations and spellings for a while. Throughout its history English has been steadily borrowing words from other lands, though borrowings of long ago have lost almost all their traces of "foreignness." The process by which foreign words are converted into English words is called Anglicizing, "making English." *Chauffeur*, for example, was once pronounced only as in French. Now it has a perfectly natural English pronunciation, with the accent on the first syllable. In time the spelling may change to conform more closely to the English pronunciation.

Many words, though, are still in the process of being absorbed into English. These tend to retain both the foreign spelling and

Monsieur Chauffeur' becomes Mister Chauf'feur.

the foreign pronunciation. Thus *entrepreneur,* a useful French word applied to those who assume the risks of business, is pronounced as though it were French, with the accent on the last syllable. *Entrepreneur* is a needed word, because the closest English equivalent, *undertaker*, has come to have an entirely different meaning.

Foreign words and phrases, in general, should be used only when there is no good English equivalent. Using foreign phrases merely to show off is always in poor taste. Using foreign words when they are obviously needed is a sign of culture. What English words could possibly take the place of these: *crochet, questionnaire, naive, rendezvous, ricochet?*

ACTIVITY 2.  Supplying Needed Foreign Words

Each of the blanks in the paragraph below is to be completed by selecting a word from the word pool. Justify your choice of the word selected by explaining the meaning of the word. Use the dictionary to check your answers.

| | |
|---|---|
| aplomb | passé |
| ballerina | première |
| debutante | repertoire |
| faux pas | résumé |
| matinee | roles |

The ———, while no longer in the ——— class, was certainly not ———. It would be a ——— to call her merely a ——— idol. In her ——— were some of the finest ——— ever given to a dancer of similar preparation. At the ——— of her latest production she carried herself with customary ———. The critics in giving a ——— of the performances again commended her artistry.

FOREIGN PHRASES

Phrases from other tongues are more likely than words to keep their original spelling and pronunciation. Many phrases have both interesting histories and present-day meanings. *Deus ex machina,* for example, is an expression for an unlikely coincidence, particularly in a novel or drama. Literally it means

Will that be à la carte or table d'hôte, sir?

"the god from the machine." In the old Greek drama, when problems were getting unusually tangled and there seemed no way to remove the obstacles, suddenly a god — Zeus, Apollo, or some other — would be lowered onto the stage from a kind of derrick. This "god from the machine" then proceeded to iron out all difficulties. Now the phrase is applied to any device that gets the characters out of their troubles through coincidence. The burning of Thornfield Hall in *Jane Eyre* is a kind of *deus ex machina*, for it allows Jane to marry Mr. Rochester.

*Laissez faire* is another phrase with an interesting history. Literally it means *let do*, that is, let people do what they want without interference. Originally it was used by economists to denote that business philosophy which emphasized freedom from all government controls. Now it is applied to any doctrine that would let things go on by themselves.

ACTIVITY 3. Matching Foreign Phrases
with English Equivalents

Match column *B* with column *A*. Consult the dictionary for the pronunciation and the meaning of each phrase. *Note:* column *B* may give a free interpretation of the spirit of the phrase rather than an exact, literal translation.

| A | | B | |
|---|---|---|---|
| 1. | carte blanche | a. | appetizer |
| 2. | cul de sac | b. | blind alley |
| 3. | dolce far niente | c. | cast |
| 4. | dramatis personae | d. | coolness |
| 5. | en masse | e. | face to face |
| 6. | esprit de corps | f. | for the time being |
| 7. | hara kiri | g. | in a body |
| 8. | hoi polloi | h. | leading lady |
| 9. | hors d'oeuvres | i. | group morale |
| 10. | modus operandi | j. | solid earth |
| 11. | prima donna | k. | suicide |
| 12. | pro tempore | l. | sweet idleness |
| 13. | sang-froid | m. | the mass of common people |
| 14. | terra firma | n. | unlimited power |
| 15. | vis-à-vis | o. | way of working |

## ABBREVIATIONS

Have you ever puzzled over the meanings of those strange abbreviations scattered through the pages of a book, initials like *i.e.*, or *e.g.?* Many of these are abbreviations of foreign phrases, like *id est* (*i.e.*) or *exempli gratia* (*e.g.*). You should know the meanings of the most common ones. Some dictionaries list them at the end of the alphabet.

| Abbreviations | Original Words | Meanings |
|---|---|---|
| cf. | *conferre* | compare |
| e.g. | *exempli gratia* | for example |
| et al. | *et alii* | and the others |
| etc. | *et cetera* | and so forth |
| ff. | —— | the following (usually applied to pages) |
| ibid. | *ibidem* | in the same place (used of quotations from books) |
| i.e. | *id est* | that is |
| op. cit. | *opere citato* | in the work cited (used of quotations from books) |
| q. v. | *quod vide* | which see (a reference, usually, to another book) |
| viz. | *videlicet* | namely |

ACTIVITY 4. Finding the Meanings of Foreign Words
and Phrases

In a dictionary, preferably unabridged, look up the meaning
and the pronunciation of the following words and phrases.

1. adagio
2. ad infinitum
3. ad nauseam
4. a fortiori
5. andante
6. a posteriori
7. a priori
8. apropos
9. arroyo
10. badinage
11. belles-lettres
12. bête noir
13. billet-doux
14. blasé
15. bona fide
16. bouillon
17. bravura

18. bric-a-brac
19. cache
20. carpe diem
21. chalet
22. clientele
23. clique
24. comme il faut
25. con brio
26. crescendo
27. debacle
28. debris
29. denouement
30. deo volente
31. double-entendre
32. ennui
33. entre nous
34. en route

35. ensemble
36. exposé
37. fait accompli
38. gratis
39. idée fixe
40. noblesse oblige
41. outré
42. pique
43. protégé
44. presto
45. pronto
46. quasi
47. reveille
48. seriatim
49. terra firma
50. tour de force
51. volte-face

# 14

# What's in a Name?

## PROPER NAMES IN ENGLISH

*When Vidkun Quisling turned traitor in the Nazi invasion of Norway, he added a new name to the English language.* Benedict Arnold *was once synonymous with traitor; now* quisling *has taken its place. The process is an old one. Names of famous places, persons, characters, in literature have been enriching English for hundreds of years.*

## STORIES OF FAMOUS NAMES

Many fascinating stories lie behind these language additions. *Gerrymander*, for example, means an unfair division of election districts so as to give one political party an advantage. The word originated in Massachusetts when the party of Governor Elbridge Gerry divided Essex County to retain their own grip on the votes. The division looked something like a dragon. A bystander commented, "Looks like a salamander to me"; whereupon a wit retorted, "More like a gerrymander," and the name stuck!

Machiavelli was a Renaissance statesman who believed that a strong central government should be maintained by any means, no matter how unscrupulous. *Machiavellian* cunning, in present-day speech, is cleverness without principle. Another interesting word is *chauvinism*. Nicolas Chauvin was a soldier of Napoleon, so outspoken in his pledges of loyalty that his comrades began to poke fun at him. Thus *chauvinism* came to mean exaggerated patriotism.

*Dunce* would be the last word, one would think, to associate with *scholar!* During the Middle Ages the enemies of Duns Scotus, philosopher, scornfully labeled his followers *Dunsmen.* From the ridicule came our present word *dunce.* *Vandalism* comes from the tribe of Vandals, whose reputation for destroying everything in their path terrified the ancient world. Word backgrounds are fascinating to study. Become word-curious and enjoy yourself while learning.

### ACTIVITY 1. Vocabulary Test Based upon Names

Each of the italicized words below is derived from the name of a person. After you have taken the test, check your answers in a good dictionary and find the stories behind the names. Unabridged dictionaries explain the origin of each word listed. Add new words to your vocabulary notebook.

1. If you received something labeled *Chippendale*, you would (*a*) take it for a walk (*b*) drive it around the block (*c*) use it as fish bait (*d*) make a salad out of it (*e*) sit on it

2. Mary bought a *lavaliere.* She wore it (*a*) on her ankle (*b*) on her arm (*c*) around her neck (*d*) around her waist (*e*) on her finger

3. A *mackinaw* is good protection against (*a*) fire (*b*) accident (*c*) cold (*d*) indigestion (*e*) sour disposition

4. The *Mercator's* projection of the world (*a*) is a globe (*b*) centers on the North Pole (*c*) was invented for the air age (*d*) has straight, parallel lines for longitude and latitude (*e*) shows only the Western Hemisphere

5. In astronomy the *Ptolemaic* system (*a*) disregarded all the planets (*b*) declared the sun revolves about the earth (*c*) tried to explain comets (*d*) studied the tides (*e*) declared the earth revolves round the sun

6. *Wedgwood* ware should be found (*a*) in the workshop (*b*) on the table (*c*) in an igloo (*d*) on the farm (*e*) in a scientific laboratory

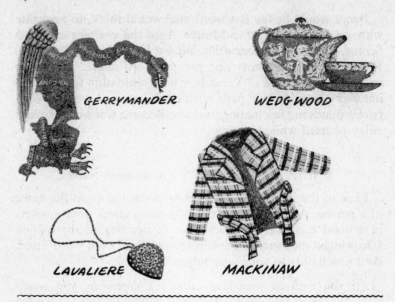

GERRYMANDER    WEDGWOOD

LAVALIERE    MACKINAW

**What are the stories behind these names?**

7. *Sheraton* is the name of  (*a*) a famous race horse  (*b*) a wine  (*c*) a kind of furniture  (*d*) a kind of glassware  (*e*) a breed of sheep

8. If someone said, "I see you're growing *sideburns*," you'd probably  (*a*) offer him some to eat  (*b*) visit the nearest barber  (*c*) get out the hedge clippers  (*d*) sprinkle them with water  (*e*) pull them out by the roots

9. If you were looking at a book in *Braille*, you'd see  (*a*) beautiful illustrations  (*b*) blank notebook paper  (*c*) raised dots  (*d*) words in a foreign tongue  (*e*) many woodcuts

10. *Pinchbeck* jewelry is  (*a*) expensive  (*b*) cheap  (*c*) semiprecious  (*d*) made of copper  (*e*) made with a safety clasp

11. If you worked for a *martinet*, you would  (*a*) resent his unreasonable discipline  (*b*) enjoy his singing at his work  (*c*) try to help him eliminate careless errors  (*d*) groan at his strained joking  (*e*) wish that he'd be more conscientious

12. If someone cried in London, "There's a *bobby*," he would be pointing to (*a*) a policeman (*b*) a hairpin (*c*) a special type of footwear (*d*) a Royal Guardsman (*e*) a fish peddler

13. As a picture a *silhouette* is likely to be (*a*) a failure (*b*) an oil painting (*c*) a lithograph (*d*) a profile (*e*) a masterpiece

14. You would hope to find *solons* in the (*a*) swimming pool (*b*) zoo (*c*) legislature (*d*) farmyard (*e*) kindergarten

15. When *mavericks* grow up, they become (*a*) horses (*b*) cattle (*c*) baseball players (*d*) writers (*e*) specialists

## NAMES FROM THE BIBLE

Two boys were playing together in the warm April sun. A man watching them declared to his friend, "Those two are like David and Jonathan." Those familiar with the Bible recognize in his remarks an allusion to the beautiful Biblical friendship of Jonathan, son of Saul, and David, slayer of Goliath. Biblical words and references abound in English. You can find explanations in the dictionary for most that you come across.

### ACTIVITY 2. Studying Words from the Bible

After you have taken the test, check your answers and the stories behind the names.

1. A *jeremiad* is a tale of (*a*) happiness (*b*) exaltation (*c*) woe (*d*) conquest (*e*) wickedness

2. A *good Samaritan* is (*a*) self-righteous (*b*) unusually clever (*c*) generous (*d*) evil (*e*) indifferent to suffering

3. A *Methuselah* is unusually (*a*) spry (*b*) near-sighted (*c*) intelligent (*d*) old (*e*) religious

4. A *Cain* is a (*a*) fisherman (*b*) farmer (*c*) murderer (*d*) philosopher (*e*) democrat

5. An *Ishmael* is (*a*) an outcast (*b*) a navigator (*c*) a friend in need (*d*) a laborer (*e*) a wealthy man

6. A *babel* is (*a*) an animal (*b*) a confusion of languages (*c*) a wall (*d*) a fruit (*e*) a war

7. A *Jonah* (*a*) brings good luck (*b*) brings bad luck (*c*) sings beautifully (*d*) runs swiftly (*e*) is a coward

8. A *Judas* is (*a*) a tyrant (*b*) a political leader (*c*) a general (*d*) a traitor (*e*) a friend of the poor

9. A *Samson* is (*a*) unmarried (*b*) bald (*c*) powerful (*d*) stupid (*e*) an awkward person

10. When a person refers to a city as a *Sodom*, he is emphasizing its (*a*) excellent water supply (*b*) fine amusements (*c*) wickedness (*d*) outstanding educational accomplishments (*e*) desirability as a home site

## NAMES FROM ANCIENT GREECE AND ROME

When scientists derived two new elements from their experiments with uranium for atomic energy, they named them *neptunium* and *plutonium* after the two planets which lie beyond Uranus in our solar system. These planets had been named after Greek and Roman gods, following the tradition in which all the other planets had acquired their names. Greek and Roman gods, heroes, places, and mythical personages have contributed a sizable number of words to English. How many can you identify?

### ACTIVITY 3. Studying Words from Greece and Rome

After you have matched column *B* with column *A*, look up the origin of all words in column *A*.

| A | B |
|---|---|
| 1. calliope | a. brief |
| 2. epicurean | b. changeable |
| 3. hector | c. devoted to pleasure |
| 4. laconic | d. disdainful |
| 5. mausoleum | e. hardy |
| 6. myrmidon | f. loud-voiced |
| 7. protean | g. loyal subordinate |
| 8. sardonic | h. organ |
| 9. spartan | i. tomb |
| 10. stentorian | j. torment |

ACTIVITY 4. Studying Greek and Roman Names

A name derived from Greek or Roman life or mythology can be found in each of the following italicized words. Define the word and trace its origin. Can you tell the story of each personage?

1. Have you purchased a post-war *atlas?*
2. Mr. Graves was appointed *mentor* of the track team.
3. A cry of "Fire!" caused a *panic* in the crowded theater.
4. The battle, though favorably reported, was in reality a *Pyrrhic* victory.
5. *Cereals* were sent to the hungry sufferers.
6. The eruption of Krakatoa was one of the most tremendous *volcanic* explosions in recorded history.
7. The speaker used the *Socratic* method to clarify his point.
8. In his home town he was looked upon as a *Croesus*.
9. His policies were *procrustean* in their inflexibility.
10. The nation unwisely disregarded the warnings of its own *Cassandras*.

ACTIVITY 5. Finding Mythological Allusions

This is for those who like mythology. Below is a trick paragraph artificially constructed to test you. In it are all the mythological allusions listed below. How many can you explain?

goddess of the dawn
goddess of the moon
goddess of the rainbow
goddesses of vengeance
god of beginnings
god of love
god of sleep (2)
god of war
god of wealth
mother of the gods
giants before Zeus
one who held the world
   on his shoulders
morning star
Muses
Muse of dancing
wife to the god of love
enchantress
   (from the *Odyssey*)
forgetful dreamers
wife of Odysseus

One day in *January*, along the very route taken by the *Titanic* in crossing the *Atlantic*, *Diana* looked in vain through the fog for the expected *auroral* display. The sea, *furiously* churning, lacked the *phosphorescence* of the tropics; yet it exerted a *hypnotic* fascination over the *Junoesque* observer. Inside the ballroom the lights, *iridescent* and multicolored, cast an ever-changing *mosaic* upon the floor. Since *martial* music scarcely lent itself to *terpsichorean* art, dreamy waltzes converted the dancers into *lotus-eaters*, lulled as if by *morphine*. For a time the *cupidity* of even the most obvious *plutocrat* was forgotten. Our heroine, more a faithful *Penelope* than a *Circe*, shuddered as though with a *psychic* foreshadowing of disaster.

## DAYS OF THE WEEK

Names from Scandinavian mythology have been embedded in our language, too; four days of the week have been named for Norse deities. Here is the complete listing.

> Sunday: day of the sun
> Monday: day of the moon
> Tuesday: day of Tiw, or Tyr, Norse god of battles
> Wednesday: day of Woden, chief of Norse gods
> Thursday: day of Thor, Norse god of thunder
> Friday: day of Freyja, Norse goddess of beauty
> Saturday: day of Saturn, Roman god of harvests

## SCIENCE AND INVENTION

Louis Pasteur's contributions to science and the prevention of disease have been told dramatically in de Kruif's *Microbe Hunters*. However, even more nearly permanent recognition is guaranteed Pasteur, for his name has been converted into an English word, *pasteurization*. Here is a kind of immortality more lasting than most monuments, for Pasteur's name will endure in popular speech. Some scientists, like Pasteur, and inventors, like Bunsen, have given their names to processes or inventions that have benefited mankind. Others, like Guillotin and Shrapnel, have contributed words that describe things hateful. Those who are associated with things outstandingly good — or pre-eminently bad — have a chance to give their own names to the language. In some words the retention of the capital reminds us of the persons honored; for example, *Roentgen ray*. Other words, like *macadam*, are less obvious.

ACTIVITY 6. Studying Words and Inventors

Look up the meaning and the derivation of each of the following names.

1. brougham
2. daguerreotype
3. derrick
4. diesel
5. Ferris wheel

6. hansom
7. macadam
8. mercerize
9. mesmerism
10. sandwich

ACTIVITY 7. Studying Words and Men of Science

Students of physics may enjoy this activity. Look up the meaning and the derivation of each of the following words. Why has it been said that science is international?

1. ampere
2. coulomb
3. Fahrenheit
4. farad
5. galvanize

6. joule
7. maxwell
8. ohm
9. volt
10. watt

## FLOWER NAMES

Many proper names are associated with common flowers. All the following flower names have proper names concealed within them. These, too, are from many nations.

begonia
camellia
dahlia
fuchsia
gardenia

gentian
magnolia
poinsettia
wisteria
zinnia

## WORDS FROM LITERATURE

In Cervantes' *Don Quixote* the principal character is forever seeking to do brave deeds of chivalry. Yet somehow the good deeds backfire, partly because the good old knight's vision is somewhat imperfect. No doubt you will recall the famous

**Don Quixote acting quixotically.**

episode of his attack on the windmills. In English the word *quixotic* means *idealistic*, *well-intentioned*, but *impractical*, like Don Quixote himself. Many other literary characters have given their names to our language.

ACTIVITY 8. Studying Words from Literature

With the assistance of the dictionary match column *B* with column *A*. Tell from what literary work each word has been chosen.

| *A* | *B* |
|---|---|
| 1. Beau Brummell | a. cruel taskmaster |
| 2. benedict | b. dude |
| 3. Dr. Watson | c. faithful assistant |
| 4. lilliputian | d. greedy, mean old man |
| 5. Pickwickian | e. hypocrite |
| 6. Romeo | f. lover |
| 7. Scrooge | g. married man |
| 8. Simon Legree | h. perfect, visionary |
| 9. Tartuffe | i. simple, goodhearted |
| 10. utopian | j. tiny |

# 15

# At Your Service

## VOCABULARY FOR SCHOOL USE

*In a recent study of the vocabulary power of college students, a Kansan professor found her students woefully inadequate. She asked her students to define* plebiscite, sovereignty, federation, *and* repudiate. *Though the words had been used over and over again in college courses, the students averaged only about 53%. Instead of clear-cut definitions they presented hazy, inaccurate, indefinite explanations. They called* plebiscite *a petition, document, slave, city person, lowest class, even the* Gallup Poll. *This word and the others the students should have been able to define.*

## A PLAN OF ACTION

To prevent yourself from being as disappointing a potential citizen, follow the following suggestions.

1. Keep a vocabulary notebook. See suggestions on pages 12–14.
2. Ask for discussion in class of words whose exact meanings are not clear to you.
3. Use lists of words at the ends of chapters. Often textbooks review new and unfamiliar words at the close of each unit.
4. Use the glossary if the book has one. A glossary is a vocabulary list usually at the end of the book. Often this section will clear up many of your incorrect ideas.
5. Don't be content with vague conceptions of important words. Curiosity about words pays dividends, social and financial as well as intellectual.

## SPECIAL USES

Look for special uses of common words. The word *harmony*, for example, has a broad general meaning applicable to many life situations. "Harmony prevailed at the council table." It has specialized meanings, too. In drawing it has a particular technical meaning; in music it has another. There is some similarity among all three, but know the differences.

The rest of this chapter will be devoted to a number of vocabulary quizzes in certain high school subjects. A few key words have been chosen from each field. By taking these tests you can get a fair idea of your vocabulary quotient in each subject. Be sure to add new words to your vocabulary notebook.

### ACTIVITY 1. Quiz in General Science Vocabulary

Select the correct alternative for each italicized word or complete each sentence with the correct alternative.

1. Oxygen supports *combustion*.

   (*a*) explosion    (*b*) burning    (*c*) suffocation    (*d*) reaction (*e*) combination of elements

2. Light is *diffused* by indirect lighting.

   (*a*) spread    (*b*) increased    (*c*) decreased    (*d*) concentrated (*e*) distorted

3. A *barometer* is used to measure

   (*a*) temperature    (*b*) wind velocity    (*c*) wind direction    (*d*) air pressure    (*e*) magnetism

4. They used a *pneumatic* drill for the purpose.

   (*a*) oil    (*b*) water    (*c*) air    (*d*) dentist's    (*e*) powerful

5. The Nile leaves behind a thick coat of *loam* after it overflows.

   (*a*) sand    (*b*) soil    (*c*) muddy water    (*d*) gravel    (*e*) oil

6. The land desperately needed *irrigation*.

   (*a*) cultivation    (*b*) rotation of crops    (*c*) supplying with water (*d*) plowing    (*e*) harvesting

7. He added *humus* to the soil.

   (*a*) decayed vegetable matter (*b*) lime (*c*) chemicals (*d*) water (*e*) clay

8. Australia suffered a severe *drought*.

   (*a*) storm (*b*) earthquake (*c*) tidal wave (*d*) lack of rain (*e*) flood

9. The substance prevented *coagulation* of the blood.

   (*a*) purification (*b*) pumping (*c*) circulation (*d*) clotting (*e*) flowing

10. The object was *immersed* in water.

    (*a*) dissolved (*b*) agitated (*c*) replaced (*d*) plunged (*e*) visible

11. Atomic energy is practically *inexhaustible*.

    (*a*) unfailing (*b*) powerful (*c*) controllable (*d*) uncontrollable (*e*) recently discovered

12. The professor lectured on *nutrients*.

    (*a*) foods (*b*) factors influencing climate (*c*) chemical elements (*d*) one-celled animals (*e*) bacteria

13. A blotter is composed of countless *capillary* tubes.

    (*a*) hair-like (*b*) closed (*c*) test (*d*) formed with rim or cap (*e*) wide

14. *Perennial* plants live for

    (*a*) -ever (*b*) many years (*c*) two years (*d*) one year (*e*) part of a season

15. *Meteorology* is the study of

    (*a*) plants (*b*) chemicals (*c*) animals (*d*) weather (*e*) astronomy

16. The sun's rays struck New York *obliquely*.

    (*a*) occasionally (*b*) at an angle (*c*) through the fog (*d*) perpendicularly (*e*) at sunset

17. *Aneroid* barometers

   (*a*) contain mercury  (*b*) contain alcohol  (*c*) contain no liquid
   (*d*) are not movable  (*e*) give temperature readings

18. The *retina* is a portion of

   (*a*) the ear  (*b*) the digestive system  (*c*) the respiratory system
   (*d*) the eye  (*e*) the circulatory system

19. The carbon particles cause the current to *fluctuate*.

   (*a*) flow evenly  (*b*) stop  (*c*) rise and fall  (*d*) increase steadily
   (*e*) decrease gradually

20. *Anemometers* measure

   (*a*) wind velocity  (*b*) air pressure  (*c*) heat content  (*d*) electric
   current  (*e*) electric voltage

ACTIVITY 2.  Checking General Science Vocabulary

How many of the following common terms in general science
can you define?

| | | |
|---|---|---|
| 1. aeration | 15. enzyme | 28. oxidation |
| 2. artery | 16. epidemic | 29. physiography |
| 3. atom | 17. focus | 30. porous |
| 4. atomizer | 18. friction | 31. pressure |
| 5. chlorophyll | 19. humidity | 32. prism |
| 6. concave | 20. insoluble | 33. protoplasm |
| 7. convection | 21. larva | 34. protozoa |
| 8. convex | 22. metamorphosis | 35. refraction |
| 9. corona | 23. microscopy | 36. refrigerant |
| 10. diaphragm | 24. molecule | 37. transformer |
| 11. dynamo | 25. opaque | 38. translucent |
| 12. electromagnet | 26. organism | 39. tropism |
| 13. electron | 27. osmosis | 40. turbine |
| 14. embryo | | |

ACTIVITY 3.  Distinguishing Terms in Art

Show by clear explanation that you can distinguish between
the words in each of the following pairs.

**Painting or caricature?**

| | |
|---|---|
| caricature, painting | modeling, carving |
| conventionalization, realism | repetition, rhythm |
| illustrator, cartoonist | symmetry, asymmetry |
| impressionism, surrealism | terra cotta, ceramics |
| lettering, printing | tint, shade |

## Activity 4. Matching Terms in Music

Each word in column *A* is associated with a word or group of words in column *B*. How many can you match properly?

| A | B |
|---|---|
| 1. cello | a. woodwind |
| 2. clarinet | b. brass |
| 3. concerto | c. percussion |
| 4. cymbals | d. strings |
| 5. opera | e. male voice |
| 6. operetta | f. female voice |
| 7. soprano | g. features full orchestra |
| 8. symphony | h. features solo instrument and full orchestra |
| 9. tenor | i. music drama |
| 10. trumpet | j. light music drama |

### Activity 5. Matching Terms in History

Match column *B* with column *A*.

| A | B |
|---|---|
| 1. belligerent | a. aggressive foreign policy |
| 2. bourgeoisie | b. agreement |
| 3. caucus | c. direct popular vote |
| 4. coalition | d. extension of national power |
| 5. confiscate | e. goods prohibited from import or export |
| 6. conservation | f. government grant |
| 7. contraband | g. middle class |
| 8. enfranchise | h. one at war |
| 9. imperialism | i. political meeting |
| 10. insurrection | j. preservation of natural resources |
| 11. jingoism | k. rebellion |
| 12. jurisdiction | l. right to exercise legal authority |
| 13. pact | m. right to vote |
| 14. referendum | n. peasant bound to soil |
| 15. regime | o. state with one political party |
| 16. secede | p. system of government |
| 17. serf | q. temporary alliance |
| 18. subsidy | r. to give the right to vote |
| 19. suffrage | s. to take private property for public use |
| 20. totalitarianism | t. withdraw |

### Activity 6. Vocabulary Quiz in Economics

Select the correct alternative for each italicized word.

1. *barter* (*a*) purchasing power (*b*) larceny (*c*) devaluation of currency (*d*) exchange without the use of money (*e*) preferred stock

2. *amortization* (*a*) inflation (*b*) depression (*c*) voluntary association of a city's banks (*d*) payment on principal of a debt (*e*) setting up of a corporation

3. *assets* (*a*) opposite of liabilities (*b*) same as liabilities (*c*) broker's loan (*d*) cartels (*e*) devalued bonds

4. *depreciation* (*a*) overcharge (*b*) decrease in value (*c*) increase in value (*d*) appreciation (*e*) arbitration

5. *dividend* (*a*) insurance premium (*b*) return for investment (*c*) maintenance costs (*d*) additional charge (*e*) reserves

6. *entrepreneur* (*a*) bank president (*b*) operator of a vehicle (*c*) doorman (*d*) clerk (*e*) owner of a business

7. *injunction* (*a*) part of speech (*b*) court restraining order (*c*) a joining (*d*) a form of rent (*e*) railroad terminus

8. *mediation* (*a*) settlement of dispute by third party (*b*) refusal to arbitrate (*c*) choosing a safe, middle-of-the-road plan (*d*) trade association (*e*) stock watering

9. *increment* (*a*) increase (*b*) decrease (*c*) repetition (*d*) customs duty (*e*) unemployment

10. *expenditure* (*a*) credit (*b*) something spent (*c*) tax (*d*) internal revenue (*e*) exchange

# 16

# When Guessing Helps

## UNDERSTANDING WORDS FROM CONTEXT

*What is the size of your vocabulary? Is it under par — about 8000 words? Or is it well above par — 20,000 words or more? If you have faithfully followed the suggestions in this book, have become word-curious, and have kept a vocabulary notebook, the chances are good that you are on your way toward acquiring a superior vocabulary. One authority estimates a vocabulary of 50,000 words as necessary to understand a good newspaper such as the* New York Times *or the* New York Herald Tribune. *As an adult will you be able to meet this requirement?*

*Obviously you have not looked up in the dictionary all the words you know. How then did you acquire most of them? The answer lies in reading and listening. Just as we can get a rough estimate of property values by examining surroundings, so we can get an idea of word meanings by examining words in their surroundings.*

## WORDS IN CONTEXT

Define *paucity*. Standing alone, it's a rather difficult word to define, isn't it? Now let's look at it in a sentence. "The *paucity* of good fiction this season has sent me back to the successes of other years in search of good reading." Does the illustrative sentence help you to guess at the meaning of *paucity*? Of course. We call the words surrounding *paucity* its context. (Pages 232–241 present a discussion of context from another point of view.) Many contexts help us to add words to our vocabulary. It is always wise, however, to look up the meaning of a new word in the dictionary, if only to verify a guess.

## WHEN CONTEXTS DO NOT HELP

"Herb was dilatory by nature." Can you guess at the meaning of *dilatory* by examining the context? Here there are no clues, and the context is of little use.

"Herb's *dilatory* habits always caused him to miss trains, be late for engagements, and annoy his friends." This sentence provides a context that enables us to guess that *dilatory* has something to do with *tardiness, being late, putting things off*.

## BE A WORD DETECTIVE!

The next time you meet an unfamiliar word examine its neighbors in the sentence. Look for clues. There are at least five ways in which a word's context may give you the meaning of the word itself.

### *Elaboration*

Suppose you came across the sentence, "The early woodsmen recklessly *denuded* the rich forests, stripping them of the finest trees." If the sentence had stopped at forests, you might be stumped for the meaning of *denuded*. However, the additional words, *stripping them of the finest trees*, present an important clue to the meaning of *denuded* by presenting additional information. Thus *denude* means *lay bare*.

ACTIVITY 1.  Guessing at Meanings through Elaboration

For each italicized word, select the correct alternative from the words that follow. Add new words to your vocabulary notebook.

1. Michael was a *brawny* longshoreman, able to toss around a one-hundred-pound bale with ease.

(*a*) old  (*b*) gray-haired  (*c*) marine  (*d*) muscular  (*e*) tall

2. The orchestra played a *medley* of songs including all the melodies from Act One of a famous operetta.

(*a*) symphony  (*b*) mixture  (*c*) concerto  (*d*) repetition
(*e*) serious collection

3. Jackson had the reputation of being a *bigot*, intolerant of all faiths and opinions other than his own.

(*a*) narrow-minded person (*b*) unbeliever (*c*) atheist (*d*) politician (*e*) enemy

4. The aviator several times placed his life in *jeopardy*, volunteering for the most perilous assignments.

(*a*) isolation  (*b*) danger  (*c*) security  (*d*) cowardly safety
(*e*) an airplane

5. Mason remained *adamant*, refusing to budge an inch from the position he had taken.

(*a*) bitter  (*b*) careless  (*c*) unyielding  (*d*) unpleasant  (*e*) vicious

6. David proved to be a *wily* opponent, cleverly taking advantage of every mistake.

(*a*) ferocious  (*b*) crafty  (*c*) fair  (*d*) unwise  (*e*) frightful

7. After his first outburst, the bull proved *tractable* enough, following his master meekly.

(*a*) wild  (*b*) colorful  (*c*) untamed  (*d*) angry  (*e*) easily handled

8. Henrietta claimed to be *omniscient*, because she heard all the news immediately from the town gossips.

(*a*) all-knowing  (*b*) curious  (*c*) indifferent  (*d*) lively
(*e*) vigorous

9. He always spoke *succinctly*, never wasting a syllable on nonessentials.

(*a*) intelligently (*b*) pointedly and briefly (*c*) loosely, though briefly (*d*) pointedly, though at length (*e*) off the topic

10. After the *carnage* had ended, observers counted thousands of victims.

(*a*) circus  (*b*) medicine show  (*c*) slaughter  (*d*) feast
(*e*) parade

### Contrast

"Frieda's usual disposition was not *morose* but gay." What is the clue to the meaning of *morose* here? Obviously the answer lies in the words *but gay*, for they tell us that *morose* must be the opposite of *gay*. Often word meanings are suggested by contrast.

ACTIVITY 2.  Guessing at Meanings through Contrast

For each italicized word select a synonym from the word pool.

| | |
|---|---|
| abundance | sea |
| baffle | silent |
| force | uncomplimentary |
| haughty | useless |
| noisy | wicked |

1. When Maxwell didn't agree freely to the plan, the others tried to *coerce* him.
2. The little man's efforts in a democracy are far from *futile*, for he can have an effective voice in his own government.
3. Roosevelt always enjoyed conversation, but Coolidge remained fairly *taciturn*.
4. Did he *balk* your efforts or try to help?
5. *Nautical* miles are different from land miles.
6. Whether his remarks be complimentary or *derogatory*, I intend to challenge him.
7. Sometimes the class is as quiet as can be; at other times it is a *vociferous* group of enthusiastic actors and public speakers.
8. Good rains bring a *profusion* of crops; scanty rains bring famine.
9. The *nefarious* plottings of Benson were upset by the fortunate opposition of the hero.
10. Far from being *arrogant*, he was humble in his dealings with others.

### Pairing Words Closely Related

If you had but a vague idea of the meaning of *pseudonym*, you'd get a good idea from a sentence like this. "Nicknames, pseudonyms, pen names — all reveal a fondness for changing one's identity and personality." The coupling of *pseudonym* with the more familiar *pen name* and *nickname* is a first-rate clue. The rest of the sentence clinches the definition: *an assumed name.*

### Activity 3. Guessing at Meanings through Closely Related Words

From the hints given guess at the meaning of each of the italicized words. Check your definitions.

1. Constant *bickering* and disagreeable squabbling spoiled their evenings together.
2. The audience's *acclamation* and wild applause gratified the artist.
3. All Scrooge's actions were mean and *despicable.*
4. The treasurer's reports were *concise* and to the point.
5. The lawyer *demurred*, disapproving the plan suggested.
6. Browning's Duchess was always *affable* and friendly to everyone.
7. The comedian was an excellent *mimic*, able to imitate many different radio voices.
8. The mountain climb proved too *arduous* and difficult for the women in the party.
9. They tried to *salvage* the sunken hull and save the metal plates.
10. The child lived partly in *reveries* and daydreams.

### Concealed Definition

Often the definition of a particular word is buried in the sentence in which it appears. "The last two *biennial* elections for governor were held in 1944 and 1946." Elections held in 1944 and 1946 must be held *every two years*. Indeed, that is the meaning of *biennial* itself: the definition of the word is hidden in the sentence. Many sentences provide such definitions.

ACTIVITY 4. Guessing at Meanings through
Concealed Definitions

For each italicized word select a synonym from the word
pool.

| | |
|---|---|
| assisting | mild |
| associate | pain-deadener |
| healthful | self-denial |
| liberal | sickness of the stomach |
| mark with spots | support |

1. An *accomplice* is as guilty as the actual criminal, even though
he may assist only before or after the crime.

2. To be *lenient* with the faults of others is to be gentle with one's
own.

3. Voluntary *abstinence* from bad habits is the best training in
self-control.

4. *Bolster* the school morale; support your team.

5. Those who are *bountiful* in one respect are usually generous
in others.

6. *Auxiliary* groups will aid the main units.

7. To *mottle* a room dip your sponge gently into the paint and
touch it to the wall at regular intervals.

8. *Nausea*, originally applied only to "seasickness," is now a
general term.

9. After he had been given an *anesthetic*, he lost all sensations
during the operation.

10. In the *salubrious* climate of southern California he soon re-
gained his physical well-being.

## The Meaning of the Sentence as a Whole

"Jesse James *perpetrated* many crimes." In this sentence we
find no elaboration, no definition, pairing, or contrast; yet we
can guess reasonably and intelligently at the meaning of *perpetrated*. What word can be substituted for it? Obviously we
need a word like *commit*. *Perpetrate*, then, must mean about
the same as *commit*. Actions can provide context, too. If Dad
takes Billy's candy away, saying, "I'm depriving you of your
candy," Billy soon learns the meaning of *deprive*.

ACTIVITY 5. Guessing at Meanings through Sentence Context

For each italicized word select a synonym from the word pool.

| | |
|---|---|
| canceled | forerunner |
| catching | returned like for like |
| disappointment | soothed |
| discouraged | stopping |
| distorted face | workable |

**Help! Police!**                    **Encore!**
**Context makes all the difference.**

1. He couldn't conceal his *chagrin* at not finding John at home.
2. The card partly *assuaged* his grief.
3. Ben made a *grimace* when he heard the unpleasant news.
4. The robin has always been the traditional *harbinger* of spring.
5. The plan seemed *feasible*, so they put it into operation.
6. After Teddy slapped Billy, Billy *retaliated* quickly.
7. Do not go near anyone with a *contagious* disease.
8. The contract was *annulled* because of obvious disagreements.
9. There must be no *cessation* in our war upon tuberculosis.
10. Edison was not *disheartened* by failure.

ACTIVITY 6. Guessing at Meanings through Context

This activity includes all the methods suggested above. From the word pool select a word to replace each italicized word. For extra credit, tell which method was used.

| deceit | hateful | overcrowding | soaked |
|--------|---------|--------------|--------|
| equivalent | hurtful | overelaborate | timid |
| excessive | made poor | peculiarities | turned aside |
| fortress | nobody | pierced | wearing away |
| harsh | noisy speech | punishment | yellowish |

1. They stormed the *citadel* with bows and arrows.

2. There was such *congestion* in the halls that members could scarcely move.

3. The tax plan of the nobles *impoverished* the peasantry, draining away all wealth and many necessities.

4. Soil *erosion* stripped the topsoil from some of our richest land.

5. Far from being *diffident*, he has boldly stepped into the limelight.

6. The tips of the shoes were *perforated*, the holes being at regular intervals.

7. The northeast winters were *rigorous* and severe to the newcomer.

8. After long confinement in the dungeon he emerged with thin frame and *sallow* complexion.

9. He rushed into the house from the storm, his clothing thoroughly *saturated*.

10. The mob growled menacingly as they listened to the speaker's unrestrained *harangue*.

11. The theft from the poor widow made the crime even more *heinous*.

12. The escaping fumes were not *noxious* but actually beneficial to the animals in the laboratory.

13. Despite Thomson's odd *quirks*, people are very fond of him.

14. The carved ceiling was too *ornate*, displeasing in its lack of simplicity.

15. Jonathan never once *deviated* from the course he had set for himself early in life.

16. Because of his own high standards of morality, Murchison spurned the *duplicity* of his comrades.

17. The trader had a virtual monopoly of salt, and charged *exorbitant* prices for it.

18. From a *nonentity* Jackson rose to the highest honor America can grant.

19. He feared *retribution* for his evil deeds.

20. The terms were *tantamount* to complete surrender.

ACTIVITY 7.  Judging Vocabulary Notebooks

Have your vocabulary notebook in class tomorrow, complete and up to date. The book will be rated by your teacher according to the following standards:

*a.* neatness and legibility
*b.* number of new words listed
*c.* exactness of word use
*d.* variety of illustrative sentences
*e.* completeness (definition, pronunciation, etymology, illustrative sentence)

## *MASTERY TEST*

If you have done the activities faithfully and have added new words to your vocabulary, the following test should be easy for you. Each of the words is taken from a preceding chapter. Write the letter of the word or expression that most nearly defines the italicized word.

1. an *avaricious* weaver  (*a*) unskilled  (*b*) skilled  (*c*) unselfish  (*d*) greedy  (*e*) vicious

2. a *pugnacious* individual  (*a*) eager to learn  (*b*) energetic  (*c*) calm  (*d*) worrisome  (*e*) ready to fight

3. a *relentless* struggle  (*a*) harsh  (*b*) brief  (*c*) easily settled  (*d*) infrequent  (*e*) unusual

4. *senile* weakness  (*a*) sickly  (*b*) pertaining to old age  (*c*) remarkable  (*d*) pertaining to men  (*e*) inhuman

5. to wear a *talisman*  (*a*) necklace  (*b*) wooden shoe  (*c*) rose  (*d*) charm  (*e*) hood

6. an *unscrupulous* bargainer  (*a*) without principles  (*b*) indirect  (*c*) wealthy  (*d*) carelessly dressed  (*e*) foolish

7. to keep *equilibrium*  (*a*) stable for horses  (*b*) a pair of racehorses  (*c*) persistence  (*d*) balance  (*e*) strict account

8. to *curtail* one's activities  (*a*) survey  (*b*) analyze  (*c*) expand  (*d*) explain to another  (*e*) lessen

9. an *edible* berry (*a*) scarlet (*b*) poisonous (*c*) round and un-wrinkled (*d*) nonpoisonous (*e*) tasteless

10. to the *detriment* of others (*a*) harm (*b*) benefit (*c*) dismay (*d*) surprise (*e*) approval

11. *corroded* metal (*a*) reinforced (*b*) eaten away (*c*) an alloy of steel (*d*) flexible (*e*) semiprecious

12. an *infallible* guide (*a*) native (*b*) pertaining to the woods (*c*) valuable (*d*) certain (*e*) worthless

13. to discard the *residue* (*a*) tenant (*b*) owner (*c*) remainder (*d*) major portion (*e*) that which is owed

14. to *swagger* along (*a*) stagger (*b*) run (*c*) skip (*d*) tiptoe (*e*) strut

15. a *scintillating* gem (*a*) impressive (*b*) used for cutting other gems (*c*) sparkling (*d*) colorless (*e*) precious

16. a *piebald* horse (*a*) lame (*b*) without a mane (*c*) black and white (*d*) tan (*e*) plow

17. a *nauseating* taste (*a*) bitter (*b*) invigorating (*c*) spicy (*d*) sickening (*e*) sour

18. the unexpected *aftermath* (*a*) after-dinner speech (*b*) postpone-ment (*c*) consequences (*d*) school problem (*e*) digest

19. an *obdurate* father (*a*) unyielding (*b*) devoted (*c*) sickly (*d*) misunderstood (*e*) long enduring

20. a *nebulous* idea (*a*) inspirational (*b*) original (*c*) straight-forward (*d*) imitative (*e*) vague

21. a *deleterious* effect (*a*) helpful (*b*) hurtful (*c*) indifferent (*d*) exciting (*e*) calming

22. an *inscrutable* expression (*a*) unpleasant (*b*) unemotional (*c*) mysterious (*d*) frank (*e*) amused

23. a *menial* task (*a*) mean and unpleasant (*b*) intellectual (*c*) simple (*d*) pleasant and desirable (*e*) absorbing

24. to *dissect* a specimen (*a*) study (*b*) photograph (*c*) cut (*d*) mount (*e*) prepare

25. to *ransack* the house (*a*) scrape the floors of (*b*) redecorate (*c*) burn to the ground (*d*) search thoroughly (*e*) demolish

26. to *withstand* criticism (*a*) comprehend (*b*) resent (*c*) publish (*d*) invite (*e*) resist

27. a *bedraggled* puppy (*a*) playful (*b*) active and quick (*c*) wet and soiled (*d*) homeless (*e*) sleek

28. *befuddled* by the reports (*a*) alarmed (*b*) quieted (*c*) aroused (*d*) confused (*e*) unharmed

29. to obey with *alacrity* (*a*) unexpected warmth (*b*) speed (*c*) delay (*d*) lack of enthusiasm (*e*) a nod of the head

30. a *pallid* complexion (*a*) lively (*b*) ruddy (*c*) heavily rouged (*d*) pale (*e*) schoolgirl

31. a bodily *contortion* (*a*) disease (*b*) lack of muscular control (*c*) twisting (*d*) attitude of despair (*e*) injury

32. an *invincible* team (*a*) colorful (*b*) unbeatable (*c*) sportsmanlike (*d*) skillful (*e*) debating

33. to *retard* progress (*a*) delay (*b*) describe (*c*) advance (*d*) explain (*e*) be interested in

34. to acquire *dexterity* (*a*) skill (*b*) method (*c*) broad outlook (*d*) interest in current events (*e*) intelligence

35. a frequent *somnambulist* (*a*) visitor (*b*) driver of a hospital vehicle (*c*) sleepwalker (*d*) insomnia victim (*e*) hiker

36. a *belligerent* attitude (*a*) comical (*b*) warlike (*c*) unexpected (*d*) resourceful (*e*) yielding

37. the old man's *cupidity* (*a*) love for reading (*b*) lack of cleverness (*c*) greed (*d*) gentleness (*e*) pride

38. an *incessant* chatterer (*a*) unceasing (*b*) noisy (*c*) annoying (*d*) harmless (*e*) gossipy

39. to *emulate* his friend (*a*) strive to surpass (*b*) attempt to help (*c*) introduce to another (*d*) invite (*e*) search for

40. to journey *incognito* (*a*) with passports in order (*b*) with identity concealed (*c*) with much publicity (*d*) unattended (*e*) rapidly

41. to trust one's *veracity*  (*a*) employer  (*b*) memory for faces  (*c*) ability to mix with others  (*d*) truthfulness  (*e*) intelligence

42. an *authentic* paper  (*a*) newsy  (*b*) copied  (*c*) devoted to sports  (*d*) genuine  (*e*) commonplace

43. a  *diabolical*  plot  (*a*) fiendish  (*b*) ingenious  (*c*) strategic  (*d*) original  (*e*) interesting

44. to *eulogize* a leader  (*a*) bury  (*b*) nominate  (*c*) imitate  (*d*) praise  (*e*) condemn

45. the  *autocrat*  of  ancient  Egypt  (*a*) explorer  (*b*) prophet  (*c*) elected president  (*d*) absolute ruler  (*e*) mechanical genius

46. a natural *antipathy*  (*a*) sympathy  (*b*) feeling of pleasure  (*c*) dislike  (*d*) understanding  (*e*) liking

47. a major *epidemic*  (*a*) disaster  (*b*) spread of disease  (*c*) work of art  (*d*) flood  (*e*) kind of election

48. a *pyrotechnic* display  (*a*) complicated  (*b*) technical  (*c*) fireworks  (*d*) spectacular  (*e*) well lighted

49. a  *bizarre*  costume  (*a*) foreign  (*b*) elaborate  (*c*) masquerade  (*d*) unusual  (*e*) rented

50. an unfortunate *pariah*  (*a*) merchant  (*b*) outcast  (*c*) dealer in rugs  (*d*) young child in India  (*e*) servant

51. an unbreakable *taboo*  (*a*) mark  (*b*) kind of pottery  (*c*) boat in South Seas  (*d*) secret message  (*e*) restriction

52. the sun at the *zenith*  (*a*) tropics  (*b*) temperate zone  (*c*) horizon  (*d*) summer solstice  (*e*) overhead

53. a  noted  *freebooter*  (*a*) furrier  (*b*) shoe  repairer  (*c*) pirate  (*d*) customs official  (*e*) tax collector

54. a  *ravenous*  appetite  (*a*) satisfied  (*b*) bird-like  (*c*) fussy  (*d*) greedy  (*e*) poor

55. an unpleasant *boor*  (*a*) kind of animal  (*b*) rude person  (*c*) industrial worker  (*d*) criminal  (*e*) uninteresting person

56. a  *sullen*  companion  (*a*) faithful  (*b*) tanned  (*c*) unsociable  (*d*) injured  (*e*) false

57. to *devastate* a city  (*a*) plan  (*b*) supply  (*c*) found  (*d*) enter in triumph  (*e*) lay waste

58. an *obstreperous* group  (*a*) noisy  (*b*) unpopular  (*c*) happy  (*d*) loyal  (*e*) destructive

59. a *querulous* patient  (*a*) optimistic  (*b*) hopeless  (*c*) inquisitive  (*d*) complaining  (*e*) helpful

60. a life of *indolence*  (*a*) insolence  (*b*) hard work  (*c*) innocence  (*d*) success  (*e*) ease

61. a *decrepit* beggar  (*a*) untiring  (*b*) poorly dressed  (*c*) worn out with age  (*d*) slovenly  (*e*) bearded

62. a trusted *emissary*  (*a*) companion  (*b*) secret agent  (*c*) employee  (*d*) overseer  (*e*) police chief

63. *nocturnal* insects  (*a*) biting  (*b*) flying  (*c*) by night  (*d*) by day  (*e*) those that prey on others

64. an *intrepid* adventurer  (*a*) interesting  (*b*) fearless  (*c*) unintelligent  (*d*) roaming  (*e*) to far places

65. a *diminutive* specimen  (*a*) correctly labeled  (*b*) temporary  (*c*) large  (*d*) very small  (*e*) precious

66. to *scrutinize* carefully  (*a*) examine  (*b*) cut apart  (*c*) conceal  (*d*) reveal  (*e*) undertake

67. to *vacillate* in deciding  (*a*) come to a quick conclusion  (*b*) waver  (*c*) compare  (*d*) reverse oneself  (*e*) nod slowly

68. an *antiquated* automobile  (*a*) well-kept  (*b*) powerful  (*c*) new  (*d*) old  (*e*) unusual in appearance

69. to show *humility*  (*a*) meekness  (*b*) pride  (*c*) talent  (*d*) a sense of humor  (*e*) self-consciousness

70. a *meager* crop  (*a*) cultivated  (*b*) of grain  (*c*) poor  (*d*) extensive  (*e*) varied

71. an *obscure* reason  (*a*) forceful  (*b*) thoughtless  (*c*) professed  (*d*) obvious  (*e*) not clear

72. to await with *timidity*  (*a*) valor  (*b*) faint-heartedness  (*c*) disgust  (*d*) anticipation  (*e*) indifference

73. a *loquacious* child  (*a*) sickly  (*b*) alert  (*c*) talkative  (*d*) unnecessarily cruel  (*e*) bright

74. an *altruistic* action  (*a*) unexpected  (*b*) unselfish  (*c*) conceited  (*d*) ingenious  (*e*) unopposed

75. to *castigate* on many occasions  (*a*) criticize severely  (*b*) complain  (*c*) publicly praise  (*d*) investigate  (*e*) laugh loudly

76. an unusual  *coiffure*  (*a*) dress  (*b*) hair-do  (*c*) proposition  (*d*) dish  (*e*) piece of furniture

77. a small *clique*  (*a*) kind of hat  (*b*) manufacturing firm  (*c*) applause  (*d*) secret vote  (*e*) exclusive group

78. the enemy's *chauvinism*  (*a*) courage  (*b*) cunning  (*c*) excessive patriotism  (*d*) unusual skill  (*e*) ability to look ahead

79. a *spartan* attitude  (*a*) weak  (*b*) cowardly  (*c*) courageous  (*d*) unwise  (*e*) intellectual

80. a *lilliputian* show  (*a*) exciting  (*b*) original  (*c*) massive  (*d*) tiny  (*e*) well-lighted

81. an *eligible* candidate  (*a*) eager  (*b*) qualified  (*c*) illiterate  (*d*) elected  (*e*) defeated

82. an *intolerable* situation  (*a*) tiring  (*b*) unbearable  (*c*) unanticipated  (*d*) extremely favorable  (*e*) complex

83. a stately *mausoleum*  (*a*) church  (*b*) school  (*c*) tomb  (*d*) lighthouse  (*e*) museum

84. a *pneumatic* pump  (*a*) water  (*b*) oil  (*c*) air  (*d*) inefficient  (*e*) for certain diseases

85. to *immerse* gradually  (*a*) dip  (*b*) become cold  (*c*) fry  (*d*) become larger  (*e*) become overheated

86. to *fluctuate* from time to time  (*a*) rise  (*b*) pierce  (*c*) rise and fall  (*d*) revive  (*e*) fall

87. a needed *referendum*  (*a*) change  (*b*) governmental collapse  (*c*) umpire  (*d*) popular vote  (*e*) memorandum

88. a deserved *increment*  (*a*) reward  (*b*) increase  (*c*) reduction  (*d*) speech of praise  (*e*) attack

89. the *paucity* of certain articles (*a*) construction (*b*) scarcity (*c*) seizure (*d*) oversupply (*e*) transportation

90. to remain *adamant* (*a*) unmarried (*b*) uncontrolled (*c*) cheerful (*d*) unyielding (*e*) vigorous

91. an *arduous* task (*a*) undesirable (*b*) complicated (*c*) easy (*d*) difficult (*e*) boring

92. a *dilatory* nature (*a*) strong (*b*) wasteful (*c*) confident (*d*) cheerful (*e*) delaying

93. to *demur* immediately (*a*) object (*b*) repeat (*c*) capture (*d*) remove (*e*) scold

94. a *diffident* girl (*a*) adolescent (*b*) clever (*c*) shy (*d*) chattering (*e*) unusual

95. a *despicable* act (*a*) contemptible (*b*) thoughtless (*c*) likable (*d*) apparent (*e*) commonplace

96. to be *lenient* with others (*a*) secretive (*b*) harsh (*c*) at ease (*d*) ill at ease (*e*) gentle

97. a *heinous* deed (*a*) official (*b*) distant (*c*) fashionable (*d*) hateful (*e*) glorious

98. a *bountiful* giver (*a*) poor (*b*) generous (*c*) conceited (*d*) unwise (*e*) selfish

99. to *harangue* a multitude (*a*) lead wisely (*b*) condemn vigorously (*c*) address noisily (*d*) mock (*e*) slay

100. a *rigorous* climate (*a*) windy (*b*) tropical (*c*) temperate (*d*) severe (*e*) unchanging

PART TWO

USING WORDS

Word Magic

# 1

# The Magic of Words

*In Shakespeare's great tragedy* Macbeth *the witches are huddled around a boiling cauldron. As they watch the liquid simmer, they chant over and over again,*

> *Double, double toil and trouble;*
> *Fire burn and cauldron bubble.*

*Like all witches and dealers in magic they believe in the power of words as charms. Whether they use the word* abracadabra *or some other strange and mystical symbol, they feel certain that the charm depends upon the word itself. Ali Baba opened a rocky hillside merely by saying, "Open, Sesame!"*

## WORD MAGIC TODAY

We snicker at such superstitions today — or do we? Words *are* really and truly magical. To be sure, we don't believe that we can call up the devil to do our bidding by saying the *Lord's Prayer* backwards, but we are influenced by word magic just the same — most of the time! For example, a boys' baseball team called the *Friends* was losing almost every game. Suddenly someone got the inspiration of renaming the team the *Avengers*. With this fiery new name the team began to win games. Was the new name at least partly responsible? Probably yes. The British Admiralty long ago realized the power of suggestion in words. They assigned "fighting" names to many of their battleships, names like *Dreadnaught*, *Intrepid*, and *Repulse*. Crews aboard these vessels identified themselves with the names.

Morale was helped. The 104th Division of the American Army was proud to be known by the name of *Timberwolves*. Boy Scouts like to be in patrols named after animals they admire. There *is* something in a name!

### Activity 1. Choosing Names

1. Suppose you were choosing a name for a football team. Which of the following would you prefer? Why?

| | |
|---|---|
| The Beavers | The Daisies |
| The Moths | The Pals |
| The Panthers | The Hermits |

2. At an amusement park the owner of a fast, exciting ride called "Brown's Roller Coaster" found that he wasn't doing as well as he should. Someone suggested that he change the name of the ride. He did and found the demand overwhelming. Which name did he choose? Why?

| | |
|---|---|
| The Witching Waves | The Thunderbolt |
| The Mystic Tunnel | The Elevated |
| Brown's Super-Ride | A Scenic Tour |

### Magic in Advertising

Among the cleverest users of words are the advertising men. Their livelihood depends upon their picking words that sell articles, and avoiding words that don't. They know that there is magic in words like *genuine* or *original*. Consequently they use them frequently. Somehow *genuine country bread* seems as though it will taste better than just *bread*. An *original copy* of an expensive hat, though a contradiction, sounds more desirable than just a *copy*. Dresses for *debuteens* seem more exclusive and unusual than dresses for *teen-age girls*.

### Activity 2. Studying Words That Sell

In each of the following pairs of words select the one that would be more likely to sell the object or the house.

1. kitchenette, small kitchen
2. hall, foyer
3. lower-priced dress, cheaper dress
4. shelfworn books, hurt books
5. five-room house, Cape Cod cottage
6. Sunset Boulevard, First Avenue
7. girls' dresses, dresses for the pigtail crowd
8. coats for heavy women, stylish-stout coats
9. Leafy Acres, Martin's Development
10. reprocessed wool, secondhand wool

~~Undertaker~~
Mortician

~~Palmer's Perfume~~
Polynesian Paradise

## ANALYZING WORDS THAT SELL

As a purchaser you should realize the ways in which you are led to buy articles. If you tried Activity 2, you found that in each pair of expressions one was more appealing. But you must realize that the more appealing word was *not* necessarily more informative. An object is not changed if we call it by another name. A swamp that is called *Sleepy Lagoon* by a real estate agent is still a swamp. Merely giving it an attractive name does not change its essential character, even though people almost believe it does. When Shakespeare declared, "That which we call a rose by any other name would smell as sweet," he was stating a profound truth. But for many people the rose would lose part of its charm if they heard it called a *weed* by a farmer who found wild roses creeping over into his lettuce patch. We are influenced tremendously by words and labels.

### ACTIVITY 3. Studying Sentences That Sell

Both selections in each pair that follows give the same information. Which would probably induce you to buy? Why?

1. *a.* This imitation-leather pocketbook is bulky and large and sells for $4.98.
   *b.* This simulated-leather pocketbook, roomy enough for all the little items you must carry these days, is priced at only $4.98.

2. *a.* If you want to be sure to get your copy of Steinbeck's new novel on publication day, place your order with your bookseller now!
   *b.* Place an order with your bookseller for a copy of Steinbeck's new novel to be published soon.

3. *a.* These women's hats are priced at $25.00.
   *b.* These sophisticated creations for the discriminating woman are exclusive at $25.00.

4. *a.* For a delicious treat try our superlative pumpkin pie.
   *b.* For a real old-fashioned Thanksgiving, try our home-made pumpkin pie.

5. *a.* Have green grass in five days with our drought-resisting grass seed.
   *b.* Our hardy grass seed is guaranteed to grow rapidly and satisfactorily.

6. *a.* Cover those unpleasant smudges and fingerprints with our one-coat glossy enamel.
   *b.* You will find our enamel a completely successful one-coat cover-all.

7. *a.* The new Greyhound Eight is the kind of car that attracts attention for its beauty.
   *b.* Your neighbors will gasp when you ride up in your new Greyhound Eight.

8. *a.* If you'd have your linens clean as mountain air, soft as down, and white as hospital bedding, try Snowbright Laundry.

   *b.* Snowbright Laundry makes your wash clean, soft, and white.

9. *a.* The Continental Railroad provides comfortable, relaxing, sanitary service.

   *b.* Relax as you ride in the spacious air-conditioned coaches of the Continental Railroad.

10. *a.* For the time when morning air is invigorating and hearty breakfasts are called for, try our hickory-smoked pork sausages, seasoned with pungent, zesty spices.

    *b.* Autumn days require good breakfasts. Try our excellent sausages, praised by all who have eaten them.

## CURIOSITY AND MYSTERY

P. T. Barnum was a master word-user. He knew that curiosity is a basic human urge and counted on it for his success. Once when his museum was so crowded that no more people could get in and no one wanted to leave, he put up a sign near an exit, "To the Egress." Of course, *egress* means *exit*, but most of the people thought it was probably some new and mysterious animal that Barnum had found. They were fascinated by the word!

Barnum was right.

They opened the indicated door and found themselves in the street. There are certain words that appeal to us even when we don't know exactly what they mean. There are certain names that catch our fancy because they suggest something adventurous, faraway, remote — words like *Samarkand*, *Cathay*, and *Bagdad*.

## ACTIVITY 4.  Studying Suggestive Words

In the following list pick out the words that appeal to you, either because of their sound, their associations, or their vague suggestiveness. Be ready to tell why each appeals.

| | | | |
|---|---|---|---|
| bayou | crystalline | gloom | murmuring |
| buccaneer | dusk | gossamer | seascape |
| cascade | forlorn | grotto | sinister |
| contraband | galleon | listener | whispering |
| crag | glen | moonbeam | windswept |

## APPETIZING WORDS

A young, ambitious discharged veteran decided to open a restaurant in a rather wealthy neighborhood. He scraped together a down payment and opened "Freddie's Restaurant." On a huge sign he printed, "Only the Best of Food Sold Here." Customers were few and far between. In desperation he sought advice from a word-wise friend. A month later his place was crowded. The reason? He had changed the sign to "The Montmartre." Below it he put "French Cuisine." On the menu he placed such phrases as *à la carte*, *table d'hôte*, and *déjeuner*. His customers ate the formerly rejected chicken hash and relished it as *émincé de poulet*. Charlie the Chef became *Monsieur Charles*. To be sure *oeufs* are *eggs* no matter what they are called, but to the customers *oeufs* taste better. Part of his success was due no doubt to his changing names, for not only did he thus entice new people into his restaurant, but he also found his own attitude changing. He became more particular about the food he served. The words had a profound effect upon him, too.

This little fable about Monsieur Charles demonstrates that a change in name does make a difference. Foreign names, to be sure, give a pleasantly mysterious suggestiveness. The French words mentioned above, an Italian word like *pizzeria*, a Swedish name like *smörgåsbord* — these help to sell food. But a clever combination of suggestive English words can make a great difference, too. Restaurants have found that they can sell more salads if they call them *garden-fresh salads*. *Brick-oven baked beans* go faster than *baked beans*. *Our own blend of highland-grown coffees* proves a better sales slogan than just *coffee*. A *barbecue sandwich* seems more desirable than a *beef sandwich*.

ACTIVITY 5.  Studying Appetizing Words

In the following paragraph select the words that help make the food *seem* more appetizing.

They certainly fed us well at camp. For breakfast we had country-style eggs, sugar-cured ham, and golden-brown pancakes. Dinner was varied; on some days juicy, rare roast beef featured the meal, while on others crisp, oven-seared pork chops or prime, inch-thick steaks brought us running. Suppers included rich farm soups with fresh-picked vegetables. Home-made muffins, mountain blueberries, and home-frozen ice cream were popular desserts.

## LABELS

Before government regulations made necessary the correct labeling of articles to be sold, misrepresentation was common. Old Western medicine men sold their "snake oil" — usually colored water — to many gullible individuals. Newspaper advertising of fifty years ago was filled with cure-alls of every description. When advertising misleads today, it is more likely to deceive through suggestion, rather than through actual false statements.

Too often, though, people want to be fooled. *Hudson Seal* coats are actually dyed muskrat and must be so indicated. Buyers of these coats know that the fur is not seal, but muskrat; yet they prefer the more desirable, though inaccurate, name.

To them the coat is *seal*, not *muskrat*. Similarly, few women will admit to owning a coat of rabbit fur (though rabbit is used for many purposes), but a purchaser will gladly acknowledge that her coat is *lapin*. Yet *lapin* is merely French for *rabbit*. Such is the power of words!

**What's in a name?**

ACTIVITY 6. Studying Substitutes for Common Objects

In each of the following a common word or phrase is concealed under a fancy label. How many of them can you call by their common names? How many can you add to this list?

1. custodial engineer
2. exterminating engineer
3. landscape architect
4. lubritorium
5. mortuary consultant
6. salon de beauté
7. tonsorial parlor
8. tree surgeon
9. waste-material dealer
10. ye olde literary shoppe

SALES PSYCHOLOGY AND WORDS

The next time you order a glass of orange drink notice how the waiter takes your order. Elmer Wheeler, advertising man, emphasizes a right and a wrong way to take the order. The inefficient salesman will ask, "Large or small?" The average man's answer is, "Small." But the wide-awake salesman says, "Large?"

Having put the suggestion into your mind, he knows you'll probably say, "Yes." Advertisers, salesmen, and public speakers know how to utilize their knowledge of human nature to work miracles with words. Keep on your toes. Actually *words are magic* if we submit ourselves to their spell. The remaining chapters of this book will show you how to handle words intelligently and interpret what you see and hear.

# 2

# Words Are Symbols

*The parade comes proudly down the street. Rank after rank passes the reviewing stand. Then suddenly a splash of color flutters in the breeze. The American flag passes by. A thrill stirs the onlookers as they proudly salute the symbol of the Republic. There are very few Americans who don't feel a surge of emotion at the sight, no matter how often they see it.*

*Let's look closer. The material of the flag may be cheap cotton or expensive linen — no matter. It isn't the material that makes the difference. The colors may be faded and washed out, rather than fresh and brilliant — no matter. It isn't the brilliance of the coloring that makes the difference. A child can draw an American flag from cheap paper and crayon in ten minutes, but it will be a flag just the same. It will affect us deeply.*

## What Are Symbols

The flag means something because it suggests something deeper. It represents the things we believe in: freedom, the Bill of Rights, our democracy itself. It is a *symbol* without material value in itself, but with tremendous spiritual value because of the ideas it represents. In a remote savage land it would have no value beyond its obvious values as gaily colored cloth. In America it has value beyond price.

Symbols are signs that we accept. Without words they convey ideas accurately and quickly. The Statue of Liberty, the American Eagle, and the Stars and Stripes are precious symbols to Americans; the Maple leaf, to Canada; the Southern Cross, to

Australia and New Zealand. Some symbols cross national boundaries. The Cross as a symbol of Christianity, the Star of David as a symbol of Judaism — these are precious all over the world.

Symbols help us communicate with others. Consider these signs-without-words and their value in communication: road direction signs, the referee's signals in a football game, and the sound man's signals to his cast during a radio broadcast. Even punctuation marks are symbols. A period says as plainly as it can, "This is the end of a sentence. Stop a moment."

ACTIVITY 1. Identifying Symbols

In each of the following identify the scene being described and point out all symbols used.

1. A baby clad only in a cloth with a date on it is greeted by an old man with a flowing white beard and a scythe.

2. A procession in long black robes passes across the auditorium of the school. Each marcher receives a rolled piece of paper.

3. A party is in progress. One person is dressed in a skeleton suit. Another wears a black cape, a pointed hat, and carries a broomstick. A third person has a white sheet draped over his shoulders.

4. An envelope is opened and the card removed. The illustrations for the card are four: a balsam tree, a poinsettia, a brilliant five-pointed star, and a jolly old red-faced gentleman with a white beard.

Symbols are signs that we accept.

5. The American flag is brought to the platform. Members of the audience rise, place their hands over their hearts, and speak in unison.

ACTIVITY 2. Matching Symbols and Things Symbolized

Match the symbols listed in column *A* with things symbolized in column *B*.

| *A* | *B* |
|---|---|
| 1. a lily | a. captaincy (U. S. Army) |
| 2. black | b. Eastertime |
| 3. green light | c. mourning |
| 4. metal golfer about one foot high | d. states |
| 5. skull and crossbones | e. tournament prize |
| 6. stars in the flag | f. purity |
| 7. two silver bars an inch long | g. Go! |
| 8. turkey | h. piracy |
| 9. white | i. Thanksgiving |
| 10. X | j. crossroads ahead |

## SYMBOLS AND REALITY

Heywood Broun's amusing essay, *The Fifty-first Dragon*, tells how a timid lad becomes a mighty dragon-killer because he thinks he has a magical charm, the word *Rumplesnitz*, protecting him against danger. When he discovers that the charm is really an unmagical word made up on the spur of the moment, he succumbs to the fifty-first dragon. Like many people today he confuses the symbol — the charm — and reality — his actual prowess. The lodge member who feels himself "a new man" when he puts on the uniform of his club or fraternity is merely paying like tribute to the power of symbols. If he submits completely enough to the spell of the uniform, he may, temporarily at least, become a somewhat different man.

In primitive societies warriors prefer the meat of tigers, stags, or boars, hoping to gain some of the fighting qualities of the animals they eat. Similarly some people today believe that they will become more intelligent by eating the brains of certain animals. Carrying a rabbit's foot or a horseshoe for luck is a reflection of the same confusion of symbol and reality. Symbols play a dominant role in our lives.

ACTIVITY 3. Studying Symbols and Superstitions

List as many superstitious symbols as you can; for example, black cats and four-leaf clovers. What is the power attributed to each?

## WORDS ARE SYMBOLS

Symbols *stand for* things or ideas. They *are not* the things or ideas. The flag stands for our country. It is not actually our country, of course. Some people confuse the symbol with the thing symbolized. They dislike all girls named Ruth, let us say, because an earlier experience with one girl called Ruth has been unpleasant. *Words are symbols* — and nothing more.

Suppose someone walked up to you and without warning declared in an even tone, "You are a miserable, contemptible, worthless loafer!" Your fists would clench and your heart would beat faster. To have those words associated with you! Yet there is nothing in the sounds themselves that makes them "fighting

Words are symbols — not things.

words." It is the meanings we have attached to them that have charged them with dynamite. Spoken in a mild tone to one who knew no English they would create not the slightest disturbance. Call someone "brave" and you flatter him. Tell him he "raves" and he is insulted. Yet there is but the slightest difference in sound between *brave* and *raves*. Remember: it's the meanings we have attached artificially to words that count. The words as sounds are neither good nor bad, neither insulting nor flattering. Words are merely symbols, handles we attach to objects and ideas for convenience.

In *Through the Looking Glass* Humpty Dumpty shows us that he understands the symbolic nature of words, though we could never communicate with each other if all of us felt exactly as he does. Alice and he are having a discussion. Alice objects to one of his words:

"But 'glory' doesn't mean 'a nice knock-down argument,'" Alice objected.

"When I use a word," Humpty Dumpty said, in rather a scornful tone, "it means just what I choose it to mean — neither more nor less."

"The question is," said Alice, "whether you can make words mean so many different things."

"The question is," said Humpty Dumpty, "which is to be master — that's all."

ACTIVITY 4. Analyzing Confusion between Symbols and Reality

In the following sentences point out the errors in thinking, particularly errors arising from identifying the word and the thing.

EXAMPLE: *"The lily is the proper name for the flower, because it is so pure and white."*

This is a nonsense sentence because the flower came first and gave the qualities of purity and whiteness to the name *lily*. There is nothing pure or white about the word *lily*.

1. I am not amazed at the ability of science to measure size, distance, and brightness of the stars. What puzzles me is how scientists found out the names of the stars.

2. I always like to go out with boys named George, for they are always a lot of fun.

3. Pigs are properly named; they are such dirty animals.

4. I like to spell my name *Grayce* instead of *Grace* because it fits my personality better.

5. "You live on the thirteenth floor of that apartment, I'm told."
"No, I don't. Please don't say that. I live on floor 12A."

6. We'll hire Timothy Adams. Somehow that name suggests thrift and honesty to me.

7. "I like your purple dress, Madge."
"It isn't purple! It's grape, violet, mauve, or plum, but it isn't purple!"

8. The word *ice* certainly fits the object; it is such a cold word.

9. I have great confidence in Dr. Abbott. Even his wife calls him *Doctor* Abbott.

10. "Your house is not legally in Minnesota. This survey puts it twenty yards over the Wisconsin line."
"Really? That's wonderful. Now I won't have any more of those cold Minnesota winters!"

## WORDS ARE NOT THINGS

Words have such a powerful influence upon all our thinking that we associate words with deeds. We tend to believe a thing is so if we see it in print. Merely printing a statement doesn't make it so, though people will stoutly defend an argument by claiming, "I read it in a book!" To be sure, most of the things we read are reliable if we confine our reading to trustworthy magazines, newspapers, and books. Yet we must accept with caution all statements that are obviously opinions rather than facts.

The power of words to rouse us or lull us into a feeling of security is best demonstrated in political speeches. Any candidate for election can say, "I shall do thus-and-so." A better test is his past record. Yet many people believe that because he has promised — in words — he will be necessarily bound to fulfill his promises. Unfortunately there is no necessary tie-up between the word and the deed.

True understanding comes through dealing with things as well as words. A man can read a thorough description of how to repair a faulty butterfly valve in an automobile carburetor. This information, however, may be of no value unless the man can identify the carburetor and the special valve, and apply the purely verbal, or word, knowledge to reality. Ability to twist and manipulate *words* does not guarantee ability to handle *reality*. Too many people can do the former job with great agility without knowing in reality what they are talking about.

ACTIVITY 5. Studying Symbols and Reality

How many of the following objects could you actually identify among a group of hundreds of objects? How many do you have a vague acquaintance with? Which ones are you entitled to speak or write about? Why? Look up in a good dictionary those words that are unfamiliar to you.

|              |           |
|--------------|-----------|
| calipers     | loom      |
| cam          | lynx      |
| gargoyle     | parchment |
| hyacinth     | Sealyham  |
| induction coil | silo    |

## CHANGING SYMBOLS

Most of the symbols mentioned at the beginning of this chapter have fairly uniform meanings. For example, the symbol of the cross on a building is seldom misunderstood. Words are not so easy to interpret. They are constantly undergoing change. Listeners and readers must constantly be on guard against surprising shifts in meaning. Words that have seemed familiar suddenly are used in a new way. Alert readers or listeners note the change carefully and enlarge their mental pictures of the words.

Merely knowing the dictionary definition of a word is not enough. During the war expert Nazi language students censored all communications going out of Germany. Yet, even though they knew dictionary definitions exactly, they let the following

**What is a bark?**

blunder go through. A captured American airman wrote the following to a friend in America.

"The Nazis are real gentlemen. They are treating me wonderfully, giving me the best of food and anything else I desire. Tell that to your friends in the Army. Tell it to the Navy. But, above all, tell it to the Marines."

Most Americans born to our language would not fail to see the point of this comment, though the Germans failed to realize that the phrase, "Tell it to the Marines," means "It's a lie!" This phrase is called an idiom (see Chapter 12, Part Two).

Another instance of confusion through misunderstanding the meaning is found in the following humorous anecdote.

A waiter approached the table quietly. "Ah, how do you find your steak, sir?" he asked in an effort to be pleasant.

"Blamed if I know," answered the diner with a good-natured twinkle. "It was so small I had difficulty in finding it at all!"

The diner chose to take the waiter's question literally (see Chapter 11), and purposely misunderstood the remark.

Be careful of these little symbols we call words. They often change under our hands.

ACTIVITY 6. Analyzing Purposeful Misunderstandings

Show how each of the following replies misunderstood the italicized word in the question.

1. Q. "Tell me, Fred, when you addressed the meeting, what did you speak *about?*
   A. "Oh, I spoke about fifteen minutes."

2. Q. "When you spoke at the dinner, whom were you *after?*"
   A. "I went after the waiter for taking my unfinished soup!"

3. Q. "*Where* did you get your hair cut?"
   A. "On my head, of course."

ACTIVITY 7. Analyzing Words in New Senses

The following common words are used in unusual ways. Point out the meaning of each of the italicized words as commonly used and as used in the sentence. Use a dictionary, if necessary; preferably an unabridged dictionary.

1. "This is the first *last* I ever used," said the cobbler.
2. He studied the *mechanics* of playwriting.
3. Though St. Anthony studied only the *book* of Nature, he was not stupid.
4. Did you plant *beefsteak* tomatoes or some other variety?
5. The tailor used a *goose* to iron the dress.
6. Within the *compass* of his eye was a lighthouse and a fishing boat.
7. She *postured* primly when she thought others were looking.
8. In the War between the States soldiers feared a *grape* barrage almost as much as cannon.
9. Your plan is *consonant* with my desires.
10. Did the publishers *marble* the edges of your dictionary?

## WORDS AND DAILY LIVING

Words affect us every minute of the day. Not only in our contacts with others do words play a part, but also in our individual thinking. A good illustration of this is the reaction of people to the change from Daylight Saving Time to Standard Time. Two o'clock of the day after the clock has been set back in October is just about the same as three o'clock of the day before. The sun is in approximately the same position and there is no noticeable difference. Yet two o'clock *seems* earlier even though it is not. The same number of hours of daylight remain, but an individual feels that he has more of the day left. This is purely a verbal (pertaining to words) distinction.

## IS A WORD A THING?

A newspaper article in the *New York Times* described a sidewalk peddler who had been forgiven a fine for peddling vegetables on Sundays by proving that the tomato is, scientifically, a *fruit*. Fortunately for him, the judge had not looked under *vegetable* in Webster's unabridged dictionary, for there he would have found *tomato* classified as a vegetable. In the past, courts have ruled that tomatoes are vegetables because they are eaten during the main part of a meal. Scientists declare that tomatoes are fruits, just as apples and pears are. What *is* a tomato? Who is right?

Both are right. The classification depends upon the purpose. If we are making a legal decision, then the decision of the court is "right." If we are studying the tomato scientifically, then the scientific classification is "right." The word *fruit* or *vegetable* is merely a convenient label tacked on to *tomato* to help us manipulate it in words. If we took a green tomato and tossed it back and forth and played with it, we could say with perfect honesty, "The tomato is a *ball*." If we decorated a banquet for Thanksgiving with all kinds of produce, including tomatoes, we could say with justice, "The tomato is an *ornament*." We classify objects for a purpose. Unless we know the purpose of a distinction, we often cannot define accurately. Unless we know the purpose the writer or speaker had in mind, we may misunderstand what he means. Whenever you see the word *is* in a statement like "the tomato *is* a fruit," ask yourself, "*Is* to whom, when, under what circumstances?"

Suppose we have a dog, Buddy, an Irish setter. We might say any one of the following:

1. Buddy is an Irish setter.
2. Buddy is my dog.
3. Buddy is a blue ribbon winner.
4. Buddy is a faithful friend.
5. Buddy is a lively puppy.
6. Buddy is a noisy hound.

What *is* Buddy *really?* He is all of these at once, and much more. We cannot fully describe that barking, happy bundle of reddish fur. We can only describe him in part by labels. To his owner Buddy is #4. To a dog lover Buddy is #1. To a judge of fine dogs Buddy is #3. To a neighbor Buddy is #5. These are all aspects of the real Buddy. No words can fully describe him for us. Mere words cannot do him justice. In fact, #6 by itself would do Buddy a grave injustice.

Despite the difficulty of fully describing anyone in words, most people make the attempt, often unjustly. We say, "John

Tommy is . . . .
Is to whom, when, under what circumstances?

is a lazy shirker," or "Roy is careless and selfish." We probably have seen only part of the real John. We may not realize that John works six nights a week after school in an effort to keep his family financially secure, and comes to school tired. Roy we may have misunderstood completely, classifying him completely from one or two actions. For the sake of economy of time and effort we must make judgments of this type, but we should realize that the judgments are not final or complete. Tomorrow's John is not today's. All of us are changing all the time. An upset stomach today makes today's Roy disagreeable; tomorrow Roy will seem the life of the party. Words merely give us at best a section of the truth.

### ACTIVITY 8. Studying Labels

1. List all the labels that might be attached to you; for example, *boy scout*, *member of the Spanish club*, *high school student*.

2. Be ready to discuss the following questions.

    *a.* In what way is the picture given by the labels incomplete?
    *b.* How can the real *you* be described?
    *c.* What labels listed would not have been true of you five years ago?
    *d.* What labels not now true might be listed for you five years from now?
    *e.* Which labels do you consider favorable?
    *f.* Which labels do you consider unfavorable?

### ACTIVITY 9. Studying Confusion of Words and Reality

Confusion of words and reality is illustrated by the following description of part of a radio comedy. See whether you can spot the error in thinking. Point out how the word and the reality have been confused.

A man is asked to comment on the new fur coat his wife has brought home on approval. "What kind of fur is it?" he asks his wife.

"Tibbar," she replies.

"Tibbar? I never heard of that fur. What is a tibbar?"

"The man told me that a tibbar is a small Asiatic mammal similar to a chinchilla."

The husband, sensing deception, declares scornfully, "There is no such animal!"

His wife replies, "Of course there is. Here is the fur!"

"The joke is on you, dear," replies her husband, having the last word for once. " 'Tibbar' is merely 'rabbit' spelled backwards."

## THE POWER OF SYMBOLS

Grandfather went to a feast at the home of a friend. The meal was delicious, the meat and gravy being particularly tasty. At the close of the meal Granddad asked his host what cut of veal he had roasted so appetizingly.

"That wasn't veal. It was goat meat. Did you like it?"

Unfortunately Grandfather could not answer, for he had already been taken violently ill. It wasn't the *meat* but the *word* that had turned his stomach, for he had never considered goat meat edible for human beings. A mere symbol had spoiled a good meal.

Words are not reality; they merely reflect reality. Yet wars have taken place over words, even though there was little real disagreement between the two opponents. Many a man has died because he has been labeled in one way or another. Hitler waged a vicious war, calling upon Germans to fight for the "Aryan race." *There is no Aryan race;* yet people believed in the word and accepted its reality, even though it had no reality. Throughout history men have shown themselves willing to do battle for a word, even a word without a counterpart in real life.

### ACTIVITY 10. Studying Fictional Words

All of the words listed below have no counterparts in real life, nothing real to which they refer; yet there is a profound difference between column *A* and column *B*. Which column is more likely to be harmless? Which column has brought great trouble to the world even though it lists words which *have no reality?* Explain the meaning of all the words and prove that they have no counterparts in reality.

| A | B |
|---|---|
| gremlin | decadence of democracies |
| satyr | divine right of kings |
| sea serpent | master race |
| unicorn | Nordic superiority |
| Zeus | pure Aryan blood |

ACTIVITY 11.  Studying a Nonsense Paragraph

The following paragraph by Mark Twain is a nonsense paragraph. (It is reprinted here by permission of Harper & Brothers, publishers.) It *seems* to say a great deal, but it actually says practically nothing because many of the words refer to objects which do not exist or which have no place in the context even if they do exist. Check each unfamiliar word and show that the passage has no basis in reality even though the words *sound* all right.

EXAMPLE: *deciduous flowers. Deciduous* is a term applied to trees that lose their leaves every autumn. Applied to flowers it is nonsense.

It was a crisp and spicy morning in early October. The lilacs and laburnums, lit with the glory fires of autumn, hung burning and flashing in the upper air, a fairy bridge provided by kind Nature for the wingless wild things that have their home in the tree tops and would visit together; the larch and the pomegranate flung their purple and yellow flames in brilliant broad splashes along the slanting sweep of the woodland; the sensuous fragrance of innumerable deciduous flowers rose upon the swooning atmosphere; far in the empty sky a solitary oesophagus slept upon motionless wing; everywhere brooded stillness, [and] serenity. . . .

SUPERSTITIONS AND CHARMS

"If you make a copy of this charm [on page 204] and carry it about in your wallet, you will be certain to ward off diseases and bad luck!"

```
A B R A C A D A B R A
A B R A C A D A B R
A B R A C A D A B
A B R A C A D A
A B R A C A D
A B R A C A
A B R A C
A B R A
A B R
A B
A
```

If someone were to give you that advice, you'd certainly reply, "I don't believe such nonsense." Yet you might pay tribute *unconsciously* to the magical power of words. For example, after telling a friend how lucky you had been, you might knock on wood to prevent some evil force from twisting your words about to bring bad luck. If you were out walking with a friend and had to go on the opposite side of a tree or post from her, you might say, "Bread and butter," to prevent bad luck. Because seven is a "magic number," we all talk about the seven seas, the seven wonders of the world, the seven deadly sins, and so on. Three, of course, is one of the most "magical numbers" we have.

Our language is filled with expressions suggesting the magical power of words. Most of these we no longer recognize as magical in origin, for they have become commonplace in use, have become mere formulas (see pages 208–210). "God bless you," said to one who sneezes, once was uttered to prevent a person's soul from slipping out through his mouth during the sneeze. Now it is little more than a polite, almost meaningless, expression.

## INCANTATIONS

In 1923 Emile Coué, French pharmacist, swept America by storm. His method for curing many ailments of the spirit and body consisted of having people repeat, over and over again, the words: "Day by day in every way I am getting better and better." Americans were fascinated by this new cure. The sentence was on everyone's lips. Then, like most sudden fads, it faded from the public's attention. Before it passed from notice, however, many people gave the system credit for unusual cures. Perhaps the repetition of certain syllables over and over produces a kind of hypnotic effect that helps cure by the power of suggestion. Medicine men in primitive tribes chant a weird song to cure their patients' ailments. They feel that the words themselves will help cure the sick. We call the repetitive chanting of magic spells *incantation*.

Nursery rhymes are a kind of survival of old incantations. The strong rhythm and obvious rhyme have been used by many a weary mother to sing her baby to sleep. Children like to hear rhymes over and over again, long after they have learned the words by heart. The content becomes less and less important. The rhyme and the rhythm are loved for their own sake. Remember some of your own childhood favorites: *Hey, Diddle, Diddle; Rub-a-Dub-Dub; A Diller, A Dollar;* and *Ding, Dong Bell.*

Not long ago advertisers on the radio became aware of the power of incantations. Many listeners enjoyed singing commercials, consisting of simple, rhythmical ditties about soap flakes, breakfast cereals, and hair tonics. Even without music the repetition of certain phrases was found to make a lasting impression that had little to do with the quality of the advertised product.

Buy .... Buy .... Buy .... B u u y  y  y.

ACTIVITY 12. Collecting Incantations

For the next week keep a listing of all incantations heard on the radio, in motion pictures, or in ordinary conversation. What is the purpose of each incantation? Is the purpose helped or hindered by using strong rhyme or rhythm or both? Why?

## SLOGANS

"Tippecanoe and Tyler, too." This was the slogan that helped elect William Henry Harrison, hero of the battle of Tippecanoe, to the Presidency in the election of 1840, along with John Tyler as Vice-President. The Whig campaign managers realized that they had hit upon a nearly perfect slogan. It was easy to remember, brief, rhythmical, and suggestive of the past glory of their candidate. In addition, it was alliterative; that is, three of the four words began with the same letter. It "caught on" and spread throughout the country. People were fascinated by the sound and the swing of the expression. It didn't *say* anything, but it *sounded* wonderful.

Most slogans try to influence us to do something. Political campaign slogans attempt to praise their own candidates and condemn the opposition. The same party will suggest, "Win with Winters," and "Ruin with Roberts." The former encourages voters to "get on the bandwagon" of their presumably victorious candidate. The latter suggests the horrible future in store for those who foolishly support the candidate of the opposition party.

Advertisers are constantly searching for slogans that capture the imagination of consumers. "Buy Burton's Biscuits" is much more likely to be remembered than "The wise customer will find it to her advantage to purchase only those biscuits sold and guaranteed by the firm of Burton." Short, concise, and rhythmical expressions lodge themselves in the back of our minds and pop out unexpectedly when we consider buying a particular article. The advertiser's goal is this linkage of his name with the article. Slogans help him.

## Activity 13. Studying Slogans

Study each of the following slogans. Put each one to the following test:

1. Is it brief?
2. Is it easy to remember?
3. Does it suggest a line of action?

Decide whether each is a good slogan.

1. It is a good and wise policy to select only watches made by Waters.
2. Remember the Alamo!
3. Wear Weskits for Warmth.
4. Shop for Shoes at Sheppard's.
5. Better Buy Bonds.
6. For economy, beauty, and style, see the new Frigidaires.
7. It's Carter's for Candy.
8. Ride in comfort with a Russell car.
9. Lowell's Lamps Light.
10. Whenever you are in need of tools for writing, consider the guaranteed Marker Pencil and Pen sets.

## MOTTOES AND PROVERBS

"*Semper Paratus*" — "Always Ready." This, the proud boast of our own Coast Guard, is a fine example of a motto, a phrase adopted as a guide, or expression of an attitude. Similarly, the boy scout motto, "Be Prepared," is an expression of the principal trait that scouting attempts to develop in its members. Like most mottoes, these suggest much more than they actually say. Schools, political parties, clubs, and fraternal groups adopt mottoes as expressions of their personal or group beliefs.

Both slogans and mottoes attempt to influence actions. Teachers place mottoes at the front of the room; for example, "A clear voice reflects clear thinking"; or "Good posture brings good health." Many expressions like "Silence is golden" or "Cleanliness is next to godliness" have become incorporated into our language. They are guides to conduct. Most educators agree that mottoes cannot easily and fundamentally influence character by themselves, for personality is developed principally through struggle and conflict. No one would deny, however, that mottoes often do have a real effect upon people, for good or evil.

Proverbs, which are often the accumulated wisdom of centuries, express folk wisdom in concise form. Often these are accepted as mottoes, as guides to conduct. "Look before you leap." "Strike while the iron is hot." "Two hands are better than one." How many times have these been quoted as undebatable truths. Yet how often do we find conflicting proverbs: "Look before you leap"; "He who hesitates is lost." All mottoes and slogans are merely words. Many are excellent when applied in one situation, but deceptive in another. The intelligent person realizes the limitations of all general expressions. He constantly reminds himself that words are, after all, merely symbols. What really count are the things symbolized, actual happenings.

## ACTIVITY 14. Studying Proverbs and Mottoes

Analyze each of the following sentences. Explain each in your own words. Do you agree with the idea presented? Why? Under what circumstances? Give an illustration to prove your point.

1. God helps them that help themselves.
2. Never leave till tomorrow what you can do today.
3. Haste makes waste.
4. Empty barrels make the most noise.
5. It is hard for an empty sack to stand upright.
6. Wisdom is wealth.
7. A burnt child dreads the fire.
8. A soft answer turneth away wrath.
9. A good name is rather to be chosen than great riches.
10. Where there is no vision, the people perish.

## WORDS AS FORMULAS

In mathematics two plus two always equals four. Not so in language. Sometimes two plus two equals one. Let us consider four words: *do, you, how,* and *do.* Each one of these words has a particular meaning. Now we'll shuffle them up a bit: "How do you do?" Does this expression mean the same as *how* plus *do* plus *you* plus *do?* Not at all. It merely means something like *hello*, a simple greeting. We have used four words to take the place of one. All four make up *one* symbol rather than four separate ones.

Our language is filled with expressions that mean less than they seem to mean. "Dear Sir" is nonsense if we take it to mean what it seems to mean. One man addressed his wife as "Dearest Maria." She saw an opportunity for a joke and scolded him for having many Marias, of which she was the dearest! If all of us were so literal, we could never again write "Yours truly" to a perfect stranger!

A young woman was trying desperately to change the tire on her automobile. A chivalrous bystander walked over to help her. "Have a flat?" he asked. Of course, he knew without asking. The question didn't say what it seemed to say. It really meant something like this, "I see you have a flat. Is there anything I can do to help?" A favorite radio joke points out the absurdity of the question if taken exactly.

A motorist struggled from beneath the wreckage of his over-turned car. As he was congratulating himself upon his good fortune, a pedestrian came up.

"Have an accident?" the pedestrian inquired.

"No, thanks," was the weary reply. "I've just had one!"

ACTIVITY 15. Analyzing Words as Formulas

The formulas in each of the following sentences are italicized. Explain why they are formulas, rather than sets of individual symbols bearing their customary meanings. What does each formula really mean?

1. *You must drop in and see us some time.*
2. *Would you be so kind* as to open the window.
3. He jotted down, "*Cordially yours*, Ted Myer," and mailed the letter.
4. *Good evening*, ladies and gentlemen, I wish to greet you on behalf of the speakers.

5. *I beg your pardon*, but I'd like to get through.

6. *May I* present to you a very good friend of mine.

7. A famous radio star closes his program with the expression, "*Obediently yours*."

8. *Happy New Year*, everybody!

9. *When you're in town, look me up; I'm in the 'phone book*.

10. We're having a fine time at Glens Falls; *wish you were here*.

## Summing Up

Words are, after all, only groups of letters that suggest certain sounds. *In themselves* they mean nothing. They mean something only because people agree to have them refer to certain objects. If everybody agreed to substitute the nonsense syllable *dilt* for *house*, then the structures we live in would be called *dilts*. There is nothing about the word *house* that connects it forever and ever to the objects to which it refers. The connection is purely by agreement.

In slogans, mottoes, and incantations, words are used in unusual ways. Often these devices induce lazy thinking, because they seem to do all the thinking for us. Just as numbers often suggest good or bad luck — like the number 13 — so words, to some people, suggest good or bad luck, even though there is nothing really magical about the words themselves.

Proof that words can mean anything we want them to mean is furnished by formulas like "Lovely evening," where the expression is not really a comment on the weather but rather a conversational opener. Toasts, congratulations upon birthdays, anniversaries, and similar occasions are formulas. We get a general pleasant reaction from simply receiving a birthday card, rather than from the specific message printed on the card.

Let us think of words as *symbols*, not as *things*.

## Activity 16. All in Fun

Realizing the symbolic nature of words many comedians concentrate their humor on twisting the symbols about "just for fun." The following jumbled sentences were popular not long ago. Read them through twice. They may seem all right the first time. By elimination, addition, or shuffling, rephrase each so that it seems sensible rather than weirdly mixed up.

1. Oh, you're only saying that because it's true!
2. It was a wonderful party. Everyone in the room was there.
3. Isn't he handsome — that other-looking fellow?
4. Two can live as cheaply as one, but it costs them twice as much.
5. There are lots of prominent people in our town, but not many.
6. Oh, look! The sea comes all the way up to the shore!
7. Well, I may be wrong, but I'm not far from it.
8. Oh, don't miss the new picture if you can.
9. She had more money than she could afford.
10. He tells one thing one day, and out the other.

# 3

# Specific and General Words

*Suppose that you got a job on a part-time basis after school, asked your new employer your salary, and were told, "You'll get a sum of money at the end of the week." You'd be disappointed, for you'd want your employer to be specific, to indicate how much you might expect to earn. You would properly resent his indefiniteness. There are times, you'd insist, when definiteness is essential!*

*Words are symbols with varying degrees of definiteness.* Marigold *is more specific than* flower. Table *gives us a fairly definite picture, but* kitchen table *is even more definite. The word* duck *is at once more definite than the word* bird *but not as definite as the word* pintail.

ACTIVITY 1. Arranging Words in Order of Definiteness

Arrange each of the following groups of words in the order of definiteness, listing the most specific word first.

EXAMPLE: *book, novel, piece of writing, romantic novel.* Since *romantic novel* is the narrowest, most definite term, and *piece of writing* the broadest, least definite, we should rearrange thus: *romantic novel, novel, book, piece of writing.*

1. skyscraper, building, Empire State Building, tall building
2. flower, aster, plant, China aster
3. animal, living thing, bear, warm-blooded animal
4. wealth, twenty dollars, money, twenty-dollar bill
5. pet, animal, puppy, Trixie
6. Californian, American, San Franciscan, Westerner

7. chess, recreation, game, board game
8. painting, work of art, painting by Da Vinci, the *Mona Lisa*
9. athlete, baseball player, member of Dodgers, Dixie Walker
10. citrus fruit, food, fruit, orange

Fir    Maple    Poplar    Elm    Tree

## GENERAL TERMS

A word or expression that includes other words or expressions within itself is called a general term. Suppose no word for *tree* existed in our language. We could mention *oak*, *maple*, *beech*, *elm*, *birch*, and *hickory*, but when we wanted to give the general idea *tree* we could not. Some languages are very weak in general terms. Basque, for example, has two different words, one for a *man's sister*, another for a *woman's sister*, but no general word *sister*. Some Eskimo tribes have different names for *snow:* for example, *snow falling*, *snow on the ground;* but they have no general word *snow*. Zulus have different words for *red cow* and *white cow*, but no general word *cow*.

English, too, in its early stages showed a lack of generalizations. Even today we speak of a horse-*stable*, a dog-*kennel*, or a pig-*sty*, but we have no general term to include all three. Can you think of a good general term which will include a *herd* of cattle, a *flock* of sheep, a *school* of fishes, and a *pack* of hounds?

### ACTIVITY 2.  Studying General Terms

In the following groups one word includes the other four. Point out the general term and explain why you feel the others are included under it.

1. hail, precipitation, rain, sleet, snow
2. brown, color, green, purple, red
3. god, Jupiter, Mars, Mercury, Venus
4. beverage, coffee, iced tea, milk, tea
5. dictator, king, president, queen, ruler
6. building, church, factory, house, hut
7. aluminum, copper, iron, magnesium, metal
8. clarinet, instrument, trombone, tuba, violin
9. bomb crater, clothing tear, hole, mine shaft, tunnel
10. nutmeg, paprika, pepper, salt, spice

### ACTIVITY 3.  Supplying General Terms

For each of the following groups of words supply the general word that includes all four. Avoid selecting *too general* a word.

EXAMPLE: *daisy, lily, nasturtium, chrysanthemum.* The general word is *flower. Plant* would be too general.

1. mare, foal, colt, stallion
2. Mars, Jupiter, earth, Mercury
3. Ford, Chrysler, Chevrolet, Plymouth
4. soldier, sailor, marine, coast guardsman
5. sturgeon, flounder, bass, perch
6. Maryland, Idaho, Oregon, Arizona
7. Brazil, Peru, Chile, Uruguay
8. table, chair, desk, sofa
9. apple, pear, plum, peach
10. mathematics, English, science, Latin

### INDEFINITE WORDS

General words are extremely useful, but they may be used so frequently they lose sharpness and clarity. Words like *thing, affair, effect, situation,* and *matter* have been run through the conversational mill so often that they are battered and worn.

Like the tired forward in a basketball game they call for substitutes, but the speech of many people supplies no substitutes. Use definite, specific words where possible.

ACTIVITY 4. Eliminating Indefinite Words.

Rephrase each of the following sentences to eliminate the indefinite, general term. Usually the improved sentence will be shorter.

EXAMPLE: *The fact is that Mary found the article on the street.*
Better: Mary found the handbag on the street.

1. What is the *state* of my patient's health?
2. About the *matter* of the canceled check may I say we are making an investigation.
3. In the present *circumstances* we find that we are unable to make the exchange.
4. The *situation* with *regard* to consumer complaints is very discouraging.
5. The *condition* which exists with *respect* to censorship cannot be tolerated.

## ABSTRACT WORDS

Some words, we have noted, refer to actual objects, like *chair*, *horse*, *rose*, and *statues*. Other words, though more general — like *tree*, *animal*, *plant*, or *bird* — still refer to real objects. There is still another group, referring to ideas that cannot be touched, smelled, tasted, heard, or seen; for example, *truth*, *justice*, *freedom*, and *wisdom*. We call these *abstract* words. Ability to think intelligently about abstract terms and to use them properly is a sign of intelligence. Someone has said that a man can be judged by his conversation. If he talks about *people* only, his intelligence is limited. If he talks about *things* rather than *people* only, his intelligence is probably much higher. But if he talks about *ideas*, then he is probably among the brightest.

Talking in abstractions, however, is not always desirable. Sometimes abstract terms are used to confuse. When someone talks about a *chair*, we know what he is talking about. When he talks about *democracy*, we are not so sure. Probably his conception of a chair does not differ importantly from ours, but his conception of democracy may be opposed to ours. We like our lawmakers and statesmen to be able to think in abstract terms, but we prefer them to come down to earth when they address us.

### ACTIVITY 5.  Analyzing Political Speeches

Two candidates for an important state office have been asked to give their definitions of democracy. Their definitions appear below. Which candidate would you vote for? Why? Why is the other candidate's definition weak?

A.  "Democracy is the concern for the individual citizen. It insists that he be given enough food to maintain his health, enough clothing to preserve his self-respect, enough wages to maintain a decent living standard. It insists that his children be educated. It maintains that his individual freedoms of expression and worship must be guaranteed, so long as his actions do not harm his fellow men. It seeks to guarantee to him 'life, liberty, and the pursuit of happiness,' but it insists that he share the responsibilities, too."

B.  "Democracy is a glorious tradition in our great and mighty land. It implies first and foremost patriotism, that whole-hearted love for the magnificent traditions of our powerful nation. Prosperity is our eternal birthright. Justice and hope and faith are with us as we scan the horizons for threats to our democratic security. Democracy is a beautiful word, and we should reverence it as we reverence our church and home."

### ACTIVITY 6.  Analyzing Editorials

Clip from the newspaper an editorial, a letter to the editor, or a report of a political speech. Underline each abstract word whose meaning is doubtful. Do you consider the writer or speaker a careless user of words? Prove.

## DEFINING ABSTRACT TERMS

Even among abstract terms there are degrees of definiteness. Both *patience* and *truth* are abstract words, but *patience* is far easier to explain. In the dictionary *truth* takes up more than twice the space allotted to *patience*. The more abstract the word the more difficult it is to define. Yet many people use these very abstract words in careless ways, as though they knew what they were talking about. *War* is an abstract word, but it is clearer in use than a word like *freedom*.

When you use abstract words, be sure you know what you are talking about. When you disagree with a friend about some issue, insist that each of you give examples of happenings in the real world which provide meanings for the important words you are using. Let each of you define such words, not in other general words, but by supplying down-to-earth illustrations. Many disagreements are merely disagreements in the use of words. To avoid unnecessary and useless disputes, debaters *define their terms* before they start. The issues can be clear only when the words are understood.

ACTIVITY 7. Studying the Need for Definitions

In the following arguments, point out the terms that need definition. Why is each argument more a battle of loose words rather than of issues?

*Argument One*

"I feel that the government is tending toward Fascism because centralized authority is emphasized above all else."

"I disagree. I feel that the trend is toward more complete democracy because a planned economy insures efficiency and greater fulfillment of democratic ideals."

*Argument Two*

"I prefer Candidate Brown to Candidate Adams because Brown believes in the management of public credit for the good of all citizens."

"I consider Brown's belief in the manipulation of public funds a disgrace and a source of peril to the economic structure."

*Argument Three*

"I didn't like the picture because the principal characters failed to show any growth of personality under the stress of circumstances."

"I thought the actors showed very much growth. They were all happy at the end and successful, too."

### Activity 8.   Defining Abstract Terms

In an unabridged dictionary look up the definitions of the following words and note some of the illustrative quotations suggested. Use each in a sentence of your own. Provide concrete illustrations from your own experience for each word selected, proving that you understand the meaning of the word *in action*.

| | |
|---|---|
| anger | intelligence |
| doubt | philosophy |
| emotion | reputation |
| generosity | skill |
| gratitude | thrift |

## Defining in a Circle

The high school freshman picked up his pocket dictionary. He thumbed through hurriedly. "Here it is! *Exorbitant* means *excessive*."

"But what does *excessive* mean?" continued the teacher.

Johnnie turned the pages rapidly. "*Excessive* means *exorbitant*." He looked up with a puzzled expression. "That doesn't help much, does it?"

Defining in a circle is the weakness not only of pocket dictionaries but also of the thinking of many people. If you were to ask a careless user of words to define *freedom*, he'd reply, "Being free, of course," without realizing that he had only said, "Black is black."

Sometimes the argument-in-a-circle may take a little longer, as in the following conversation:

"What is *happiness?*"
"*Happiness* means *having a good time*."

How to get nowhere: define in a circle.

"What do you mean by *having a good time?*"
"*Having a good time* means *enjoying oneself.*"
"*Enjoying oneself?*"
"Yes, you know — *being happy.*"

And there we are right back at the beginning!

### ACTIVITY 9. Studying Circular Definitions

Prove that the following attempts at definition are not really definitions at all. Restate each definition to prove that you know the meaning of each italicized word.

1. *Cowardice* is the quality possessed by cowards.
2. *Hypothesis* means *theory; theory* means . . . *hypothesis.*
3. *Victory* refers to the victorious conclusion of a war.
4. A *hypocrite* is one who is hypocritical toward others.
5. One who is *demonic* acts like a demon.

## GENERALIZATIONS

Little Paul let out a cry of pain. He had touched the radiator and found it very hot indeed. The next day, toddling in another room, he again touched a radiator. Again he cried in pain as the hot coils burned him. After that he avoided radiators. He had learned to associate pain and radiator.

Most of us gain experience in the same way. We find, on one occasion, that melons that are as hard as rocks are unripe. The next time we try, we find again the hard melon unripe. We then make a generalization, a broad sweeping statement, "Hard melons are not ripe." We have added to our store of knowledge.

There is danger in this procedure, too. Generalizations are easy to make, but to be sound they must be based upon long observation of a great number of instances. If little Paul were old enough, he might have declared, "All radiators are hot." This is, of course, not true. Radiators cool off during the day; they do not operate during the summer; they may be turned off or broken. Little Paul's generalization, while useful to him, would have been inadequate.

Similarly, we might find a novel by Kenneth Roberts about the Revolutionary War; then another by him on the same subject. A generalization, "Kenneth Roberts writes only about the Revolutionary period," would obviously be unsound, for we'd have to know all his other work before we could generalize.

Generalizations can be troublesome when applied to people. If we find a Portuguese untrustworthy, we cannot then assume that all Portuguese are not to be trusted. If we find a handful of Danes to be sharp business men, we cannot conclude that all Danes are tricky people to deal with. Snap judgments of this kind are useless, even dangerous. People of one group resemble people of other groups rather closely. No generalization about a particular trait in a particular group has any scientific basis. (See stereotypes, pages 268–270.)

### Activity 10. Studying Generalizations

Criticize the reasoning behind the following generalizations. Why is each scientifically unsound?

1. Last Monday I found a dollar bill in the mud. This Monday I made 100 in a history test. Monday is my lucky day; I'm going to make important decisions only on Mondays.

2. I noticed that an Albanian was convicted of the crime. All Albanians are criminal types.

3. All three of our dogs have been black and gentle. I guess all black dogs are gentle.

4. I received a package of twenty Jefferson nickels from the bank. The buffalo nickels must be completely out of circulation.

5. Frank is an excellent hockey player and basketball player. He can excel in any sport.

6. All Alice's children are tall. All of them eat "Mighty Wheat Flakes" for breakfast. "Mighty Wheat Flakes" makes tall people.

7. This year we bought a Christmas tree that dropped all its needles. This was a bad year for Christmas trees.

8. I didn't study for the history test and passed anyway. I never have to study to pass a test.

9. Austrians are not to be trusted, for I know an Austrian who is unreliable, whose promise is worth nothing.

10. Lightning has struck the telephone building and the City Hall. Lightning never strikes twice in the same place.

ACTIVITY 11. Studying Commonplace Generalizations

The following statements are often heard. Supposedly they contain the wisdom of centuries. Apply to each one the following questions:

1. What is the danger of accepting each generalization as absolute truth?
2. What exceptions to each can be noted?
3. Upon what occasion can you imagine each one being said?

1. Men are all alike.
2. All politicians are interested in bribes.
3. Every man has his price.
4. All women are fickle.
5. All those who are outstanding literature students are poor in mathematics.
6. All teachers enjoy giving homework.
7. All students hate school, and are happiest at vacation time.
8. All Americans chew gum and use slang frequently.
9. Good athletes are poor students.
10. "Winters are getting milder. Why, when I was a boy. . . ."

# Tone and Context

*The pupils watched intently as the air was slowly sucked out of the jar by the vacuum pump. The ringing of the alarm clock grew fainter and fainter; finally, it died away altogether. The pupils could see that the alarm was still ringing, but no sound came through. The science teacher paused a moment, and asked for the conclusion. Ted raised his hand and declared, "Evidently sound cannot travel through a vacuum. There is no sound as we know it without the air to carry it."*

## How Words Live

Ted's observations of an important scientific demonstration can be applied to words, too. Just as there is no sound in a vacuum, so words cannot exist in a vacuum. Words must be used to become alive; in use, all kinds of strange things happen to them. Dictionaries tell us what words *should* mean, but as we use them we fit words to our own purposes. A dictionary is like a collection of seeds. The words, like seeds, are in a state of suspended animation. They are alive but unchanging — almost lifeless. When we plant seeds and water them, tremendous changes take place. In a short time the seeds are transformed into new plants. So words are changed tremendously when we use them. From quiet, inactive letters on a page, they become living, breathing, effective symbols. They may soothe us in grief, rouse us to anger, encourage us in our struggles, or quiet our wrath.

Words are more powerful than the atomic bomb because, without them, man could not have unlocked atomic energy. Without their intelligent use, he will not be able to control his discovery. They stand ready as faithful servants or tyrannical masters. Like the "chain reaction" of atomic explosives, they may start a succession of explosions out of all proportion to the original use or intention. Words have tremendous power. Use them carefully.

### ACTIVITY 1. Studying Directive Language

The following is an excerpt from a speech delivered by Adolf Hitler at the peak of his power, in March, 1941. The occasion for the speech was a memorial address in honor of the German soldiers. In analyzing the speech point out Hitler's scorn for the Allies, his blaming them for the war, and his appeal for home-front action. Pick out the words and phrases best calculated to arouse the emotions of his audience.

As twelve months ago in this consecrated hall we turned our thoughts to our heroes, there lay behind us the thoroughly successful beginning of a war that Germany did not want, but that was forced upon us by the same forces that were responsible before in history for the great war of the peoples in 1914 to 1918. . . .

In complete misjudgment of the situation, in a sadly false estimate of their own and Germany's power, and in complete ignorance of the will and determination of the new German leadership, they [England and France] expected a second crushing of our people would be as easy as the first attempt. . . .

The German people have recovered everything that once was sacrificed in a foolish delusion. So today we can recall with lightened hearts the sacrifice of life in the World War. But in the illustrious events of the present we must not overlook the vast spiritual powers for which the German people and its soldiers must thank the heroism of their ancestors.

The soldiers of the World War did not fall in vain. If at that time the sacrifice was not immediately crowned by success, their heroic conduct left a heritage that an ever worthy German generation will prize with deepest emotion and that paralyzes the memories of our enemies.

It is perhaps the consciousness of strength that enabled the German people to achieve such greatness. The people feel they are carrying out the will of heroic ancestors. . . .

So we enter the year 1941, cool and determined to end what started the year before.

### ACTIVITY 2. Studying Directive Language

Each of the following sentences is urging us, directly or indirectly, to do something. Point out for each whether you consider the appeal direct or indirect. For the latter, indicate what readers are being directed to do.

EXAMPLE: *The soup needs salt.* If this were said at the table, it would be an indirect appeal for someone to pass the salt.

1. Visit Maine, "Vacationland."
2. Beware of the dog!
3. Our lawn has just been seeded. Please!
4. Motorists: Children should be seen and not hurt.
5. Our coffee is a special blend of South American highland-grown coffees.
6. "The baby is sleeping," whispered Marie.
7. Have you ever in your life seen grapefruit as big and as juicy as ours?
8. On the sign was painted "Winding road ahead."
9. It's very stuffy in here.
10. The reviewers have called *Cass Timberlane* Lewis's best book since *Arrowsmith*.

### "BAND WAGON" DEVICE

When someone wants us to do something, he is likely to appeal to our desire to be "one of the crowd." He cleverly identifies his listener with himself, or his reader with a great mass of people who are doing the same thing. He says, in effect, "Get on the band wagon. Everybody's doing it. Let's march forward together to a new prosperity." This is directive language which urges that we act in common with a great number of other people.

Hop on the band wagon.   Everybody's doing it!

ACTIVITY 3.  Studying the "Band Wagon" Device

Show how each of the following sentences uses the "band wagon" device by urging you to do something *with somebody else*.

1. All of us are parading this Saturday. Are you joining us?
2. We shall defeat the specter of want and hunger together.
3. Read the *Daily Clarion* — circulation 87,500.
4. It will be our concern that no one in our city is unemployed.
5. This is your team; support it.
6. Everyone in town is seeing the football game. Will you buy a ticket?
7. Forty thousand people are supporting my candidate. Join this group of intelligent Americans.
8. We Parkerville citizens have to stick together.
9. Shall we accept this defeat at the hands of an irresponsible minority? Never!
10. We need a new car. The Browns, Joneses, and Smiths all bought new automobiles.

## WORDS LIVE BY USE

A word has no meaning unless it is used. The four-letter word *fire* is defined in the dictionary, but it doesn't begin to have life until it is used. Then it may mean almost anything from the colloquial "*fire* an employee" to the figurative "*fired* with enthusiasm." It may give sad news, "The *fire* is out, Dad"; or it may suggest terror and panic, "*Fire!*" It hasn't one, two, or a dozen meanings. It has thousands of meanings depending upon the actual situation, the tone of voice, accompanying gestures, or the intention of the user. In the dictionary it lies idle. In action the word is a living, changing symbol.

ACTIVITY 4. Studying a Word in Varied Uses

In each of the following sentences the word *trip* has a different meaning. Explain its meaning in each sentence. Note that some meanings will be quite general while others will be very specific.

1. When was your last *trip* abroad?
2. You cannot *trip* me up by that trick.
3. He tried not to *trip* as he entered.
4. The children *tripped* along ahead of the others.
5. He enjoyed the *trip* of children's feet.
6. Let's go on a *trip* to Mexico.
7. No. I prefer a *trip* to Alaska.

THE IMPORTANCE OF TONE

"Watch out!" A man thoughtlessly walking in front of an oncoming car would jump back immediately if we cried out our warning, but he would be responding more to the *tone* of our voice than to the actual words. The message would be understood in any language because the voice itself would convey the warning, "Danger!" On the other hand correct English in a normal tone might be ineffective if phrased like this: "Pardon me, sir, but the approach of that automobile is likely to endanger your life."

The voice is a remarkably adaptable instrument. It can suggest deep and complex emotions merely by a change in tone. Young children are sensitive to tone, for they listen less to *what* is said than to *how* it is said. Dogs learn simple commands by the *tone* their masters use. A voice is *monotonous* when it keeps *one tone*. How important our manner of speaking is!

In print, tone is indicated partially by symbols like question marks and exclamation points, but these are poor substitutes for the living voice. Writers realize the difficulty and have their characters speak *sneeringly* or *cheerfully*, thus indicating the tone of voice used by the people in the book. A play comes to life when the actors understand their roles and adapt their voices and tones accordingly. The endless variety of ways in which *Hamlet*, for example, can be presented makes the play worth seeing over and over again, for every actor interprets the part differently, delivers the great soliloquies with different emphases. Teachers can tell whether students understand what they read by having students read aloud. The emphases assigned to words, the rise and fall in inflection — these reveal comprehension or ignorance.

By our way of speaking words or phrases we can make them mean something entirely different from their apparent meaning. "Al, you old loafer" may merely be an affectionate greeting. The phrase "You're wonderful!" can mean many things. It can be literally true when spoken by the heroine to the hero after her rescue from the villain. But it can mean just the opposite when it is said by the wife in the comedy to the husband who has just wrecked the living room trying to hang a picture. The clue is in the *tone*.

Henry, you're just wonderful!

ACTIVITY 5. Modifying Tone to Suit the Purpose

By reading aloud with the proper tone convey each of the meanings suggested below.

1. Read the phrase "He's smart" to mean:
   *a.* He's stupid.
   *b.* He's fresh and impertinent.
   *c.* He's unusually brilliant.
   *d.* It's he, not Cliff, who is smart.

2. Say the phrase "I can see" as it would be said by:
   *a.* The blindfolded player in "blind man's buff."
   *b.* A former blind man just after a successful eye operation.
   *c.* A mountain climber to whom a distant peak has been pointed out.
   *d.* A debater who has just agreed with his opponent on one point.
   *e.* An indignant old lady who has just been offered glasses.

3. Read "I don't want John to come" to indicate:
   *a.* That you want Ben to come, instead.
   *b.* That you want John to stay at home.
   *c.* That it was you, not Anne, who didn't want John to come.
   *d.* That you are indignant because someone has declared you don't want John, and you really do.
   *e.* That you are emphasizing again your dislike of John.

4. Read "Where's your invention?" to indicate:
   *a.* That you believe there never was an invention.
   *b.* That you have seen other inventions and now want especially to see this one.
   *c.* That you feared it might have been stolen.
   *d.* That you want to see the invention, nothing else.

5. In the play *Macbeth* Lady Macbeth waits uneasily downstairs as her husband is upstairs murdering the King. She fears that Macbeth may fail at the last moment. She fancies she hears noises. At the end of her speech she sees Macbeth coming downstairs after the deed. Part of her speech is quoted.

"Hark! I laid their daggers ready; he could not miss them. Had he not resembled my father as he slept I had done't. My husband!"
How should she deliver the dramatic words "My husband"?

## Quotation Marks and Tone

Several "comedians" attempted to monopolize the conversation.

Have you ever seen a sentence like the foregoing, in which the use of quotation marks around a word or a phrase changed the meaning of the sentence? Newspapers often use this device to indicate scorn, contempt, disbelief, or ridicule. In an expression like *the "progressive" candidate for mayor*, the quotation marks mean something like *so-called, false*, or *pretended*. If such a phrase were read aloud, it would have to be pronounced scornfully. Thus quotation marks sometimes indicate tone.

## Gestures

Just as tone changes word-meanings, so gestures or facial expressions may alter completely the apparent meaning of a sentence. A needed criticism or suggestion given with a smile and a light tone is taken without offense. A much less serious criticism given without the smile may hurt feelings. Children, sensitive as they are to tone, are more aware of the significance of slight gestures and expressions than many adults.

Words are symbols and so are gestures. The sign languages of the Indians and of the deaf consist of symbols. In the former, whole ideas are expressed by symbols; for example, the gesture of drawing the bow and killing a buffalo. In the latter, individual letters are indicated by a set of carefully prescribed gestures.

Even with our fully developed language we use gestures constantly. Ask someone to describe a spiral staircase without using his hands! Simple directions are often given in gesture: for example, "Come here!" "Go away!" "In this direction." Athletes, too, have elaborate gestures to help in playing the game. Gestures may change the meanings of the words we use. If a friend tells us something we find difficult to believe, we merely say, "Really?" and by uplifted eyebrows indicate we don't believe him at all. Although gestures are not used as frequently as they used to be in oratory, a good speaker uses a few simple gestures to emphasize his points. If he doesn't overdo the gestures, he adds effectiveness to his speech.

RADIO VOICE

BEDTIME

DESPAIR

EXQUISITE

GARRULOUS

PENSIVE

RAPTURE

**Words are symbols and so are gestures.**

ACTIVITY 6. Studying Gestures as a Form of Language

For each of the following sentences indicate the gestures or expressions that may be substituted.

1. The supper is delicious, Mrs. Hostess, but I can't eat another thing.

2. I feel very sorry for you in the experiences you had to undergo.

3. It's too cold in the classroom, Mrs. Brown.

4. I am very fond of cherry ice cream topped with whipped cream and grated nuts.

5. Stay where you are until the dance is over.

6. He's the one who did the job, you mark my words.

7. Is that story true? It sounds unbelievable.

8. I'm not so sure that the answer given was the correct one.

9. Come over to our banquet table, if you can slip away for a moment.

10. The airplane made a sudden power dive to test the wing strength.

11. And then the ghost walked slowly up the stairs.

12. We finally arrived, thoroughly exhausted.

## INTENTION AND ATTITUDE

Our purpose determines what we do with our words. Consequently, before we can fully understand anything we read or hear we must know the purpose of the speaker or writer and his attitude toward us. Intention and attitude determine the changes words undergo in use. In unscrupulous hands words become deadly weapons. If the attitude of the speaker toward us is one of contempt, his words will reflect that state of mind. Often we have no clue to the author's purpose, but must decide for ourselves. If we read a book of humorous anecdotes with the same seriousness we reserve for textbooks, we are wasting our time. On the other hand if we study textbooks as casually as we read light novels, we are mistaking the writers' aims completely, as well as failing to get lasting benefit from the books.

The tone of the book sometimes gives no clue. Many writers seem to be admiring their characters while in reality they are poking fun at them. We call this *irony*, and its product, *satire*. *Gulliver's Travels* is classified as satire, for the author, Jonathan Swift, is ridiculing man and his foolish habits. Many people read *Gulliver's Travels* without realizing satire is intended. The irony is so well done that they are fooled. This is quite understandable in young people, but adults who make the mistake should know better.

Some magazines treat their readers as though the readers were children, incapable of understanding anything above the elementary school level. Other magazines give their readers credit for intelligence. The purpose of the first type is usually only effortless entertainment. As you read, ask yourself, "What is the intention of the writer? What is his attitude toward me, the reader?" Only then can you expect to read intelligently, to evaluate correctly, and to understand words in action.

ACTIVITY 7. Analyzing Intention in an Editorial

A. Cut from the daily newspaper an editorial. Decide which of the following purposes the author had in mind when he wrote the editorial, and prove your point.

| | | |
|---|---|---|
| to commemorate | to entertain | to instruct |
| to condemn | to evaluate | to move to action |
| to criticize | to explain | to praise |

B. Discuss the attitude of the writer toward you. By his choice of language does he give you credit for intelligence, or does he contemptuously "write down" to you?

ACTIVITY 8. Analyzing Intention in Books

What is the purpose behind the writing of each of the following books? Discuss briefly the importance of knowing the purpose as you read.

1. an adventure novel
2. *Care of Tropical Fish*
3. a collection of humorous cartoons
4. a collection of informal essays
5. a collection of poetry
6. *Gulliver's Travels*
7. a history textbook
8. a play in book form
9. a travel book
10. *Winning Words*

## THE IMPORTANCE OF CONTEXT

"The principal called me down." What does the sentence mean? Each of the words has a dictionary definition of its own, yet the meaning of the expression is doubtful. Does it mean that the speaker has been summoned before the principal for some reason? Or does it mean that the speaker has been reprimanded, "called down"? No one can tell. Something is lacking. The missing clues would be supplied by the *context, the word or words immediately surrounding the expression*. We have noted that words do not exist in a vacuum. The words surrounding another word or expression are called the context. Out of context, without its associated words or phrases, a word loses its meaning. The expression "Don't bother!" may mean "Do bother!" if the speaker is merely trying to be polite to a host who has offered to serve cake and tea. We cannot tell the exact meaning unless we know the context. (The context here includes a living situation as well as words.)

Most words in the dictionary have more than one meaning. The only way to tell the meaning of a particular word is by the context. The noun *air* has twenty definitions in *Webster's New International Dictionary*. Only through context can we tell which *air* is meant; for example, "Burns took an old Scottish *air* and composed beautiful words for it." All the words in addition to *air* in the sentence just quoted provide its context. They tell us which *air* is meant; Burns would compose beautiful words for a *melody*. So *melody* and *air* are synonyms here. Different contexts are provided for *air* in each of the following:

1. He *aired* his views on the subject of unemployment.
2. *Air* pressure is normally 14.7 pounds per square inch at sea level.
3. Station WDCH is on the *air*.
4. A warm *air* from the south quickly melts the snow.
5. She certainly gave herself *airs* at the party.
6. He went about the job with the *air* of one accustomed to hard work.

Other contexts would provide still other meanings for *air*.

ACTIVITY 9.  Analyzing the Importance of Context

Show how each repeated word varies in meaning in each of the three sentences.  Use the dictionary to help you with new uses of familiar words.

1. *a.* The *score* was 4–3, with St. Louis in the lead.
   *b.* *Score* the steak before frying it.
   *c.* The conductor of the symphony memorized the entire *score*.

2. *a.* Count Rumford was an outstanding scientist in his *field*.
   *b.* The shortstop couldn't *field* the ball cleanly.
   *c.* The coal *fields* of Pennsylvania are extensive.

3. *a.* Patten had the reputation of being a *hack* writer.
   *b.* Hardy hired a *hack* at the station.
   *c.* Le Beau *hacked* at the door until he made an opening wide enough for his hand.

4. *a.* Penrod had just a little *down*, but he tried to shave, anyway.
   *b.* Sheep were grazing peacefully on the *down*.
   *c.* Carnegie Tech made a first *down* on Notre Dame's four-yard line.

5. *a.* "Asleep in the *Deep*" was the mariner's favorite song.
   *b.* The naval uniform is a *deep* blue.
   *c.* The argument is too *deep* for me.

6. *a.* Morgan paid his bills by *check*.
   *b.* "*Check!*" cried the player for white in the chess tourney.
   *c.* The visitor lost his hat *check*.

7. *a.* Godfrey won Nancy's *hand* in marriage.
   *b.* On the one *hand* I agree; on the other, I'm not so sure.
   *c.* Gissing knew the poverty of London at first *hand*.

8. *a.* Lou Gehrig played hard, but he played the *game* fair.
   *b.* Teddy Roosevelt had a reputation as a hunter of big *game*.
   *c.* I'm *game* to try it. Are you?

9. *a.* The dog was removed from the *pound*.
   *b.* They *pounded* the fortress with hammer blows.
   *c.* He paid five *pounds* for it in London.

10. *a.* Paul Revere called the country folk to *arms*.
    *b.* The baby was soon in the *arms* of Morpheus.
    *c.* The *arm* of the law extends to every corner of our land.

### Activity 10. Studying Context

Show how each of the italicized words, normally pleasant, has an unpleasant meaning because of the context.

1. He was a *friend* to every thief and gunman in the city.
2. The monster's *mother* appeared to attack Beowulf.
3. We have encouraged laxity and now the *flowers* of evil are blossoming everywhere.
4. The city has become the *home* of gamblers from all over the country.
5. The rat-a-tat of the machine guns was an ominous *lullaby* to the soldiers.

### Context and Part of Speech

We cannot classify the part of speech of a word until we have seen it in use. All we can say is that a word is commonly used as a noun, a verb, or an adjective. Its use may change its part of speech. Thus, *but* is generally used as a preposition or as a conjunction, but in the following sentence it is used first as a verb and then as a noun: "*But* me no *buts*."

ACTIVITY 11. Studying Changing Parts of Speech

Each *well* in the following sentence is used as a different part of speech. Tell what each *well* means.

"*Well*," she sighed, as a tear *welled* in her eye, "the *well* doesn't work *well* any more, and I'm not *well* enough to fix it."

### CHANGING CONTEXTS

"We use the latest type of illumination." What kind of lighting equipment does the proud speaker of the foregoing sentence have in her home? Electricity? Fluorescent lighting? Gas? Kerosene? Candle? No one can tell unless we assign a time to the sentence. Uttered in 1600 the sentence might refer to

*1901*          *1911*

*1914*          *1948*

How do you like our new car?

candles; uttered in 1948 the sentence might refer to fluorescent lamps. Quoted out of context the sentence is meaningless. (See pages 164–171.)

## Context in Time

*Sentences change in meaning as times change.* The Magna Carta, often called a democratic document, would be rather undemocratic by our standards, for the bulk of the people were not given the right to vote. Yet by the standards of the thirteenth century the Magna Carta was democratic. The Greeks of the time of Pericles believed in *democracy*, too, but they did not give the vote to slaves, nor even to women. The word *democracy* has changed tremendously with the passing of time. "I believe in democracy" would mean one thing if uttered by an ancient Greek, another if uttered by an American of 150 years ago, and still another if professed by an American of today. Before we can be certain of what a word or sentence means we must place it in *time*.

## Context in Place

*Sentences have different meanings in different places.* Using the word *democracy* again, we would find different interpretations for it throughout the world. In 1918 at the end of the first great war *democracy* became a popular word, yet its meaning varied a great deal from place to place. Each nation had its own idea as to what constituted "democracy," and the definitions, in many cases, excluded the interpretations of other nations. "I am a democrat" meant one thing if spoken by a Pole, another if spoken by a Hungarian, and still another if spoken by a Frenchman. Before we can be certain of what a word or sentence means we must assign it a place. Most of our conversation does not have to be so explained because our listeners know the context of time and place. However, in disputes, disagreements, and debates we demand that facts be clearly labeled as to source so that we can judge the facts presented. There can be no real agreement if two opposing parties have two different contexts in mind as they argue.

## The Speaker and Context

*Sentences have different meanings when said by different speakers.* We noted that "I am a democrat" meant different things to people in different places. However, even if two Americans living in the same place were to make the statement, the meaning would be different for each. A member of the Republican party making the statement would mean *democrat* with a small *d*, that is, a believer in the fundamental tenets of democracy as he understood them. A member of the Democratic party making the statement might mean *Democrat* with a capital *D*, that is, a member of the party so labeled. Before we can be certain of what a word or sentence means we must know something about the speaker, his likes, dislikes, prejudices, and background. When we read a biology textbook, we'd like to be sure that the writer is an authority on the subject. When we listen to a political speech, we'd like to know the speaker's political affiliations. If he is violently biased on one side or another, we'd like to know that, too. Particularly in controversial issues is it necessary to know *who is talking*.

### ACTIVITY 12. Studying Changing Contexts

Explain how the meaning of each of the following statements would be changed if contexts were changed.

1. "I enjoy a good book," if said by
   a. a college professor of English
   b. a mystery "fan"
   c. a child

2. "I fight for the rights of the people," if said by
   a. a dictator
   b. a leader of a political party
   c. a prosecuting attorney

3. "We went for a ride Sunday," if said by
   a. an American farmer about 1890
   b. an American businessman ten years ago
   c. a famous aviator

4. "That's my favorite picture," if said by
   a. a visitor to a museum
   b. a confirmed moviegoer
   c. a woman looking at a photograph album

5. "That weapon is a deadly one," if said by
   a. a modern scientist
   b. a Roman soldier
   c. a British archer at the time of Robin Hood

## THE USE OF AUTHORITY

"Shirley Thompson recommends the use of our vitamin pills. Buy some now and know the vitality of movie stars like her."

You have all seen advertisements similar to the foregoing, in which a motion picture star or other celebrity recommends a product. You might even have said to yourself, "If Shirley Thompson recommends it, it must be good!" The advertisers have attempted to provide a favorable context for the advertising by having a popular star recommend it. Many people accept the context without question. But wait a moment. Is Shirley Thompson qualified to recommend the product? Just because she is a capable actress does not necessarily mean that she is a brilliant scientist, able to discuss the relative merits of vitamin pills. We might treasure her opinions about acting, but her recommendation of vitamin pills is worth no more than ours, unless she has had special training. Similarly, a scientist had better not offer advice on acting, unless his qualifications and training extend to that field, too. Often political speakers use the weight of authority to bolster up their own speeches when they have no ideas of their own. By quoting Lincoln, Webster, Washington, and Jefferson, they give the impression of being unusually well qualified — but anyone can quote authorities. Incidentally, this is an illustration of the "band wagon" device in action.

When you have to make a decision, go for help to those who are acknowledged by leaders in that field to be authorities. And remember to allow for changing contexts of time and place.

### ACTIVITY 13. Studying Authorities

From the group listed at the top select the person who would most likely be qualified to present an opinion about the truth or falsity of each of the sentences given.

| | |
|---|---|
| arctic explorer | English teacher |
| art critic | geographer |
| astronomer | geologist |
| baseball coach | historian |
| biologist | mountain climber |

1. The origins of the American Revolution were economic in part.

2. Some of the largest cabbages in the world are raised in northern Alaska.

3. The Pennsylvanian rock formations contain coal, petroleum, and natural gas.

4. Many words may be used either as adjectives or as adverbs; for example, *slow* and *fast*.

5. Many one-celled living things can be classed as either plants or animals.

6. Some of the Alpine summits are nearly as difficult to scale as Mt. Everest.

7. Generally speaking, it is best to sacrifice a man to second base when there is a man on first with none out.

8. Our solar system seems to be moving in the direction of the star Vega.

9. The French Impressionists contributed a fresh appreciation of color to paintings.

10. Most of the land masses on the globe lie north of the equator.

## QUOTING OUT OF CONTEXT

"In many respects this play is an excellent drama, a brilliant piece of work, but its weaknesses make it dull and uninteresting on the whole."

The drama critic wrote his review, saw it printed the next day. Three days later he read something that made him rub his eyes and look again. There, in a full-page advertisement ballyhooing the play he had condemned, were several quotations. One of them had his signature. It read, "This play is an excellent drama, a brilliant piece of work." The critic was disgusted and angry. He noted that once again advertisers had quoted him *out of context*. True, he had called the play *excellent* and *brilliant*, but he had added many *buts* to indicate clearly his disapproval of the work as a whole. Yet the advertisement gave the impression that the critic had praised it wholeheartedly.

Quoting out of context is all too common. Many things we say sound very bad — out of context. We may say, "Ted is careless about things of no importance, but extremely alert when it counts. I like him." Someone listening may send the tale back to Ted, but quote us as saying merely, "Ted is careless." Much trouble has been caused and many friends lost because people have taken only part of a conversation or letter and quoted it as though the fragment were all of it. Some try to justify quoting out of context by saying, "Well, he said it, didn't he?" "Of course," we reply, "he said it, but he said many other things too that make the short sentence you gave very misleading." The *it* is not the same if taken out of its proper context.

### ACTIVITY 14. Studying Quoting out of Context

Each of the following sentences would be changed considerably if the words in parentheses were omitted. Explain how the meaning would be altered if we quoted just the part not in parentheses.

1. I found *Silas Marner* slow reading (in spots, but my general impression of the book was very favorable).

2. Mathematics is the most difficult subject for me (next to Spanish and history).

3. (I cannot agree that) *Julius Caesar* is better than *Macbeth*.

4. The marine was terrified at the thought of advancing; (yet when the order came he rushed forth courageously with the rest).

5. (Compared with hockey), soccer is a dull game. (Compared with most games it is exciting and fast moving).

6. (Bill foolishly felt that) a high school education isn't necessary for success in business.

7. (This novel doesn't quite become) a powerful study of American life.

8. (Unwisely I insisted that) Aram acted selfishly.

9. (Don't think for a moment that) I have no concern for the rights of others.

10. (I kept repeating that) I just couldn't understand algebra. (Later I realized that I'd been mistaken.)

5

# Connotation vs. Denotation

*Jess and Ben were having an argument over words. Jess asserted vehemently, "No two words in the English language are exactly alike."*

*"Not even synonyms?" questioned Ben scornfully.*

*"No, not even synonyms," replied Jess equally disdainfully.*

*"How about the words* vision *and* sight? *You can say a man has good* vision *or good* sight. *The words mean the same!"*

*"Do they? Suppose I said, 'Ben, my wife is a* vision, *but yours is a* sight!' *Would they be the same?"*

*Ben realized that he had lost the argument and wisely kept silent.*

Jess was right, of course; no two words in English are exactly alike. There is always a shade of difference, no matter how slight. Synonyms can be approximate substitutes for each other, but each word has a shade of meaning entirely its own. The dictionary considers the following words synonyms: *close, end, conclude, finish, complete, terminate.* All of them have the same general idea; yet a sentence could be devised for each that would exclude the others; for example, you can *close* the door, *conclude* a treaty, *finish* a job, *complete* the meaning of a sentence, *terminate* a contract, and *end* the uncertainty by making a decision. In the foregoing sentence each of the synonyms is used in a special way. No one of them could reasonably be substituted for any of the others. Synonyms are alike — up to a point. Good general dictionaries and synonym dictionaries attempt to show differences by including illustrative sentences containing the synonyms. (See pages 118–133 for a discussion of synonym discrimination.)

ACTIVITY 1. Studying Synonyms in Action

In each of the following sentences choose from the list of synonyms in parentheses the one word that best completes the meaning of the sentence. Show why the others do not quite "fit."

EXAMPLE: *Although he had been away for years, when he approached his house, everything suddenly seemed to become (close, confidential, familiar, intimate).*

Familiar is the desired word here. *Close* and *confidential* are too farfetched. *Intimate* suggests much greater privacy than the street could possibly provide. *Familiar* has the correct meaning.

1. The ex-champion's muscles became ——— from lack of exercise. (*limp, flimsy, loose, flabby*)

2. The photographer specialized in ——— camera shots. (*frank, open, candid, plain*)

3. The characters in this novel are ——— and bear no intentional resemblance to actual people. (*fabulous, fictitious, mythical, legendary*)

4. The prisoner was ——— under the laws pertaining to espionage in time of war. (*slain, murdered, executed, assassinated*)

5. A mild ——— blew in out of the west. (*gale, blast, breeze, tornado*)

6. The ancient Spartans sought to eradicate from the boys any traits they considered ———. (*effeminate, ladylike, womanly, feminine*)

7. Demetrius and Lysander were ——— for the hand of Helena. (*opponents, adversaries, rivals, antagonists*)

8. Medieval monks spent a great deal of time ——— ancient manuscripts. (*copying, imitating, mocking, aping*)

9. He was unreasonable because he expected nothing short of ——— in his employees. (*excellence, merit, virtue, perfection*)

10. The spectators were gripped by sudden ——— and stampeded when the cry of "Fire" was raised. (*dismay, panic, consternation, dread*)

ACTIVITY 2.  Studying a Word with Many Synonyms

From the list of words below supply the proper synonym for each use of the word *run* in the sentences listed. Why is it each synonym is different from the others, though all are synonyms of the one word *run?*

| | |
|---|---|
| brook | path |
| epidemic | race |
| flowing | route |
| ladder | score |
| migration | trip |

1. The Dodgers made a *run* in the first inning.
2. The hunters waited by the deer *run* for their prey.
3. The *run* of salmon up the Columbia River is an annual event.
4. The first *run* of sap in maple orchards usually occurs in February.
5. A *run* of influenza terrified the country.
6. The train made the *run* in six hours.
7. The *run* of the Miami Special is through Jacksonville.
8. One will seldom find a *run* in nylon stockings.
9. The battles of Bull *Run* were hotly contested.
10. The sprinter entered the mile *run* to test his endurance.

## CONNOTATION AND DENOTATION

Dictionaries supply only part of the meaning of a word. The strict dictionary definition we call *denotation.* The extra meaning that a word acquires in use we call *connotation. Vision* and *sight* have similar denotations, but vastly different connotations, as Ben found out to his dismay. Connotations are harder to describe because they change so frequently in action. Large dictionaries attempt to meet the problem by inserting short sentences illustrating the meaning of a word in use. Even this procedure is inadequate because words have so many different connotations. We can learn denotations by memorizing dictionary definitions. We learn connotations by reading intelligently and listening intently to note how words are used. *Both are necessary to intelligent vocabulary building.*

People often make amusing mistakes by learning denotation only. One person told the driver of a bus, "Please *procrastinate* me at the next corner." The bus driver was flabbergasted. The passenger finally admitted that he had looked the word up and found it means "to put off." Unfortunately the word means "to put off" only in the sense of *time*, "to put off doing something."

Another boy looked up the word *trite* and found it means *commonplace*. He wrote on a composition, "Tomorrow at the picnic we'll all meet at the *trite*." Unfortunately it isn't that kind of *common place!* Still another student wrote, "While going to school, Munson made his *contemporary*." The boy had looked up *contemporary* and found that it meant "living at the same time," so he merely substituted the denotation and went completely off. *Contemporary* refers to a person "living at the same time as another." For example, "George Washington was John Adams' *contemporary*." To learn denotations only is not enough.

### ACTIVITY 3. Studying Misused Words

In each of the following sentences the italicized word is incorrectly used. By checking with a dictionary decide which word in the word pool is correct for each sentence. For each, point out why you think the writer had learned the *denotation* but not the *connotation*. Use the word correctly in a sentence of your own.

EXAMPLE: *Alice's actions made a permanent stamp upon him.* In one sense, when speaking of leaving a mark on cloth or paper, for example, *stamp* and *impression* are alike in denotation and connotation, but in this instance, dealing as it does with the human personality, their connotations are different.

| | |
|---|---|
| *a.* abrupt change in feeling | *f.* dishonor |
| *b.* absolute | *g.* foreign |
| *c.* approve | *h.* ordinary |
| *d.* clear | *i.* susceptible |
| *e.* crown | *j.* wall |

1. After the clouds had disappeared, the day became *distinct*.
2. The blow fell heavily on the *diadem* of his skull.
3. Is that a United States or an *exotic* stamp?

4. He caught a chill and experienced a *caprice*.
5. A birthday is not a *mediocre* day; it's a special day.
6. Mr. Alexander did not *ratify* his daughter's actions.
7. He feared the evil deed would *infamy* his good name.
8. He was very *capable* to colds.
9. The Mikado was *certain* ruler of 70 million people.
10. Instead of using paint he decided to paper each *parapet* of his room.

## How Connotations Vary

"The American sailors refused to give up. They had hearts of *Quercus*."

"The floor was sturdy; it was made of select *Quercus*."

"The *Quercus* is monarch of the forest."

"Great *Quercuses* from tiny acorns grow."

By now you have probably guessed that *Quercus* is the same as *oak*. But is it? *Quercus* is the scientific name; *oak*, the popular name. They cannot be interchanged successfully, can they? Somehow the word *Quercus*, though it means, according to the dictionary, the same as *oak*, doesn't have the rich suggestiveness of the word *oak*. *Oak* does much more than simply define. It suggests lasting strength, grandeur, serenity. Both words have the same strict meaning (or denotation), but they differ tremendously in their connotations.

## Scientific and Poetical Words

Science, because it requires exactness and precision, prefers to use words of slight connotation. *Quercus*, we noted, was more specific than *oak*, and not so suggestive. *Felis domestica*, the scientific name for the common house cat, is much more specific than *cat*, for the latter may refer to an African lion, a Bengal tiger, a leopard, a puma, a cougar, an American mountain lion, a person, a game, a whip, or a boat. Science cannot thrive upon such indefiniteness. Consequently scientists have devised names that may not be beautiful but are exact.

**Felis Domestica and his feline cousins**

Poetry, on the other hand, seeks to present a mood, suggest an atmosphere, describe an emotion. Consequently, highly suggestive words like *solitary*, *wintry*, *life* are common in poetry. Wordsworth's poem *To the Daisy* would be ridiculous if he had used the scientific name and called it *To the Bellis Perennis*.

Both types of words have their uses. When we seek facts and specific information, we insist upon words with slight connotation. We object when a political speaker avoids telling us specifically what he intends to do and uses only vague, highly connotative words like *home*, *mother*, and *country*. But we'd also object if our poets and writers gave us only denotative words like *Quercus* and omitted beautiful and suggestive words like those in the following lines taken from Walter de la Mare's *The Listeners*.

> And his horse in the silence champed the grasses
> Of the forest's ferny floor.

Almost an entire scene is suggested by those few words.

Activity 4. Studying Popular and Scientific Words

In each of the following sentences indicate which word you would prefer. Does the sentence call for the exact scientific term or the popular suggestive term? Explain.

EXAMPLE: *Spring must be here. I saw my first ——— today. (robin, bird, Planesticus migratorius)*

Obviously *robin* is the choice. "The first robin" as a sign of spring would be nonsense if we substituted the scientific term. We desire the pleasant suggestiveness of *robin*. It is specific enough and still suggestive enough for our purposes. *Bird* is too general.

1. The student decided that the specimen belonged to the order of the ———. (*Lepidoptera, winged insects, butterflies*)

2. Poe's most famous poem describes the entrance of a mysterious ———. (*raven, Corvus corax, black bird*)

3. I'd like to plant some fruit trees this year. I like particularly ———. (*apple, Pyrus Malus, Mackintosh apple*)

4. In the museum the skull was labeled ———. (*dinosaur, Tyrannosaurus Rex, giant lizard*)

5. The lawn was covered with ———. (*dandelions, Taraxacum officinale, yellow flowers*)

6. "That group of stars up there," commented the old farmer, "is ———." (*Ursa Major, the Big Dipper, a constellation*)

7. His eyesight is excellent, like that of a ———. (*hawk, bird, Accipter velox*)

8. In certain parts of our country it is dangerous to go swimming because of the great numbers of ———. (*Agkistrodon piscivorus, snakes, water moccasins*)

9. Throughout pestilence and wars, the Flemish farmhouse stood as solid as a ———. (*rock, metamorphic rock, mineral*)

10. The amoeba belongs to the phylum of ———. (*protozoans, tiny animals, animate objects*)

## ACTIVITY 5. Studying Poetic Words

In each of the following poetry selections point out the words that are richly suggestive and connotative. Rephrase each in prose. Which do you prefer, the prose of the poetic version? Why?

EXAMPLE: *Night's candles are burnt out, and jocund day*
  *Stands tiptoe on the misty mountain tops.* (*Shakespeare*)
Rephrased *in prose:* The night is over, and the stars have faded. Another happy day is breaking over foggy mountains.

1. Sweet day, so cool, so calm, so bright,
     The bridal of the earth and sky;
   The dew shall weep thy fall tonight,
       For thou must die. (*George Herbert*)

2. With how sad steps, O Moon, thou climb'st the skies!
   How silently and with how wan a face! (*Sir Philip Sidney*)

3. It is an ancient mariner,
     And he stoppeth one of three. (*Coleridge*)

4. That orbed maiden with white fire laden,
     Whom mortals call the moon. (*Shelley*)

5. The castled crag of Drachenfels
     Frowns o'er the wide and winding Rhine. (*Byron*)

6. But, look, the morn in russet mantle clad,
     Walks o'er the dew of yon high eastern hill. (*Shakespeare*)

7. The skies they were ashen and sober;
     The leaves they were crisped and sere. (*Poe*)

8. And not by eastern windows only,
     When daylight comes, comes in the light,
   In front, the sun climbs slow, how slowly,
     But westward, look, the land is bright. (*Clough*)

9. And the night shall be filled with music,
     And the cares, that infest the day,
   Shall fold their tents, like the Arabs,
     And as silently steal away. (*Longfellow*)

10. The great brand
    Made lightnings in the splendor of the moon,
    And flashing round and round, and whirl'd in an arch,
    Shot like a streamer of the northern morn. (*Tennyson*)

## CONNOTATIVE WORDS AND OUR EMOTIONS

"Boys, we're going home!" The sergeant's message was greeted by cheers from a hundred throats. "Home!" each soldier thought. No wonder the joyful cries rang out. As each soldier gathered his belongings together, the one word *home* dominated his thinking. "Going home" is a phrase that thrills anyone away from his native land.

Strangely enough, though there are many synonyms for *home*, not one has as much power to move us as this simple word. *Mansion, house, dwelling, domicile, abode, residence* — all of these supposedly mean the same as *home*, but what a difference! "Going to my residence" is a poor substitute for "going home." Where does the difference lie? Not in the strict dictionary definition, certainly, but in the host of associations that have gathered through the years around the word *home*. These are the connotations. These make the word *home* infinitely richer than the word *house*. *Home* stirs us; *house* leaves us cold. Our minds are influenced by denotations, but our hearts are moved by connotations. An unscrupulous speaker, like Adolf Hitler, can use that power for evil, by introducing words like *fatherland*, *Greater Germany*, and *master race*.

### ACTIVITY 6.  Studying Connotative Words

In each of the following groups select the word or expression that seems to you most connotative, suggestive, or emotional. If your selections differ from those of your classmates, discuss the possible reasons for disagreement.

1. pater, male parent, father, daddy
2. automobile, family buggy, car, Ford
3. holiday, celebration, Christmas, anniversary
4. America, country, nation, people

5. wizard, magician, sleight-of-hand artist, necromancer
6. shack, hut, cabin, hunting lodge
7. sister, relative, sis, step-sister
8. commencement, graduation, happy occasion, bright beginning
9. weed garden, flower garden, rose garden, wild garden
10. book, novel, best seller, masterpiece

### ACTIVITY 7. Studying Wartime Connotations

Each of the following words took on richer connotations because of the war. For each discuss its additional wartime suggestiveness and point out whether the word acquired pleasant or unpleasant connotations.

1. aggressor
2. appeasement
3. defeatist
4. freedom
5. hoarder
6. hostage
7. isolationist
8. price controls
9. rationing
10. underground

## THE RIGHT WORD

"In the painting a beautiful lady held a lily in her delicate fist." Somehow the sentence doesn't sound right, does it? Every word is correctly used according to its denotation or dictionary definition; yet one word clashes. We don't associate the masculine, powerful "fist" with a delicate, beautiful lady.

**The lady held a lily in her delicate fist.**

Many people misuse words constantly because they rely solely upon the narrow dictionary definitions. A feeling for words is gained by studying the dictionary definition and the *word in action*. One without the other is unsatisfactory. We can say, "The strong man *wept*," but we'd hesitate to say, "The strong man *blubbered*." *Wept* is dignified; *blubbered* is comical. Both mean *cry*, but each suggests a different kind of crying. Using the right word requires judgment, not merely memorization.

ACTIVITY 8. Pointing out the "Wrong Word"

In each of the following sentences one word obviously does not belong, because its connotation clashes with the picture presented. Point out the word and tell why you consider it unsatisfactory, even though its dictionary definition might make it seem suitable. Suggest a substitute.

EXAMPLE: *Beside the aircraft carrier even a light cruiser seemed petite.* The wrong word is obviously *petite*. The word may be applied to a small, dainty woman, but it can scarcely be applied to a cruiser, no matter how small it might seem by comparison. A good substitute would be *small*.

1. The knight dashed in on his magnificent nag.
2. The stately old gentleman waltzed into the room.
3. "Watch out for that car!" he murmured.
4. The defeated candidate wore a sour expression on his visage.
5. A welder carried some posies home to his wife.
6. Tiny icicles fell and struck the ground with a crash.
7. Ted is a very dear acquaintance of mine.
8. The dignified hostess gulped down her food.
9. The puppy splashed daintily through the puddle.
10. The travelers glared at the colorful sunset over Mt. Washington.

ENGLISH IS NOT LOGICAL!

A minister from the kingdom of Afghanistan was attending a dinner at Buckingham Palace in England. As he escorted one of the ladies in to dinner, he turned to the picture galleries and commented to his companion, "All these pictures are worthless — absolutely *worthless*." His companion was shocked for a moment, but suddenly she realized that he had meant *priceless*, not *worthless*. He had made the mistake of assuming that, since *price* and *worth* are partial synonyms, so *priceless* and *worthless* must be, too. Unfortunately they mean exactly the opposite, for the former means "valuable beyond price" and the latter means "of no value whatever." Another foreign visitor complimented his hostess on the quality of the *feed* she had served him. He failed to realize that *feed* is used for animals, not for human beings. Logically, *feed* seemed as good a word as *food*. Meanings depend upon *use* not *logic*. The only way to learn English meanings is to read and listen attentively to those who use words with discrimination.

ACTIVITY 9. Reviewing Connotation and Denotation

Discuss the difference in meaning between each of the sentences in the following pairs. Point out how connotation influences meaning.

EXAMPLE: a. *I order you to take these to the warehouse.*
b. *I suggest you take these to the warehouse.*

Sentence *a* is likely to arouse resentment because it states an order directly. Sentence *b* says the same thing, but says it gracefully. The connotation of *suggest* is much more pleasant than that of *order*.

1. *a.* Like a shepherd he carefully watched over the people in his care.
   *b.* Like a cowboy he carefully watched over the people in his care.

2. *a.* The old gentleman struck me as being eccentric.
   *b.* The old gentleman seemed insane.

3. *a.* He spent his time in lazy idleness.
   *b.* Enforced unemployment wearied him.

4. *a.* Princeton routs Dartmouth, 12–6.
   *b.* Dartmouth is nosed out by Princeton, 12–6.

5. *a.* The water lay stagnantly quiet in the swamp.
   *b.* The water lay peacefully silent in the bayou.

6. *a.* The rain beat a merry tattoo on the windowpane.
   *b.* The rain struck madly against the window.

7. *a.* He learned slowly, but retained what he learned.
  *b.* It took time for anything to penetrate his thick skull.

8. *a.* He ruthlessly rose to the top by defeating all his competitors.
  *b.* By clever bargaining and shrewd planning he made his mark in the world.

9. *a.* Her thrift and careful economies enabled her to save a tidy sum.
  *b.* Her own stingy miserliness deprived her of the pleasures of living.

10. *a.* He lived bravely as he pleased and refused to let himself be narrowed by others.
  *b.* He disregarded all rules of decent conduct and lived only for his own pleasures.

11. *a.* When I look at him, time stands still.
  *b.* His face would stop a clock!

12. *a.* He wore an outlandish and ridiculous costume to the masquerade.
  *b.* His masquerade costume was whimsical and unusual.

13. *a.* The army retreated in mad disorder.
  *b.* The army withdrew to previously prepared positions.

14. *a.* The old colonel was gruff and rugged.
  *b.* The old colonel was rude and crabbed.

15. *a.* His appetite was excellent.
  *b.* He gorged himself and stuffed himself with food.

16. *a.* He is slightly misstating the facts.
  *b.* He is a liar.

17. *a.* I was unable to do last night's homework.
  *b.* I am unprepared.

18. *a.* He squandered his money quickly.
  *b.* He had nothing but contempt for money.

19. *a.* He thoughtfully planned every move before he acted.
  *b.* He fearfully held back until the last moment.

20. *a.* My sister is one of the neatest people I've ever seen.
  *b.* My sister is one of the fussiest people I've ever seen.

# 6

# Unpleasant Connotations

*"Tommy plays with girrulls. Tommy is a sissy." How many little boys since time began have been upset at this heartless chant of other little boys. How many have become desperate, trying to erase the name of* sissy, *a dread label that no little boy wants pinned to him. Too, how many girls have tried to live down the name of* tomboy, *carelessly applied to all girls who play baseball or climb trees at an early age. Sissy and* tomboy *are two words we meet early in life. For many people they are the first experience with unpleasant connotations.*

## SMEAR WORDS

"Smear words" are words of unpleasant connotation, words that have acquired their bad reputation through use. Words like *sissy* and *tomboy* are universally accepted "smear words." Some words, however, have bad connotations, not in general, but only to some individual because of his unhappy experience with them. A boy who cuts himself severely with a hatchet will always associate pain and discomfort with the word *hatchet*. The boy who has used the hatchet on scouting trips looks upon the word with pleasure and fond remembrances. To some people the word *kerosene* is pleasant, suggesting farm kitchens, country surroundings, out-of-door living. To others the word *kerosene* has unpleasant associations, because of the strong smell, a past burn, or poor lighting. Many words cannot be classified definitely in one way or the other because individual reactions vary.

### ACTIVITY 1. Studying Individual Likes

Which of the words in the following list have for you a pleasant connotation? Unpleasant? Try to trace the origin of your likes or dislikes.

| | | |
|---|---|---|
| boy | girl | park |
| cat | hike | pine tree |
| dishes | horse | soap |
| dog | insect | suit |
| fire | matches | sunlight |
| football | mountain stream | trout |
| garden | newspaper | turpentine |

## LABELING

Words change. The word with former unpleasant associations, like *mugwump* in American political history, may be harmless today. However, at any given period of time some words are generally accepted by all people in a given group as words with unfavorable connotations. *Fascist* and *dictator* represent ideas that are thoroughly hated by every democratic American of today. A speaker who doesn't like someone attempts to capitalize upon this current dislike by calling the person he doesn't agree with a *dictator* or a *Fascist*. We call the device *labeling*. The label may or may not be true, but if a charge is made we are entitled to know the basis of the charge, so that we may be able to judge the truth or falsity of the label.

Labels tend to have unfavorable, but vague, connotations. The most serious charge against the use of labels is encouragement of loose thinking. The label becomes a substitute for thought. Such labels as *un-American* and *radical* mean one thing to Mr. A and still another thing to Miss B. It is the fuzziness of real meaning that makes labeling, for the most part, a thorough source of confusion rather than light.

### ACTIVITY 2. Defining Labels

Write down in your notebook your own definition of each of the following labels. After you have completed the definitions, compare your definitions with those supplied by the rest of the class. Why is there such disagreement? What does this variety of interpretations prove about the use of labels in argument?

| | |
|---|---|
| 1. bureaucracy | 6. left-wing |
| 2. communist | 7. loafer |
| 3. dreamer | 8. reactionary |
| 4. foreigner | 9. socialist |
| 5. idealist | 10. tyrant |

ACTIVITY 3. Studying Labeling

Point out how each of the following words may label through bad connotations.

| | |
|---|---|
| 1. autocratic | 6. ne'er-do-well |
| 2. coward | 7. pompous |
| 3. insolent | 8. self-centered |
| 4. makeshift | 9. shiftless |
| 5. miser | 10. slipshod |

## SLANTING

"Only five hundred attend meeting."

"Five hundred people throng to meeting."

Here we have two typical newspaper headlines, each one giving exactly the same facts but each *implying*, or *saying indirectly*, something different. The first is saying, in effect, "The meeting was a failure — only five hundred came." The second is saying, "The meeting was a success — five hundred people crowded in." The word *only* in the first headline tells us the newspaper thinks, or wants us to think, that fewer came than expected. The word *throng* in the second headline tells us that, in the newspaper's opinion, the meeting attracted a large and eager group of people. A neutral report of the meeting would be the simple direct statement, "Five hundred attend meeting." This last statement allows the reader to draw his own conclusions, doesn't attempt to force an opinion upon him.

The device of taking a simple account or report and giving it an emotional bias is called *slanting*. When you report to your dad about a high school game and say, "We trimmed them,"

Orderly withdrawal or rout?

you are using the emotional word *trimmed*, which implies a lopsided score. "We defeated them, 20–12," would be a straightforward and less emotional description. The former expression *slants* the facts, implying a much greater victory for your team than the score itself warrants. A member of the opposing team reporting to his dad might say, "They just nosed us out." This slants the facts in the other direction, saying, "We should have won, but they were lucky and barely won the game."

Facts are facts, but the way in which people interpret or slant the facts tells us a great deal about the people themselves. A newspaper with Republican sympathies will report an event quite differently from a newspaper with Democratic leanings, even though each is starting with the same facts. The first will tend to display prominently the names of Republican leaders, Republican successes. The second newspaper will emphasize Democratic predictions of success. Often a wide-awake observer can judge the political sympathies of a newspaper, not by its editorial page alone, but by its slanting of partisan news and its placement of political news on the front page.

ACTIVITY 4. Studying Slanted Headlines

Discuss the difference in suggested meaning of each headline in the following pairs. Point out how each starts from the same facts but gives a different picture by the choice of words that slant the meaning in one direction or another.

1. *a.* Violence grips capital.
   *b.* Minor outbreaks checked in capital.

2. *a.* Crowds cheer thrilling play.
   *b.* Mild applause greets play.

3. *a.* Barker leaves employ of steel mills.
   *b.* Barker fired.

4. *a.* City snowed under by first storm.
   *b.* Light snow falls in city.

5. *a.* Weary runner barely makes finish line.
   *b.* Runner gamely spurts at finish.

6. *a.* Merely 25% fail to vote.
   *b.* Nearly 25% fail to vote.

7. *a.* Martin believes in government controls.
   *b.* Martin believes in government dictatorship.

8. *a.* Three hundred club members parade in strength.
   *b.* Twelve hundred club members shun parade.

9. *a.* Workers forced to reject terms.
   *b.* Workers spurn terms.

10. *a.* Charges against Burnett cannot be proved.
    *b.* Charges against Burnett cannot be disproved.

### ACTIVITY 5. Writing Slanted Reports

To understand how slanting can confuse your thinking, try slanting. Below are listed ten literal, factual descriptions or reports. Slant each one, first to give a favorable picture, and then to present an unfavorable one. Show how the same fact can give vastly different interpretations.

EXAMPLE: *Dr. Renner is unanimously elected President of the Republic.*
   Favorable: Dr. Renner is overwhelmingly acclaimed President without one dissenting vote.
   Unfavorable: Dr. Renner is elected President. All opposition has been stifled.

1. The Benton baseball team loses to Center High School by a score of 5–4.

2. Johnson's new novel sells 1000 copies on publication day.

3. A sales tax is urged to eliminate revenue deficits.

4. Nelson is chosen outstanding athlete by a ten-vote lead over Wilton.

5. The bus lines accept the terms laid down by the transit commission.

6. Jordan's department store closes down permanently.

7. Stocks drop one point on the average.

8. Marvin wins mayoralty election.

9. The newspaper has a circulation of 30,000.

10. One inch of rain fell in the city yesterday.

## ACTIVITY 6. Writing Longer Slanted Reports

Report some school contest; for example, a baseball, football, basketball game, or some other. Write the description first as a prejudiced observer for the home team and then as an unbiased reporter for a large newspaper. Show how differences in emphasis provide completely different pictures.

## ACTIVITY 7. Writing Literal Reports

Each of the following statements is a slanted report of some event. Rephrase each so that merely the cold facts are given.

EXAMPLE: *The orator made so favorable an impression on his audience that he encouraged lively debate at the end.*

> Factual report: At the end of the speech the audience engaged in lively debate. (The debate may have been favorable or unfavorable to the orator. The factual statement doesn't try to interpret.)

1. The senator has timidly refused to support the Oaks Resolution.

2. Barely 200 people signed the petition.

3. Our gallant team fought bravely against odds but lost out at the end.

4. The editorial scandalously and unreasonably attacked the administration.

5. The novel is a brilliant exposé of our slums.

6. Dickinson, an unfair bargainer, swayed the audience to his viewpoint.

7. Thomas failed miserably in his attempt to secure a new school for his neighborhood.

8. The poor speaker made so pitiful a sight that the audience listened out of kindness.

9. Burns is successful in every respect, for he has made $100,000 in the paint business.

10. Councilman Ives courageously took a positive stand on the road problem, voting for the new highway.

## EDITORIALS AND NEWS REPORTS

Since an editorial is an obvious expression of opinion, some slanting is unavoidable. However, the body of a straight news report should give *facts*, not *opinion*. Slanting in a news report is misleading. Careful newspapers clearly indicate statements of opinion in news reports by including sources of opinion, by using quotation marks, or by placing editorial comment in brackets. Unsupported wild statements, the use of vague identities like "reliable sources" or similar unverifiable informants, are weaknesses.

### ACTIVITY 8. Studying News Reports and Editorials

Compare a news report and an editorial. Point out unslanted statements of fact and slanted statements. Can you detect any slanting in the news reports? Do you approve or disapprove of this? Exactly what statements of opinion are included? Are they so labeled?

### ACTIVITY 9. Finding Fair and Unfair Editorials

From your own reading of the newspaper select a pair of editorials, one that you consider fair; the other, unfair. If possible, find two editorials on the same subject, preferably from two different newspapers. Compare them. Point out how the unfair editorial introduces "loaded" words and omits material to make its side more convincing. Show, too, how the fair editorial attempts to give both sides of the question.

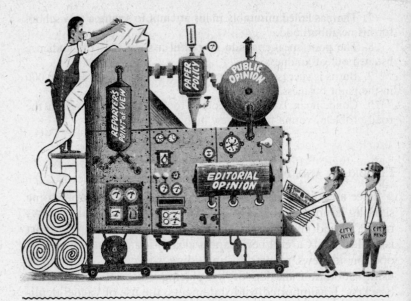

**The newspaper in the making**

ACTIVITY 10.  Finding Slanted News Reports

From your reading of the newspaper find a news report that you consider one-sided, slanted to present one point of view only. Point out how this slanting gives an erroneous impression.

ACTIVITY 11.  Writing a Letter to the Editor

Using as your title *A Needed Change*, write a letter to the editor of your school newspaper discussing some problem of school, local, or international importance. Point out the change needed and suggest remedies. Seek to influence your readers to your point of view by selecting your facts and choosing words with the "right" connotations.

SLANTING THROUGH OMISSION

"Those mushrooms make a fragrant, tempting stew, but unfortunately they are a poisonous species."

If you were planning a meal with mushrooms, you'd certainly want to know *all* the facts. You would not be interested so much in the word *fragrant* as in the word *poisonous*. Yet you might be misled by the first half of the sentence if you did not have the important second half beginning with *but*. *Fragrant* and *tempting* by themselves suggest food treats. With *poisonous* they lose any appetizing quality they may have.

This is farfetched, you say. No one would quote only part of such a sentence, leaving one of the most important facts out altogether. Probably no one would — with mushrooms, but people are doing it all the time with other words. All of us tend to select the favorable qualities of those we like, and the unfavorable qualities of those we dislike. In anger we often forget that Bert Towne is a human being, with the faults and virtues of most of us. When we have quarreled with him, we tend to think only of his stubbornness, his quick temper, and his carelessness. We forget his loyalty, his generosity, and his inability to hold a grudge. In ill-advised moments we may even confide his failings to others, in an effort to bolster up our own pride. Later, when Bert has won his way into our affections again, we regret those hasty statements, observations which may have been *true* factually, but which were really *false* because they gave an incomplete picture of Bert.

Political campaigns tend to use the technique of slanting through omission. One candidate charges the other with great carelessness, laxity, and inefficiency, forgetting conveniently the good points of his opponent. Newspapers that have a pronounced bias against one party may omit favorable facts in a report about the party, presenting a lopsided report, slanted through omission. Those who wish to make sweeping statements about one race, group, or religion select only certain facts and omit other facts that would balance the picture, present a truer report. Slanting through omission is one of the most difficult tricks to detect because we must be in possession of all the facts before we can judge. Whenever we read reports that present a person as all good or all bad, we should ask for more facts. Sometimes the deliberate omission of important facts tells voters a great deal about a candidate.

#### ACTIVITY 12.  Studying Slanting by Omission

Show how the following statements would present an unfair description of Mr. Adams if the material in parentheses were omitted.

Mr. Adams' views may be considered un-American (only if a concern for the rights of others is un-American). He is concerned that tne benefits of democracy be available to the lowliest thief (as well as to the most fortunate American). He does not believe in any government (if it means slavery).

#### ACTIVITY 13.  Studying Slanting by Selection

Mr. Carter likes all the activities and things listed below.

| | |
|---|---|
| checkers | being thorough in his work |
| chow mein | lounging about the house |
| football | lying in bed late |
| handball | mowing his lawn |
| hiking | playing cards |
| hockey | reading detective stories |
| roast beef | resting frequently |
| swimming | working late at the office |
| whipped cream | writing for magazines |

By selecting only some of the items at one time "prove" that Mr. Carter is a lazy idler, a hard worker, a lover of food, an athlete. Which one of these truly represents Mr. Carter? How could one give an accurate picture?

#### ACTIVITY 14.  Studying Selection in News Reports

The following items were jotted down by a news reporter at a fire scene.

| | |
|---|---|
| colorful sky | people scurrying back and forth |
| fire sirens clanging | smoke drifting lazily upward |
| fleecy clouds in east | sunset |
| house on fire | woman screaming |

Which items might be selected to give an impression of the noise and confusion of the fire? Which might be selected to suggest the quiet and serenity of the background? Why is selection actually unavoidable? Would you omit some of the description here? Which items? Why?

### ACTIVITY 15. Studying Slanting by Selection

Anne received the following marks on her report card.

| | | | |
|---|---|---|---|
| *algebra* | 96 | *history* | 95 |
| *drawing* | 70 | *hygiene* | 71 |
| *English* | 92 | *mechanical drawing* | 68 |
| *French* | 98 | *public speaking* | 72 |

Which marks would a friend emphasize in telling about Anne's achievements? Why? How could Anne's marks be slanted unfavorably by omission? Which marks are needed to present an honest picture of Anne as a student?

## BAD CONNOTATION IN ADVERTISING

We have already noted that advertisers, those wide-awake practical psychologists, understand words better than most of us. They know how to play upon our emotions to sell their goods, often without any appeal to the intellect. They understand the public's sensitivity to words, and use that sensitivity to frighten, persuade, encourage, and challenge us to buy. Most of the words they use are pleasant words, words that conjure up visions of happiness, success, beauty, and affection. Occasionally, however, they introduce words that suggest unpleasant events, things that may happen if we fail to buy their products. A dancing school, instead of emphasizing the joys of dancing, may suggest the unfortunate results of not learning to dance by using the word *wallflower*. Since the word suggests loneliness and unattractiveness, many people resolve immediately to learn to dance, to avoid the unpleasant name of *wallflower*. Thus the suggestion has its intended effect. Suggested health remedies emphasize the evils of *athlete's foot*, *halitosis*, or *pyorrhea*. Correspondence courses beg readers to avoid *blindalley jobs*, *illiteracy*, and *failure*. Since people want to be healthy, popular, and successful, these suggestions bring results. Before acting on impulse intelligent people, realizing that the evils may exist, consider their own needs and abilities and then decide whether the advertised articles will help them. They refuse to be stampeded into action merely by a word.

### ACTIVITY 16. Studying Connotation in Advertising

Keep a scrapbook for the next week, cutting from the newspaper all advertising containing words of bad connotation. Analyze each advertisement. Does it give facts, suggest a real remedy? Or does it try to stampede everybody into buying the product regardless of real need?

## A MISUNDERSTOOD WORD

One of the commonest words in the English language is one of the most dangerous. It is used hundreds of times a day and seldom means the same thing twice in succession. Babies learn it as one of their first words, and often misuse it as adults do. In this paragraph so far it has been used twice. Have you guessed it yet? The word is *is*.

"Dangerous!" you scoff. "How so?"

Examine these two sentences closely:

> An amoeba *is* a one-celled animal.
> Helen's brother *is* selfish.

Both uses of *is* are clearly different. The first one is a statement of fact, capable of verification when someone gets out a microscope. The second one is a statement of opinion, incapable of verification because opinions differ widely. The first *is* is an equal sign. The second one means something like "seems to me," so that we really mean, "Helen's brother *seems to me* selfish." A careful thinker and speaker tends to qualify direct statements of the second type by adding an explanatory "in my opinion" or "I feel." Unfortunately not all speakers take such pains for exactness. As a result we have many *is* sentences in which *is* is misused. You as listener and reader should be able to separate the statements of fact from the statements of opinion. You should realize that when a speaker says, "Mr. Burns *is* a reactionary" he is really saying, "Mr. Burns *seems to me* to be a reactionary." He isn't proving the label merely by stating it.

Besides stating opinions *is* may be used to state facts incorrectly. This, too, is a serious abuse of the word. If we say, "Green *is* the complementary color of blue," we are misstating a fact. The truth is that green is the complementary color of red. Statements of fact can usually be checked. Authorities can tell us whether or not a porpoise *is* a mammal, but no authority can tell us whether or not Tim *is* a snob.

Even statements of fact are subject to change as our knowledge advances. Fifty years ago textbooks declared, "Neptune is the outermost planet in the solar system." Today we realize such a statement is false, for the planet Pluto has been discovered far out in space beyond Neptune. If textbooks declare today, "Pluto is the outermost planet," then they ought to add *according to our present knowledge*. To be accurate, books which present facts, scientific or otherwise, should declare, "These facts are accurate so far as is known." We might take the same care in our own speaking and writing.

## ACTIVITY 17. Studying Uses of *Is*

Classify each of the following sentences into one of the following groups:

1. Statement of fact: true, according to present knowledge
2. Statement of fact: false
3. Statement of opinion: may be true or false

In which of the sentences is the word *is* used most intelligently and truthfully? Which statements inform? Which attempt to persuade emotionally? Which mislead?

1. Thompson *is* a coward.
2. A gallon *is* equal to two quarts.
3. Jupiter *is* the largest known solar planet.
4. Victor *is* a pompous and insolent fool.
5 Angel cake *is* tastier than fruit cake.

6. Ordinary pine wood *is* heavier than water.
7. Merrill's novel *is* the best fiction volume of the season.
8. Aluminum *is* lighter than steel.
9. A word *is* a symbol, not a thing in itself.
10. Mildred *is* self-centered and conceited.

## STEREOTYPES

"Did you hear the story of the Scotsman who was so tight he beat his son because he bought an all-day sucker at four in the afternoon?"

The speaker chuckled and sat back, waiting for the expected laugh. But one member of the party, a soldier in uniform, looked puzzled.

"Do you know," the soldier remarked, "I just can't see anything funny in jokes about Scotsmen any more. I was stationed in Scotland during the early part of the war and never once met any evidences of stinginess or miserliness. I think the usual picture is a lie!"

The soldier had suddenly realized one of the most important truths anyone could learn — that there is no such thing as a "typical" Scotsman, Irishman, Englishman, or Chinese. Every individual of every nationality is distinguished from every other member of the same group by his own personality. You are proud to be an American. Yet look at Alex over there. He, too, is proud to be an American, but he is unlike you in every respect. The word *American* includes you both, but how different you are in appearance, attitudes, and likes. In every group there are tall and short, lazy and industrious, bright and dull, honest and dishonest. No one should make a general statement about any group — but people do.

The Scotsman has been associated with stinginess, the Irishman with an ungovernable temper, the Englishman with a poor sense of humor, and the Chinese with sly cunning. Though an individual Englishman might lack a sense of humor, so might an individual Spaniard, Norwegian, Italian, or American. Most Englishmen have a sense of humor neither better nor worse than that owned by the majority of mankind. The good and

Do these stereotypes exist in your mind?

bad traits have been fairly evenly distributed over the globe. Yet these peculiar ideas affect people's thinking.

A metal cast used to print thousands of copies of a newspaper is called a *stereotype*. We apply the word *stereotype* to any false notion about a group of people. The person who identifies all living Chinese with the imaginary, shrewd Chinese in his mind is employing a *stereotype*, for he is making all Chinese of the same mold as the one in his mind. (See page 220 for the danger in making generalizations about any group of people.)

Many stereotypes have been created by the motion pictures or by light fiction. Let's consider one for a moment, the *professor* as shown on the screen. A popular motion picture not long ago depicted a group of professors working on an encyclopedia. Though they were shown as kindly and lovable, for the most part they were impractical dreamers with false sets of values. Immediately the audience mentally observed, "Absent-minded professors." Yet real professors may be businessmen, scientists who make atom bombs, and even men about town.

Sometimes the stereotype is good-humored, as in dialect jokes or the professors' daydreaming, but often stereotypes do serious damage by maliciously confusing thinking. If a candidate is of foreign birth, sometimes his opponent at election will identify him with the stereotype of the ignorant immigrant or the grasping foreigner. If he is a businessman, he may be typed as shrewd and heartless; if he is a labor leader, he may be typed as revolutionary and unstable. Intelligent voters will cast aside these false pictures and demand to know the truth: *What has this man done thus far? What will he probably achieve in office?* These are the questions that count.

### ACTIVITY 18. Studying Stereotypes

Each of the groups in column *A* have been victims of stereotyping. Match column *A* with the usual association in column *B*. Point out why the stereotypes are inaccurate.

| A | B |
|---|---|
| 1. American heiresses | a. dreamers |
| 2. athletes | b. barbers |
| 3. Chinese-Americans | c. laundrymen |
| 4. gruff old men | d. poor students |
| 5. Italian-Americans | e. holiday haters |
| 6. mothers-in-law | f. hearts of gold |
| 7. newsmen | g. fast talkers |
| 8. poets | h. foreign titles |
| 9. teachers | i. poor cooks |
| 10. young brides | j. meddlers |

### ACTIVITY 19. Finding Stereotypes in Newspapers, Periodicals, and Motion Pictures

Start a "stereotype page" in your notebook. Keep a listing here for the next week of all stereotypes encountered in your reading, your listening, and in seeing motion pictures. Look particularly for stereotypes in the treatment of the news, local and international. One week from today your list will be called for in class. Be ready to discuss how each stereotype operates.

# 7

# Pleasant Connotations

*The jury debated the fate of the woman defendant. They reviewed the evidence, all of which seemed to point clearly toward the young woman's guilt. All but one of the jurymen were ready to turn in the obvious verdict of "Guilty." The one juror who held out was asked to explain on what basis he was asking for a "Not guilty" verdict. "Gentlemen," he declared, "she can't be guilty. She is a* mother!" *The other jurors quickly pointed out that the fact she was a mother had nothing whatever to do with the merits of the case. The twelfth juror had confused in his mind the mental image of* mother, *carrying all its suggestions of self-sacrifice, tenderness, and reliability, with an individual woman. The glory associated with the* word *had been transferred in his mind to a* person. *The defendant may or may not have been a good mother, but that cannot change the fact of her guilt or innocence.*

## PRESTIGE WORDS

Through the years many words have attained favorable connotations. *Home, country, America,* the name of our home town, the name of our high school — all these are words of pleasant suggestiveness. A speaker who uses them is likely to earn our good will because he has called to mind pleasant memories. Too often, though, he dulls our sensibilities and plays upon our emotions rather than our intellects. Instead of asking us to think, he tries to put our brains to sleep. He urges us to listen to pleasant sounds and accept these for truths. Often he uses words like *freedom* and *happiness*, words so general that they can mean all things to all people. In short, he tells us little, while seeming to say a great deal. The "prestige words" he uses keep us happy — but uninformed! (See pages 215–218 for additional treatment of abstract terms used carelessly.)

ACTIVITY 1.  Studying Prestige Words

Analyze the following political speech. Which words are "prestige words," used, not to inform, but to lull listeners into a mood of lazy and pleasant acceptance? Sum up what the speaker has actually said.

My party's platform emphasizes the importance of the full life, the good life, health, happiness, and security. We have chosen a candidate whose fearless integrity and glorious good name have brought nothing but honor to our strong and respected party. He is a man of sound principles and unswerving loyalty to the finest ideals. He gives not only lip service but faithful devotion to democracy. He is a fighter for the right, for the protection of the little man. In short, he is perfectly equipped to fulfill the tremendous obligations of high office. May I present to you my candidate, Mr. Wilton.

TRANSFER

Johnnie, aged nine, wore his new cowboy suit. It was supper time. Johnnie's mother urged him to eat all his vegetables, but Johnnie stubbornly refused. At last, in desperation, Johnnie's mother declared, "You're not a real cowboy. All real cowboys eat their vegetables!" Johnnie quickly gobbled down the vegetables!

What had happened? Suddenly Johnnie, wearing his cowboy suit, transferred to himself all the virtues of a cowboy as he understood the word *cowboy*. In his eyes the glory of the uniform was transferred to himself and he had to act the part. Little Johnnie *became*, for a time, a "real cowboy."

This transfer of glory from an object to a person is not restricted to children. A favorite trick of speakers who wish to persuade audiences to action is to have the national anthem and the flag salute followed almost immediately by their talk. Members of the audience, still pleasantly stimulated by the pledge to our country, unconsciously transfer some of the prestige to the speaker, undeserving though he may be. Some speakers use introductory music to put their audience into a proper mood. Pleasant responses to the music are transferred to the speakers. Alert audiences refuse to let themselves be swayed by this clever device, but listen even more carefully to what the speaker has to say. They know that even un-American Bund meetings before the war displayed the American flag prominently, together with pictures of Washington and Lincoln.

Transfer operates in our own lives frequently, often harmlessly. When the baseball team we support wins a game, we unconsciously transfer some of the honor to ourselves. When our friend wins an award, we bask in reflected glory. The juror described above, who disliked finding a mother guilty, was transferring the prestige of the word *mother* to the person. Transfer becomes a dangerous device when someone attempts to move us to action by using emotion, not reason.

### ACTIVITY 2. Studying Transfer

Show how transfer operates in each of the following brief speeches. Point out how the prestige of one symbol is transferred to a person.

1. As a father my candidate respects the home and all it stands for.

2. My friend is not guilty. Besides he was a lieutenant in the U.S. Army.

3. As the organ chimes die away, let me beckon your thoughts to serious matters. Have you considered your health lately? My product is the answer to many of your health problems.

4. The income tax evasion charge is baseless. My client is generous to everyone. He has given thousands to charity.

5. After we have pledged our loyalty to Old Glory, let us resolve that we shall maintain an honest government by voting for my candidate.

6. Alec Burns, formerly All-American fullback from Illinois, will talk to you about our new building project.

## SLANTING FAVORABLY

The previous chapter pointed out how factual news events or reports may be slanted in one direction or another, either by choosing emotional words or by omitting some of the facts. The same candidate for election will be described entirely favorably by one group and entirely unfavorably by another. The truth usually lies somewhere in between. If a candidate enjoys sports, his own party will emphasize his all-round athletic prowess. The opposition may imply that he will make a poor executive because he spends so much time in unimportant activities.

Newspapers that favor the present administration tend to emphasize successes rather than failures. A congressional victory is featured prominently and clearly labeled "victory." Opposition papers may give the event less prominence and perhaps call it a "strategic victory" for their own party. Even people who try to be fair start with a point of view. You might find it difficult to report factually a high school game won by your own team. You'd find yourself tempted throughout to use the words *stirring*, *thrilling*, *courageous* to apply to your own team. It takes maturity and judgment to write without slanting. It is important to recognize slanting, however, and to make allowances for prejudices and likes.

### ACTIVITY 3. Studying Slanting in a Newspaper

During the next week examine the political reporting of two newspapers known to have opposing points of view. Compare reports of the same political events by noting placement of news, use of connotative words (including both "prestige" and "smear" words), omission of some details and stressing of others, and use of transfer device. Why is it important for all citizens to read more than one paper, if not on the same day, at least occasionally?

## PRESTIGE WORDS AND ADVERTISING

Since advertising has as its basis the implied suggestion, "Buy my product," it uses every device known to further sales. The most common and fruitful is the use of "prestige words," words that suggest pleasant results: improvement in appearance, success, popularity. If the product is a necessity, made to appeal to people with low incomes, the advertising will stress *economy* and *durability*. If the product is a luxury, made to appeal to the high-income group, the advertising will stress "snob appeal," using words like *exclusive*, *unique*, and *individualized*.

Advertising, like many political speeches, tends to appeal to emotions rather than to reason. Consumers often neglect facts and buy articles because of words. Beauty preparations stress words like *charm*, *glamour*, *well-groomed*, *vivacity*, and *attractiveness*. Breakfast foods include words like *tasty*, *refreshing*, *wholesome*, *nourishing*, and *hearty*. Vitamin preparations mention *vigor*, *pep*, *vitality*, *strength*, and *alertness*. We are constantly bombarded by words like *sparkling*, *fragrant*, *aristocratic* — all good, suggestive English words, but none necessarily factual in these contexts. To be sure, products may be all that is said for them, but consumers should want to know more before they buy. For example, before buying so-called "economy-size" boxes — containing large quantities of a product — consumers should try the product in a small box first. A large economy-size box on the shelf is no economy if it isn't used.

ACTIVITY 4. Studying Connotative Words in Advertising

In the following description of a new automobile pick out the words that are strongly connotative, words that give a very favorable picture of the automobile described. Are these words factual here? What additional information would you want before you would purchase an automobile?

The new Granger is a joy to behold. Picture if you can its sturdy chassis, streamlined frame, roomy interior, and powerful motor. Imagine yourself sinking deep into its luxurious upholstery as you depress the clutch and start off. Mile after mile of thrill-packed adventure along new unexplored roads will be yours economically in the new Granger. Your best easy chair at home cannot give you the comfort provided by the spacious front seat large enough for that extra passenger. Come down to see the newest model. You'll thank me for inviting you.

### Activity 5.  Studying Advertising Appeals

From the newspaper select three advertisements that attempt to appeal to some basic human emotion by using strongly connotative words with pleasant associations. What *facts* are presented in each of the articles? Is enough actual information given to warrant your purchasing the article?

## Euphemisms

In ancient times navigation was a dangerous occupation at best. When the seas were stormy, vessels were tossed about and lost. One body of water that sailors hated to sail upon was the sea we now call *The Black Sea*. In those days, however, it had another name — *Pontus Euxeinus*, or "Sea that is hospitable to strangers." What prompted the sailors to call a sea they hated by such a flowery name? It was an impulse as old as mankind, to avoid putting the unpleasant into words, and perhaps even encouraging the unpleasant to become more pleasant. It was the same impulse that caused Eric the Red to call his ice-capped island *Greenland*, that caused more modern navigators to change *Stormy Cape* to *The Cape of Good Hope*. We call the device of saying something disagreeable in pleasant or indirect words *euphemism*.

### Softening Reality

One of the principal functions of euphemism is to soften the hard blows of reality. The most bitter and inescapable reality of all, death, has perhaps the most euphemisms. People hate the harshness of the simple word *die*, and substitute instead more indirect expressions like *pass on*, *pass away*, *go west*, or *go to a better world*. Some euphemisms are humorous and in questionable taste, expressions like *kick the bucket* or *fade out*. Others depend upon the occupation of the deceased (a word which is in itself a euphemism). A dead actor has *made his last curtain call*. A dying cowboy *heads for the last round-up*. Whether the tone is grave and serious or gay and flippant, euphemisms attempt to lighten the blow that has to fall.

Other minor tragedies of living have their euphemisms, too. A man would rather be *laid off* than *fired*. A boy would rather be charged with a *fib* than a *lie*. *Deranged* is a softer word than *insane*. During the war our government preferred to use the term *selective service*, though most people kept the more direct, briefer *draft*.

### Disguising Occupations

Certain occupations, like engineering, suggest intellectual pursuits, high salaries, and respect from the community. Others, like the simplest forms of manual labor, though necessary and important in community life, tend to be looked down upon. Consequently, new terms are constantly being coined to give higher-sounding titles to these occupations. The word *engineer* is often used to transfer some of the prestige from the admired *engineering* to scorned manual jobs. Somehow *custodial engineer* seems like a much better job than *janitor*. *Exterminating engineers* seem more important citizens than *rat killers*. *Sanitary engineers* gain more respect than *garbage collectors*. People now hire *domestic help* rather than *servants*, for the latter term implies too much inequality for our democratic America.

To give "tone" to their businesses barbers become *tonsorial artists;* hairdressers become *beauticians;* undertakers become *morticians;* and tree trimmers become *tree surgeons*. Instead of

**Barber**          **Tonsorial Artist**

pawn shops we note *loan offices*. Candy shops become *candy studios*. Garages are often *lubritoriums*.

Sometimes, though, euphemisms confuse. Instead of *used*, retailers have invented terms like *reconditioned*, *rebuilt*, *reused*, *repossessed*, and *reprocessed*. Some consumers buy such goods without realizing that they are secondhand and should be sold for considerably less than new goods.

ACTIVITY 6. Studying Euphemisms for Occupations

The following euphemisms are noted by H. L. Mencken in *The American Language* and *Supplement One* of the same book. Match the occupation at the right with the euphemistic title at the left.

| | | | |
|---|---|---|---|
| 1. aisle manager | | a. | fishmonger |
| 2. collection correspondent | | b. | cobbler |
| 3. demolition engineer | | c. | press agent |
| 4. household engineer | | d. | bill collector |
| 5. podiatrist | | e. | house wrecker |
| 6. public-relations counsel | | f. | box-office clerk |
| 7. realtor | | g. | corn doctor |
| 8. sea food caterer | | h. | floorwalker |
| 9. shoe rebuilder | | i. | real-estate agent |
| 10. treasurer | | j. | housewife |

EUPHEMISMS AND GOOD TASTE

At any period in history certain words find themselves avoided in polite conversation as being too coarse, disagreeable, or brutal. To be sure, fashions change, and yesterday's outcast may be admitted into today's society. For example, a century ago the word *leg* was felt to be somehow indecent, so the word *limb* was substituted. People even spoke of the *limbs* of a chair. English visitors to the America of that time found themselves making many social blunders because they did not realize that the word *leg* was to be avoided. The word has since returned to polite speech.

Changes are taking place constantly. *Coffin* has been replaced by *casket*; *graveyard* by *cemetery* or even *burial abbey*. *Soiled linen* is often used for *dirty clothes. Expectorate, perspire,* and *intoxicated* are felt to be mild euphemisms. Conversation is studded with words that say mildly or indirectly what another age might have blurted out. Sensitive people avoid profanity, though perhaps they may, in unguarded moments, use expressions like *heck, darn, deuce,* or *dickens.* These, too, are euphemisms.

Sometimes euphemisms seem unnecessarily "elegant" and affected. The words *retire* for *go to bed* and *dine* for *eat* are euphemisms of doubtful value. Most modern writers prefer the direct, simple, and common words, rather than the pretentious *retire* and *dine.* The intelligent speaker knows how to adapt his vocabulary to the sensibilities of his audience. Some euphemisms are kindly expressions of human sympathy, lubricants that help conversation to run smoothly. Others are needlessly indirect. The alert listener recognizes euphemisms, understands the part they play in communication, and chooses wisely. In formal writing euphemisms should be used sparingly.

### ACTIVITY 7.  Studying Euphemisms

Each of the italicized words in the sentences below is a euphemism. Explain each and point out why a euphemism was used.

EXAMPLE: *The army suffered a thousand <u>casualties</u> in the first battle.*
*Casualties* is a euphemism for *dead and wounded.* It is a less emotional word and states an unpleasant fact without using direct and harsh words.

1. The *sales-promotion expert* addressed the meeting of salesmen.
2. The victim of the accident *breathed his last* at 3 P.M.
3. After the war Europe was filled with *displaced persons.*
4. He had to have two molars *extracted* by the dentist.
5. Business suffered a *temporary setback* during the last two months.
6. The hotel installed a swimming pool for the use of its *guests.*
7. The play had a *brief stay* of three evenings.
8. The *floral technician* arranged the decorations for the wedding.
9. The *Grim Reaper* called Ben Munson at last.
10. MacIntyre *lost out* in the last election.

# Two-Value Judgments

*"I want to be an Indian."*

*"I'm going to be a cowboy."*

*And so a game of "cowboys and Indians" gets started. Some of the group have to be willing to be the "bad" Indians so that the "good" cowboys will have someone to fight. Whether the game be called "cowboys and Indians," "cops and robbers," or "G-men and gangsters," there are always two rigid divisions, two opposing forces, the entirely good and the entirely bad.*

## HEROES AND VILLAINS

The child's world is simple. There are good people and bad people, good things and bad things, good ideas and bad ideas. There are no "in-betweens." Children's literature emphasizes this division. In fairy tales the fairy prince is always brave, handsome, and unselfish. The princess is beautiful, kind, and gentle. The witch is mean, old, and coarse. The stepmother is wicked, scheming, and self-centered. Not once is there a hint of anything less than perfection in the good people or a hint of a good streak in the wicked. Fairy tales are beautiful and charming, but no one pretends that they are true.

Adventure stories for young people follow the same pattern. The hero courageously overcomes all obstacles, wins the beautiful girl, and they live happily ever after. The villain tries at every hand to defeat the hero, but is at last destroyed through his own vileness. Every good trait is assigned to the hero; every bad trait, to the villain.

Some adult fiction tends to follow the same artificial pattern, as do many motion pictures. The human weaknesses that characterize even the best of us are conveniently slighted or omitted. Certain stock characters, or types, repeatedly return with little variation. Many adventures befall the characters, but the characters change little, if at all. Just as in child dreamworlds, there is the same sharp division into the good and the bad.

### ACTIVITY 1. Studying Characterization

Select a novel or a motion picture with commonplace plot and characterization. Choose two characters and show that each is entirely good or entirely bad. Contrast these with characters that grow, characters that are neither perfect nor completely villainous. Books that you have read in school will provide you with many real-life characters.

## MANY-VALUE JUDGMENTS

A little reflection proves to us how untrue the simple division into good and bad can be. Consider the people you know. They are all fairly good people in all probability; yet you would be the last to claim perfection for any of them. All-too-human failings probably have nestled here and there among the fine qualities, so that no one you know could be called faultless. It's probably a good thing, too. Guinevere spoke for most of us when she objected, in the *Idylls of the King*, to the unhuman perfection of King Arthur:

> He is all fault who hath no fault at all,
> For who loves me must have a touch of earth.

Similarly, even villains have occasional good impulses. Childish adults are never prepared for this. When an archvillain like Adolf Hitler showed a fondness for children, people said, "He can't be bad; see how he likes children." Of course, we know that most of his actions resulted in suffering and loss, though he might have had a few decent traits in him. We find people to be somewhere between total perfection and total villainy. A realization of this helps us become more nearly mature.

### ACTIVITY 2. Studying Varied Qualities in People

Choose some person of national or of international importance. List his traits as you think of them, trying above all to be impartial and fair. Into one column, place all the traits you consider favorable; into another, place unfavorable traits. Which predominate? What is your general estimate of the man or woman? How does your picture agree with that given by a classmate? From the differences in your lists what conclusions can you draw about the difficulty of making clear-cut judgments?

### ACTIVITY 3. Studying Changing Judgments

Suppose you were an Italian citizen at the time Mussolini came into power. From your knowledge of history list adjectives pro and con describing him at the height of his power. Then draw up another column listing the adjectives pro and con after the second World War. What differences between the two listings might be noted? What conclusions can you draw about the permanence of judgments?

## TAKING SIDES

An old witticism has it that there are three sides to every argument, your opponent's side, your side, and the truth! Jocular though it is, it emphasizes an important point to remember: there may be an in-between ground separating one point of view from another. Debating, by its very nature as a contest, makes all arguments seem two-sided. "_Resolved:_ That homework in high schools should be abolished." Here the question seems to be either the complete abolition of homework, or its retention as at present. The debate overlooks, for the purposes of the contest, the in-between ground: the possibilities of modification in homework, its partial abolition, its extension, or other likely changes. Sometimes there are but two alternatives —— as in voting for or against an amendment. Then you must weigh all the available pros and cons on both sides.

## ACTIVITY 4. Studying a Debate Topic

What are the two sides represented in the following debate topic? What middle ground, disregarded for the purposes of debate, might be considered?

*Resolved:* That school teams should be abolished in favor of intramural athletics.

## TWO-VALUE JUDGMENTS IN ACTION

"If you're not with me, you must be against me. If you don't support my plan, you're obviously an enemy." In wartime such statements are necessary for survival. In peacetime they hinder the processes of democracy, which depend upon thought and honest disagreement. S. I. Hayakawa, in his book *Language in Action*, calls such thinking *two-valued orientation*, the belief that there are only two possibilities: the good or the bad. Thus not long ago we heard dictatorship opposed to anarchy; for example, "If you don't want complete lawlessness (anarchy), you'll have to choose the only alternative, dictatorship." Such thinking rules out all the other possibilities, democracy pre-eminently. A problem may have a hundred possible solutions, not just two.

Those who believe in the two-sided approach to life always see events and people either as *good* or *bad*. Like the child with his fairy princes and wicked stepmothers, these people immediately classify everyone and everything without evaluating as intelligent individuals should. They label as evil and contemptible all persons who disagree with them in politics or economics, who belong to another church, live according to a different philosophy, have different attitudes. They applaud persons most like themselves, regardless of other qualities.

What people with a two-sided point of view fail to realize is that all of us may be classified in an infinite number of ways. Thus the immature become confused when a person whom they had mentally labeled "good" is found to have other political beliefs or religious affiliations.

As we noted when we studied the word *is*, classifications are never entirely true. Of course, we must make choices, decide whether a given action is good or bad, practical or impractical, but to feel that there is only one alternative to disaster or one solution to every problem is to invite trouble.

#### Activity 5. Studying Faulty Judgments

Each of the following statements might be made by one with a two-value approach to life. Show how each is faulty.

1. He's a foreigner. You can't trust him.
2. He can't be a criminal. He belongs to my club.
3. If you don't agree with me, you must be a Communist.
4. The dog couldn't have turned on its master. A dog is man's best friend.
5. Old beet tops must be poisonous. My mother said they weren't fit to eat.

## Two-Value Judgments and Words

Chapter 11 in Part One emphasized the difficulty of finding antonyms or opposites to many words. Some words, like *gray*, *grin*, and *building*, have no direct opposites. Others have many words which are opposed partly but not fully. *Dry*, for example, has the direct opposite *wet* and the partial opposites, *dank*, *moist*, *damp*, and *soggy*. For some pairs of words we can construct a whole series of words between the two extremes. Our description of a character in a novel can suggest a range of adjectives. Between *beautiful* and *ugly* we may supply many transitional words: *beautiful, lovely, pretty, attractive, plain, unattractive, homely, ugly*. There is a great gap between *beautiful* and *ugly*, but there is much less difference between *beautiful* and *lovely*, *pretty* and *attractive*, *homely*, and *ugly*. The intervening words show the steps by which we come from *beautiful* to *ugly*. The person who thinks in terms of two values only would insist that if the novel's heroine weren't *beautiful* she'd have to be *ugly*. Common sense tells us that she can be described in any number of ways. Indeed, modern authorities insist that no person need be described as *ugly*. Not all girls can be described as *beautiful* but all can earn the label *attractive* or *pretty* by neatness, alertness, and pride in appearance. Two-value judgments rule out this possibility.

### ACTIVITY 6. Reshuffling Words

Rearrange the words in each of the groups below so that there will be a gradual change from one extreme to the other. Since this is one of the most difficult activities, requiring a keen knowledge of words, you will find it interesting to compare your rearrangement with those of your classmates. Discuss reasons for the placement of each word.

EXAMPLE: *chilly, moderate, sultry, warm, hot, cool, cold*. Since *hot* and *cold* are the extreme words, place *hot* at one margin of your paper and *cold* at the other. Which comes closest to *cold*? *Chilly*? Very well, place *chilly* next to *cold*. Your completed job might look like this:

hot   sultry   warm   moderate   cool   chilly   cold

If the day is not *hot*, it need not therefore be *cold*. It may be *warm*, *moderate*, or *chilly*.

1. affection, aversion, bitterness, friendship, hate, indifference, liking, loathing, love, scorn.
2. calm, clamor, murmuring, outcry, silence, tumult.
3. black, bright, brilliant, dim, dull, gleaming, shady, glowing.
4. of average means, penniless, poor, rich, starving, wealthy, well-to-do.
5. dwarfed, high, lofty, low, towering.

### ACTIVITY 7. Supplying Intermediate Words

Supply the words that belong between each of the following extremes. Use Activity 6 as a guide. This time, instead of rearranging, supply the words yourself in their proper order.

1. energetic, lazy
2. enormous, small
3. expert, bungling
4. fat, thin
5. ferocious, mild
6. healthy, ill
7. humiliate, exalt
8. squander, hoard
9. swift, slow
10. wise, foolish

# Subjective vs. Objective Writing

*He struggled to his feet, turned a red face to the speaker, and with eyes flashing shouted, "It's a lie!"*

*He felt the anger rising within him until he felt he must do something. Indignantly he accused the speaker of lying.*

Both sentences describe the same incident, but how differently each reports it! The first gives us all the facts, all the information that a person present at the meeting could fairly record. The second gives us the man's feelings, his inner emotions. Reporting of observable facts is called *objective writing*. Reporting of emotions and feelings is called *subjective writing*.

ACTIVITY 1. Labeling Subjective and Objective Writing

Label each of the following statements subjective or objective. Give your reasons for each decision.

EXAMPLE: *Little Teddy stamped upon the floor and cried long and loud.* This is objective writing because observable facts, rather than inner feelings, are given to the reader.

1. Cold resentment gripped him.
2. He experienced a feeling of surprise at the unexpected comeback of his team.
3. He was eager to make a success of his new job.
4. The audience vigorously applauded the performance.
5. The critic was displeased with the star's performance.
6. A flowerpot crashed to the sidewalk with a thud. Max looked up to see a face unexpectedly thrust over the window sill.
7. The immigrant felt homesick and lost in the new environment.

8. Though the temperature went down to zero, the snow kept falling.

9. The little boy was happy to receive a perfect mark on the test.

10. The Tigers lost by a 4–3 score.

## OBJECTIVE VS. SUBJECTIVE

Objective writing allows the reader to use his head, to think for himself. It says, "Here are the facts; interpret them." It gives the reader a picture: "Little Howard pressed his nose against the bakery window. He looked from one cake to another. Finally, he turned away and sighed." The description hints that Howard would like very much to eat one of the cakes placed enticingly in the window, but *it doesn't say so*. The reader is expected to supply Howard's emotions and hunger. Objective writing is usually forceful and readable.

Subjective writing, on the other hand, describes inner emotions directly. Poor writers often resort to this type of writing because it is easy to turn out. Story characters can be described effortlessly — and boringly — by a few adjectives like *sophisticated, blasé, cheerful, clumsy, charming*. A more alert writer will *suggest* sophistication, cheerfulness, or clumsiness by noting a few actions that reveal these traits. Much good subjective writing has been done by some of our greatest writers. Young writers, though, tend to overdo it or do it poorly.

ACTIVITY 2. Matching Subjective and Objective Statements

Group *A* contains objective statements of incidents. Group *B* contains subjective descriptions of the same events. Match the letters with the proper numbers. Which do you prefer in each instance? Why?

*A*

1. He yawned, opened one eye at the speaker, and closed it again.

2. She dropped the dish she was carrying, ran to the door, and cried, "Johnny!"

3. He sank deeper into the chair, and gradually lowered the book to peer into the darkness from which the sound came.

4. "Is there any news?" she asked slowly, her eyes on the doctor's face.

5. She skipped around the room, humming a light tune to herself.

6. He winced a bit and gritted his teeth as the doctor applied the cast.

7. "I've got it," he cried, leaping to his feet and upsetting the table.

8. He scratched his head, looked into space, and bit the end of his pencil.

9. As she looked at her son among the graduates, she threw back her shoulders, and smiled to herself.

10. He banged his fist on the table and shouted, "I refuse!"

*B*

a. A feeling of pride surged through her.

b. She felt happy and carefree.

c. He was elated at his discovery.

d. In his anger he became stubborn.

e. He was bored by the talk.

f. The problem puzzled him.

g. Severe pain shot through him.

h. The noise terrified him.

i. Anxiety nearly overwhelmed her.

j. The arrival surprised her.

ACTIVITY 3. Analyzing Good Subjective Writing

The following poem by Elizabeth Barrett Browning is an example of good subjective writing. It is one of a series that Mrs. Browning wrote to her husband, Robert Browning, who was himself a great poet. It presents a mood and expresses inner emotions so directly that we are made to share in the experience. Its honesty and sincerity are apparent. As a love poem it has few equals in our language. After you have read it, prepare to answer the following questions.

1. Why is this called subjective writing?
2. What emotion is being described?
3. Why is subjective expression more essential in poetry than in prose?

How do I love thee? Let me count the ways.
I love thee to the depth and breadth and height
My soul can reach, when feeling out of sight
For the ends of Being and ideal Grace.
I love thee to the level of everyday's
Most quiet need, by sun and candle-light.
I love thee freely, as men strive for Right;
I love thee purely, as they turn from Praise.
I love thee with the passion put to use
In my old griefs, and with my childhood's faith.
I love thee with a love I seemed to lose
With my lost saints, — I love thee with the breath,
Smiles, tears, of all my life! — and, if God choose,
I shall but love thee better after death.

### ACTIVITY 4.  Writing a Subjective Report

Select some event or occasion that you remember with
pleasure, terror, or some other strong emotion. Describe your
own reactions to the event. Use words that describe your emotional state. Try to make the reader share your experience.

## OBJECTIVE WRITING AND THE EMOTIONS

Though objective writing does not describe emotions directly,
still it can arouse emotions. "Child threatened by strange, incurable disease." In the newspaper a headline like the foregoing,
although a statement of fact, can upset readers greatly. Cold
facts may stir warm emotions. Thus objective writing, while
seemingly unconcerned with emotions, may play upon the
emotions.

Often clever propagandists realize this. While pretending to
be calmly relating facts, they select facts that inflame, give one
side of the story only. Their reports may be objective — but
incomplete. During the American Revolution, for example,
Tories presented one set of facts, patriots another. Though both
may have tried to be objective, both suggested different lines
of action.

ACTIVITY 5.  Studying Objective Writing that Stirs Emotions

Each of the following statements is an objective statement. Point out how each arouses an emotional response in the reader.

1. Twenty-seven were killed in the latest mine disaster.
2. Scientists discover new bacteria to fight tuberculosis.
3. Cars collide; four hurt.
4. Operation on famous singer is unsuccessful. Old ailment returns.
5. City council rejects plan for new schools.
6. Candidate Bagby is a millionaire. His opponent rose from poverty.
7. William Rogers, former district attorney, defends convicted criminal.
8. City employees parade along Main Street as thousands look on.
9. My candidate has supported all legislation for highways and civic improvements.
10. Hanson of the Chicago Cubs hits a home run with two on to win the game.

ACTIVITY 6.  Writing an Objective Report

Describe an exciting event you have witnessed — an unusual show, an accident, a game, or some other happening. Make your reader *feel* the sensations of excitement you felt as you watched, but describe only what you could see or hear, not your own reactions to the event.

FACTS AND INFERENCES

"Mary Lou has been rushing around all day, busily working on a dress and chattering to everyone. She must be going to a dance tonight."

What difference can you detect between the first and second sentences quoted above? The first is a statement of fact, objective fact, as reported by someone in Mary Lou's house. The second is far different. It may or may not be true. Though it is based upon a fact, it is not necessarily a fact itself. We call the second sentence an *inference*, a conclusion or opinion presumably based upon facts. Inferences may be unreliable.

All of us constantly draw inferences from facts and observations. If we should see two girls of college age parading around the street in queer costumes, stopping pedestrians to put foolish questions to them, we might infer that the girls are insane, or at least eccentric. Actually they might be the embarrassed pledges of a college sorority, forced to do something unusual for initiation. "There's more to this than meets the eye" is often a sound observation. Inferences should not be treated as facts until they have been verified. Calling Wilkins a scoundrel doesn't prove that he is one. (See pages 255–257 for discussion of "smear words.")

ACTIVITY 7. Distinguishing between Facts and Inferences

Decide whether each of the following statements is a fact or an inference. For each inference point out how it might be unreliable or untrue.

1. Mr. McGregor is a stingy neighbor.
2. Secretary Lewis supported the resolution.
3. Three plus four equals seven.
4. Ann's sister is a spiteful person.
5. Peters is absolutely without a conscience.
6. The temperature dropped to 30 degrees in the city.
7. Jack made the football team.
8. Jack made the football team through favoritism.
9. Marigolds must have caused my sneezing spell.
10. Marigolds are commonly grown in gardens.

MANY INFERENCES FROM ONE FACT

"Ted has been pacing back and forth all evening, sitting down only to rise again almost immediately and resume his pacing."

What inference might we draw from the description of Ted? We might say, "Ted is a nervous type of person." Is that the only inference possible from the facts? Hardly. Ted might have received bad news, might be worried about the results of an

Who'll make it four?

examination, or might be trying to work out a difficult problem in mathematics. We don't know which inference is correct until we verify it. Similarly if we see a man acting mean, we might infer that he is a habitually mean person. Actually he might be a fine citizen, temporarily upset, forgetful, or accidentally forced to act as he does. To form accurate judgments we must observe many situations to test our first inferences.

ACTIVITY 8.   Drawing Inferences from Facts

Each of the scenes briefly described below encourages the drawing of inferences. One possible inference is included for each scene. Suggest at least one other possible inference for each incident and demonstrate its plausibility.

EXAMPLE: *The gardener bent low over the small seedling. Suddenly he straightened up and called to his wife, "Martha, would you come down a moment. There's something here I'd like you to see." (The gardener's first seeds had sprouted.)*

The suggested inference is possible, but it is only one of many possible inferences. Perhaps the gardener had succeeded in growing a new, hybrid species. Perhaps he had found his wife's engagement ring, lost since last summer. He might even have found a worm and decided to go fishing! All are possible.

1. The new teacher glanced around the room and called upon Jimmy to recite. Jimmy struggled to his feet, red-faced, was silent a moment, and then sat down. (*Jimmy was not prepared.*)

2. Mrs. Leeds watched her daughter walking slowly down the aisle on Mr. Leeds' arm. Suddenly Mrs. Leeds burst into tears. (*She didn't approve of the bridegroom.*)

3. As his teammates called for the ball Arthur turned, paused, and tried for the basket himself. (*Arthur wanted all the glory of winning.*)

4. Little Sue grasped her doll in one hand and stalked away, her nose in the air. (*She was a spoiled child.*)

5. I couldn't find my tie this morning when I went to put it on. (*My little brother must have worn it to school.*)

6. Lilian said that she couldn't go to the dance with Al. (*Lilian doesn't like dances.*)

7. Rita has only a few books in her home. (*Rita doesn't enjoy reading.*)

8. The stranger walked up to one car in the used-car lot, looked at the body and tires. "How old is this car?" he asked. (*The stranger was comparing the car with his own.*)

9. Dan shook his head as the student-salesman asked him to buy a ticket for the championship game. (*Dan has no school spirit.*)

10. Mr. Hawkins has a fine house, a powerful car, and a large bank account. (*Mr. Hawkins is very happy.*)

## SELECTING THE BEST INFERENCE

Even though several inferences may be drawn from one set of observations, usually only one fits the facts. The man who lit a match to see whether his gasoline tank was empty inferred later — from his perch in a tree! — that the combination of match and gasoline vapor caused the explosion. This is a fairly reliable inference, supported by scientific experiment. Similarly if we find that our dog becomes ill whenever we feed him a certain kind of food, we may reliably infer that the dog food is responsible. Absolute accuracy, however, requires the scientific method — with control groups and careful experimentation. Since most of us must make decisions from day to day, we have to learn the trick of selecting the best inference from many.

ACTIVITY 9. Selecting the Best Inference

For each of the following incidents three inferences are suggested. Select the one that is most probably correct and give your reasons.

*Remember :* all inferences are subject to change when more facts become known.

EXAMPLE: *Mr. Abbot usually works every Friday. The Friday before Christmas I saw him in one of the department stores gaily doing his Christmas shopping. He probably wasn't working because*

> *a. he had been discharged.*
> *b. he was sick.*
> *c. he had been given the day off to go shopping.*

Inference *c* is the most likely, though all are possible. If *a* were true he would probably not be gay. If *b* were true, Mr. Abbot probably would not be shopping. Thus *c* seems most likely, though we cannot be absolutely certain from the facts.

1. Mr. Wheeling is painting the outside of his house this year.
   *a.* He inherited a great deal of money.
   *b.* The paint had been given to him.
   *c.* The house needed painting.

2. Clara was late to school today for the second time this week.
   *a.* Her grandmother in California must have died.
   *b.* She overslept again.
   *c.* Her dog was lost.

3. Alex wrote his mother just once a week from camp.
   *a.* He was wrapped up in other activities.
   *b.* He was seriously ill.
   *c.* He cared little for his parents.

4. The score was 7–4 against Elmville. Norris, weakest batter on the Elmville team, was scheduled to go to the plate.

   *a.* He hit a home run to win the game.

   *b.* He was replaced by a pinch hitter.

   *c.* He hit a long double to left field.

5. On a hot summer afternoon Walter and Mickey, aged ten, were walking along despondently. Suddenly Walter cried out. There at his feet lay a shiny quarter. "Come on, Mickey; let's go."

   *a.* They deposited the quarter in Walter's savings account.

   *b.* They went to the ice cream parlor.

   *c.* They went to an expensive motion-picture theater.

6. Two men hadn't seen each other for thirty years, since their college days. At their reunion they were busily talking all evening.

   *a.* They spoke about current business trends.

   *b.* They spoke about "the good old days."

   *c.* They spoke about a popular motion picture.

7. Barney, who had just moved north from Florida, was reading one December evening. Suddenly his mother called to him, "Barney, it's snowing! Come look at your first snow."

   *a.* He watched in wonderment.

   *b.* He didn't stir from his chair.

   *c.* He looked out a moment and then went back to the book he was reading.

8. Wilson, a star halfback on the football team, was made shortstop on the varsity baseball team.

   *a.* The coach plays favorites.

   *b.* Wilson is a good all-round athlete.

   *c.* There was no other talent available.

9. Ground had been broken for a huge new department store. The steam shovels were busily at work. A crowd gathered, looking on at the scene.

   *a.* An accident had occurred.

   *b.* One of the shovels had broken down.

   *c.* The crowd was idly curious.

10. During a heavy storm suddenly the lights went out.

   *a.* A fuse in the house had blown.

   *b.* Wires were down somewhere.

   *c.* The power company was experimenting.

POINT OF VIEW AND JUDGMENTS

A popular anecdote tells of the famous Hollywood star who had been telling his companion all about himself for three boring hours. Suddenly, realizing perhaps that he had been monopolizing the conversation, he turned to the poor companion and said, "We've talked enough about me. Let's talk about you. What did you think of my last picture?"

Obviously our point of view influences our judgments. We are likely to be more tolerant of faults in those we like and ruthless in discussing the faults of those we dislike. Even objective judgments are always slanted by the point of view adopted. Historians find writing without bias an extremely difficult job. They find their sneaking admiration for one tyrant of history or another causing them to play down faults and play up successes. So in our daily living we find it easy to forgive the faults of our friends.

We are human. A point of view is necessary. Those without opinions are colorless. However, as citizens we must realize how point of view influences the statements of others. We must discount some of the praise given one candidate by his managers, and some of the faults ascribed to his opponent. When you analyze a statement, ask yourself, "Who said it? Did he have a special ax to grind? How did his special point of view influence his judgment?"

**It's all in the point of view.**

# USING WORDS

### Activity 10. Studying Point of View

Point out how each of the following statements might have been biased because of the point of view of the speaker.

1. "My new discovery will revolutionize house planning and eliminate drudgery," insisted the inventor.

2. The Prince of Homelandia declared flatly, "The cultural contributions of Homelandia to world progress have not been equaled by any nation of similar size."

3. "Our team is probably the best in the city," declared the student.

4. The Palmer salesman declared that the Palmer automobile was the most economical and serviceable on the market.

5. "My daddy is the smartest man in the whole world," declared the little boy proudly.

6. "Our candidate for governor is not only an outstanding citizen but a legislator of rare skill and good judgment as well," repeated the speaker.

7. "Benson's cereals give more energy per serving than any other cereals," the advertisement stated.

8. The billboard urged, "Keep our town the most progressive town in the state."

9. "That plow is old-fashioned. Try this new, improved model," suggested the salesman.

10. "I believe the town ought to buy my property for the proposed park. And this spot would be ideal for a school site." The owner paused and put his finger on the chart.

# 10

# Metaphor

*"I fell down in history today, Mom," said Bart to his mother.*
*Little Marian, who was sitting at the table, spoke up with con-*
*cern, "Did you hurt yourself when you fell, Bart?"*

*Bart explained that he had not actually fallen, that he had*
*earned lower marks for the day, that it was just a manner of*
*speaking. Marian, like many people who have not learned to*
*distinguish metaphors in action, was puzzled. Yet her own speech,*
*childish though it is, is filled with metaphors, for they are the*
*very basis of our language.*

## HE IS WHAT HE ISN'T

A metaphor is usually defined as a comparison stated without
the words *like* or *as*. For example, we call a hero a *lion in battle*.
Of course, he isn't actually a *lion*. We mean that in battle he
shows the fine qualities of lions: courage, strength, recklessness.
*Lion*, as we have used it, is a metaphor. Metaphors are frequently used in poetry, but they are very common in ordinary
speaking and writing, too, though often we forget the original
comparison. When Bart declared that he had *fallen down* in
history, he was comparing his lowered marks with an actual
physical fall. He didn't realize the literal interpretation of his
remark until his little sister, unfamiliar with this common expression, took his statement *literally*. The next chapter will discuss further the differences between *literal* and *figurative*
language.

## ACTIVITY 1. Analyzing Metaphors

Each of the following sentences contains at least one metaphor. What things are being compared? What basis is there for the comparison?

1. Miss Pross was a tigress in her battle with Madame Defarge.
2. "The road was a ribbon of moonlight over the purple moor." (*Noyes*)
3. His thinking was confused and muddy.
4. Amateur poets often refer to the pearly teeth, silken hair, and rosy cheeks of their dream girls.
5. The trees were two sentinels against the sky.
6. Time stole her beauty.
7. "In manufacturing chlorophyll the leaf is a sun-trap," declared Mr. Peattie.
8. Friendship is a bond, a sacred trust.
9. The eyes are windows of the soul.
10. Tom, who played guard for Navy's football team, was called "The Rock of Gibraltar."

## METAPHORS FROM VERBS OF ACTION

One of the most fruitful sources of metaphor in English is our plentiful stock of colorful verbs. Bart's use of *fall* in the expression "To fall down in history" is metaphorical. When we *dive* into a good book or *break* into song, we are using *dive* and *break* metaphorically. Try to picture yourself "*diving* into a book," if you take *diving* to mean what it seems to mean.

## ACTIVITY 2. Studying Metaphors in Action-Verbs

Each of the following sentences contains a metaphor based upon a verb of physical action. Point out the metaphor and explain why you consider it metaphorical.

EXAMPLE: *The scientists stumbled upon the discovery. Stumbled* is used metaphorically here because it means in a strict sense *tripped, staggered.* The word suggests *to come upon by chance or accident.*

1. The partners continued to run into debt.
2. The weary soldier sank into a dreamless sleep.

3. Steinbeck leaped into prominence with the publication of *The Grapes of Wrath*.

4. Don't be too eager to rush into print.

5. The opposing debater neatly walked into the trap.

6. The mining town sprang into existence overnight.

7. Squire Cass flew into a rage over Dunsey's actions.

8. Romeo fell in love with Juliet at first sight.

9. She eased her way into the club even though she was unwanted.

10. Goodrich hit upon a new method of processing rubber.

## CONCEALED METAPHORS

Just as Bart didn't realize that he had used a metaphor, so many of us use metaphors unconsciously. Many expressions have become so commonplace that we forget each was a daring metaphor when it was first used. The common statement, "to run out of ink," is made by people who consider themselves completely unpoetic and literal-minded. Yet, if we analyze it, we find that it is really an unusual metaphor with the word *run* used in an unaccustomed way. Metaphor is so important that it has been called the very well of language creation, for we add to our stock of words every time we make a new and striking comparison.

### ACTIVITY 3. Analyzing Concealed Metaphors

Each of the following italicized expressions is a concealed metaphor. Explain why each is really a metaphor. Substitute for each a strictly literal expression. Which do you prefer? Why?

1. The financier *discarded* the idea as fundamentally unwise.

2. One of the purposes of this book is to help you *build* a vocabulary.

3. Tom passed his *tenderfoot* test in the Boy Scouts.

4. When she *caught* his attention, she *dropped* her eyes.

5. He *buckled* down to work and *outdistanced* his rivals.

6. After the war new buildings *blossomed* on every side.

7. Holmes *shadowed* the suspect through the streets of London.

8. His wife *threw* him a warning glance at the table.

Can you detect a metaphor?

9. I'm so *tied down* I won't be able to *slip* out of the office before six o'clock.

10. "He *came* to *look upon* the *low ebb* of morals as an *outcome* of *bad taste*." (*Jespersen*)

## ANIMAL METAPHORS

"Linda is a cat," affirmed Anne and thus conveyed to her feminine listener more in a word than she could in volumes. To be sure, Linda isn't a four-footed member of the feline species in reality, but Anne felt, rightly or wrongly, that Linda and cats have enough traits in common to justify the label.

Man's observations of the traits of his fellow creatures have served him well in language. The names of many animals have been used to suggest human traits. Everyone knows that a *foxy* person is *clever*, but few realize that this is a metaphor. Even legendary animals like the chimera and the basilisk, and half-legendary animals like the chameleon and the salamander have been used to express ideas. Is a *chimerical* idea a good one? Would you like someone to give you a *basilisk* stare? Would you trust someone who is a *chameleon* in his thinking? Look up the words. Would a man like to marry a *shrew* or a *vixen*? And the girls — would they like to have mates who were *waspish* or *viperous*? Not unless they were *bears* for punishment!

### Activity 4. Using Animal Metaphors

Fill the blank in each of the sentences below, by choosing one of the adjectives listed. Before deciding which to use, consider the traits of the animals and their suitability for the sentence.

EXAMPLE: *After a long period indoors, the young child was frisky and* ————. *Coltish* might be supplied here because a colt, or young horse, is lively, frisky, and glad to exercise his muscles.

| | |
|---|---|
| bearish | leonine |
| canine | mousy |
| cat-like | parrot-like |
| elephantine | serpentine |
| kittenish | sheepish |

1. After he had made the mistake in class, his expression was ————.
2. The massive prosecutor stepped into the courtroom with ———— tread.
3. The road curved in and out of the mountain in a ———— manner.
4. Little children tend to be ———— in their repetition of sounds.
5. Toby's devoted attachment to his master was ———— in its unselfishness.
6. Zeus is always pictured as a ———— old man.
7. The thief stole into the room with ———— steps.
8. She became playful and ————.
9. Mrs. Cruncher was a quiet, ———— woman.
10. His friends sensed a gentle heart underneath his gruff and ———— exterior.

## Body Metaphors

Our own bodies provide a fruitful source of metaphors, perhaps because we are most familiar with ourselves. We see a mountain rising into the sky, and decide to hike across its *shoulder*. New York calls its long, narrow lakes the *Finger* Lakes. Many Arkansans live in the *foot*hills of the Ozarks. Others live in the *heart* of Little Rock. All around us man has given metaphorical body names to common objects because of a real or fancied resemblance.

### ACTIVITY 5. Analyzing Body Metaphors

The following expressions are all metaphors taken from parts of the body. For each tell why the metaphor was chosen and discuss its appropriateness.

1. the *eye* of the potato
2. a *head* of cabbage
3. the *leg* of a chair
4. a *red-cheeked* apple
5. *knee-action* wheels
6. the *jaws* of a clamp
7. the *teeth* of the gale
8. a *chest* of drawers
9. an *ear* of corn
10. an *arm* of the sea
11. a *neck* of the woods
12. an *elbow* in the road
13. the *mouth* of the river
14. the *nose* of the airplane

If body metaphors were taken literally . . . .

## METAPHORS FROM SPORTS AND VOCATIONS

Each man sees life through his own experience. A horse enthusiast, a fighter, and a lawyer filed statements of bankruptcy at the same time; yet each one described his bad luck differently. The first man said that he had "come a cropper." The second declared that he had been "knocked out" by bad luck. The lawyer merely said that his struggle had been a "lost case." Thus each one used metaphors from the sport or vocation he knew best.

ACTIVITY 6. Analyzing Sports and Vocational Metaphors

In column *A* appear metaphors that had their origins in particular sports or other activities. Explain each and then match each with the proper activity in column *B*.

*A*

1. He's a *bushleaguer* in politics.
2. He launched a *broadside* at his opponent.
3. His plans were *checkmated*.
4. The idea was *dissected* for flaws.
5. We're out *of the red* at last.
6. Mr. Micawber *planted* the idea in David's brain.
7. He *mapped* his day's activity in advance.
8. His plan *backfired*.
9. His face *clouded over* at the news.
10. His store is a *gold mine*.

*B*

a. surveying
b. agriculture
c. gas or oil engine
d. weather
e. chess

f. baseball
g. business
h. surgery
i. naval warfare
j. mining

THE POETRY OF FOLK NAMES

When scientists see a certain common swamp plant, they call it *Arisaema triphyllum*, but when everyday folk see it, they call it *Jack-in-the-pulpit*. Like so many other labels for flowers and birds, *Jack-in-the-pulpit* reveals the poetry of many common names, for this is an effective metaphor. Anyone who has seen the plant's resemblance to a preacher in his pulpit can never forget the unusually appropriate name. Some names are sweet and gentle, like "love-in-a-mist" or "bleeding heart"; others are strong and expressive, like "farmer's curse" or "adder's tongue." All are clever metaphors.

## Activity 7. Studying Flower Metaphors

Each of the following plant names is a metaphor. Select five and by checking with the picture in a dictionary, or a flower guide, decide whether the plant is well named.

1. baby's breath
2. bluebell
3. buttercup
4. cattail
5. crabgrass
6. Dutchman's breeches
7. goldenrod
8. Indian pipe
9. jewelweed
10. lady's slipper
11. larkspur
12. lily of the valley
13. long purples
14. moccasin flower
15. Queen Anne's lace
16. snow-on-the-mountain
17. spider lily
18. star of Bethlehem
19. trumpet vine
20. Turk's-cap lily

## Activity 8. Studying Concealed Flower Metaphors

The flower names listed in column *A* are metaphors, although their original meanings are not apparent. By looking up the word derivations in a good dictionary, match the original metaphorical meanings in column *B* with the names in column *A*.

| *A* | *B* |
|---|---|
| 1. amaranth | a. golden flower |
| 2. anemone | b. immortality |
| 3. aster | c. lion's tooth |
| 4. chrysanthemum | d. of the rainbow |
| 5. dandelion | e. rock breaker |
| 6. iris | f. rose tree |
| 7. pansy | g. star |
| 8. rhododendron | h. thought |
| 9. saxifrage | i. unfading |
| 10. tansy | j. wind |

## Metaphors in Word Derivation

Just as we found metaphors concealed in common speech, so we find metaphors concealed in the Latin or Greek derivations. Activity 7 pointed out little-realized metaphors in names of plants. Word derivations, or etymologies, have treasures of

Egregious

metaphors concealed in them. The word *egregious*, for example, means "outstanding, in a bad sense." If we take it apart we find it consists of *ex* — "out of" and *greg* — "herd." Consequently, something *egregious* "stands out from the rest of the herd." *Outstanding* is its present literal meaning. Similarly, *precocious* means "developed early" as a "precocious child." But the word consists of *pre* — "before" and *coc* — "cooked." Someone *precocious* is "pre-cooked." These are truly fossil metaphors embedded in our language.

### ACTIVITY 9. Studying Fossil Metaphors

Each of the following words is a metaphor in its original, etymological sense. By using either a good dictionary or an etymological dictionary, discover the metaphor in its original form.

| | |
|---|---|
| 1. accumulate | 6. imminent |
| 2. delirious | 7. insult |
| 3. depend | 8. legerdemain |
| 4. eccentric | 9. lunacy |
| 5. grotesque | 10. pulverize |

### MIXED METAPHORS

"I smell a rat; I see him floating in the air; but mark you, I will nip it in the bud." Confused metaphors may be funny rather than effective. The originator of the quotation started out with a common metaphor, "I smell a rat," but then proceeded to mix his comparisons. We may speak of a *rumor* as "floating in the air," but not a *rat!* We may talk of a *plot* "nipped in the bud," but not a *rat!* Usually, metaphors to be effective must be consistent.

However, we do use mixed metaphors often without realizing it because we don't know or fail to realize the original meaning of the word. Thus we may *sail* a *steam*ship, *man* factories with *women*, or *land* in the *water* after falling from a boat. If we were overcautious, we would not speak of a *dilapidated wooden* house, for in the Latin *lapis* referred to *stone*. These uses are not considered incorrect because the metaphors have become so weakened through constant use that they have lost almost all their metaphorical meaning. Thus *sail* has lost almost all connection with sailing vessels. Even airplanes and kites may be said to *sail*.

## PICTURESQUE PHRASES

"We lived on a bull's-eye," said an officer who escaped from heavily bombed Corregidor, and thus in a few words compressed all the terror of being shot at in a comparatively small area. Metaphorical expressions are being coined all the time. If we say, "The searchlights bored holes in the darkness," or "The cool night air vacuumed up the day's heat," we are coining metaphors, striking, effective, and brief. Watch for concise and picturesque expressions in your daily reading.

### ACTIVITY 10. Recording Picturesque Phrases

Keep a record of all picturesque phrases found in your reading for the next week. Copy the expressions intact and note the source of each. Be ready to explain why you consider each effective.

# 11

# Figurative Language

*"The tent was a mile high. We ate about a hundred hot dogs and drank about a gallon of lemonade. There must have been a million people at the circus!"*

*Thus did Johnnie describe to his mother his experiences at the circus with his uncle. Of course, his mother knew the tent was tall but not a mile high. She worried that Johnnie might have overeaten, but she knew that even Johnnie's appetite would not take a hundred "hot dogs." She knew, too, that a few thousand, rather than a million, better represents the number of people at the circus. Yet she knew Johnnie wasn't lying; he was merely using figurative rather than literal language. She knew perfectly well what he meant, even though he exaggerated numbers.*

Literal language states a fact and means just what it says; for example, "He was six feet nine inches tall." Figurative language suggests the truth colorfully but indirectly. It does not mean exactly what it says; for example, we might say, "He was as tall as a skyscraper"; or "He was a giant"; or "He was about a hundred feet tall." All suggest unusual height, but they do it indirectly. These are figurative rather than literal statements. Metaphors, discussed in Chapter 10, are good examples of figurative language.

### Activity 1.  Analyzing Figurative Language

Assume that you are a foreigner learning English. What difficulties might each of the following sentences hold for you? Why? Rephrase each so that an intelligent foreigner would have no difficulty understanding the meaning at first sight.

1. She was frightened stiff at the trembling curtains.
2. The grass danced in the breeze.
3. The report is something a reader can get his teeth into.
4. In her anger her eyes shot sparks.
5. His trousers were several yards too long for him.
6. He opened a can and had it for supper.
7. Ice water ran in her veins.
8. In one hour Ted must have asked his dad a billion questions.
9. The pages of history describing the French Revolution are written in blood.
10. The clock told him it was time to leave.

## SIMILE

Just as metaphors compare seemingly unlike objects, so similes attempt the same job. Similes, however, use *like* or *as* to make certain that the readers or listeners realize a comparison is being made. A simile more cautiously says, "He's as big as a house," while a metaphor comes to the point and says, "He's a house." People use similes constantly to improve the effectiveness or colorfulness of their language. Everyone has heard the expression, "March came in like a lion, but went out like a lamb." How much more effective this is than a direct, literal attempt to describe March's changing weather!

A simile, like any other form of language, is fresh and appealing the first few times it is used, but it, too, can become threadbare with constant use. A tired, worn-out simile is called a cliché. *Red as a rose* was striking the first time it was used, but it has long since lost its charm. The following expressions are clichés and should be avoided: *bright as stars, blue as the sky, fresh as a daisy, sweet as sugar.* Compare these with the following striking simile from New England: "It was as cold as the north side of a January gravestone by starlight." Did that make you shiver?

### ACTIVITY 2. Composing Similes

Complete each of the following similes by inserting the comparison that you consider most effective. Be ready to give reasons for your choice. Do any clash with the picture suggested? Are any completely inappropriate? Can you suggest alternates of your own?

1. Inside the cavern sat the leader, quiet as a (*stone, mouse, snowball, busy intersection*).

2. His heart was as hard as (*marble, a stepmother's slap, a 1907 prune, velvet*).

3. The July day was as hot as (*the devil's kitchen, a burning coal, a pudding, a wooded glen*).

4. She was as graceful as (*a bear, a gazelle, a fairy tale, a cloudy day*).

5. The old man felt as lonesome as (*a miser, a bell-buoy at sea, a young girl, a tree*).

6. In despair he groaned like (*a lion, a door on rusty hinges, an engine getting up steam, a lonely coyote*).

7. Scrooge was as pitiless as (*the sun, driving sleet, a window, moonlight*).

8. The book was as precious to him as (*jewels, oranges, friendship, oxygen*).

9. He sprang away quickly, like (*a watchspring, a mountain brook, a pawing horse let go, an old man to his dinner*).

10. They prowled around the house like (*stealthy cats, strange intruders, friendly assistants, plodding sentinels*).

## HYPERBOLE

One of the commonest forms of figurative language, particularly among young children, is the use of exaggeration, or *hyperbole*, as it is called. Johnnie's description of the circus was filled with hyperbole. This device is used for emphasis, but may lose emphasis if it is overdone. The word 'colossal,' for example, has lost its strength through overuse. Often we use hyperbole without being aware of it ourselves. Thus we say, "I was scared to death." If that were literally true, we wouldn't be here to make the statement. Hyperbole is effective — in small doses.

### ACTIVITY 3. Recognizing Hyperbole

Each of the following sentences has at least one example of hyperbole. Pick it out and tell why it is hyperbole. Rephrase each sentence without the hyperbole. Which do you prefer? Why?

EXAMPLE: *I was tickled to death to see him.*

Literal: I was *happy* to see him.

1. I'd give the world to see Ted before he leaves for South America.
2. I was thunderstruck when I saw the bill.
3. As the shadow came nearer, Bill was petrified with fear.
4. "If you'll marry me," he declared, "you'll make me the happiest man in the world."
5. You should have seen the two boys playing. It was a circus.
6. Through sleeping on the hard cot I found my legs paralyzed when I wanted to get up.
7. After an exhausting day shopping, Mother and Bob were nearly dead.
8. Dad hit the ceiling when he saw the broken window.
9. There she sat, crying her eyes out.
10. The waves, mountain high, crashed on the deck of the schooner.

**Dad hit the ceiling when he saw the broken window.**

### ACTIVITY 4. Studying Concealed Hyperbole

Each of the following italicized expressions is really a hyperbole, though constant use has dimmed its figurative meaning. Explain why each is a hyperbole by calling attention to its literal meaning.

EXAMPLE: *By all means try to come.* Taken literally, *by all means* would imply overcoming obstacles and coming no matter what happened. Actually the expression means little more than "Come, if you can."

1. I'm *delighted* to meet you.
2. A game of tennis *exhausts* me.
3. You're *absolutely* right.
4. The mishap *enraged* old Thomas.
5. I *love* ice cream.
6. The rider was a *daredevil.*
7. His excellent manners *charmed* the group.
8. I'll be down to see you *in a moment.*
9. We buy, sell, and repair *anything.*
10. Buddy *loathes* spinach, though he'll eat it occasionally.

### UNDERSTATEMENT

The opposite of *hyperbole* is *understatement.* The former seeks emphasis by suggesting more than is meant; the latter suggests less than is meant. "Not a few people came" means that a great many came. "Your story is not entirely true" means that it's rather inaccurate. "I did fairly well on the test" is a modest report of a good mark. All of these seem to say less than they mean. Even slang and colloquial expressions use understatement a great deal; for example, "not half bad" means "very good." Occasional use of understatement is good for variety and emphasis, but too frequent use weakens communication.

### ACTIVITY 5. Recognizing Understatement

Each of the following sentences has at least one example of understatement. What does each sentence *literally* say? After

explaining each, indicate whether you consider the use effective in transmitting the idea.

1. Even among wealthy people malnutrition is not uncommon.
2. He made a rather high mark in his history test.
3. "The report of my death is slightly exaggerated," declared Mark Twain.
4. I was more than a little pleased to see the report.
5. He was none too gentle with the criminals.
6. "Now you're telling a story," Paul's mother declared sadly, after hearing Paul's explanation of the disappearance of the cookies.
7. The English climbers found the attempt to climb Mt. Everest a bit tiring.
8. "I'm a fairly good chess player," declared the state champion.
9. The war was an unpleasant business.
10. The attack on the heavily protected fortress proved a discouraging prospect to the men of the Fourth Division.

HAVING A LITTLE TROUBLE!

**Understatement**

## IRONY

Knowing word meanings isn't all there is to understanding language. We have found hyperbole saying more than was meant, understatement saying less. Irony, another important use of figurative language, means almost the opposite of what it says! Sometimes it is conveyed by the tone of voice, as in "He's a *fine* fellow" meaning "He's not a likable person."

Sometimes a special combination of words gives the true meaning. "This is a *nice* mess" means that everything is wrong. Only someone unaccustomed to our language would miss the true meaning. Sometimes the irony goes over the head of the listener, who takes a scorching statement as a compliment. Often the speaker's intentions must be clear before we can determine whether a statement is literal or ironical.

### ACTIVITY 6. Studying Irony

Analyze the following sentences. Decide what the irony consists of in each sentence. Say each aloud as it should be said. Rephrase each so that the same message is transmitted literally, rather than ironically.

1. Antony kept saying at the funeral of Caesar, "Brutus is an honorable man."
2. This rainy, unpleasant day is the ideal time for our picnic.
3. The farmer looked at the scorched corn, muttering, "This is a pretty picture."
4. "You have a real ability for breaking dishes," commented the bride sadly.
5. After the car had splashed water on her, she observed to her friend, "That driver was a real gentleman."
6. Mr. Brown was so generous he gave each of us ten cents and an apple for working eight hours for him.
7. "Yes," declared the Jacobin grimly, "the guillotine is a cure for headaches."
8. "Stick close to your desks and never go to sea,
   And you all may be Rulers of the Queen's Navee."
   (*W. S. Gilbert*)
9. That's a fine way to treat a friend.
10. "You're early," greeted Jack's wife angrily, as she looked back at her cold dinner.

## METONYMY AND SYNECDOCHE

Two other uses of figurative language, *metonymy* and *synecdoche*, are common despite the strange-looking labels we have applied. Metonymy is the substitution of a closely associated word for another; for example, we say *the Crown* when we mean *the King*, or *the White House* when we mean *the President*. Literally understood, the following would be nonsense: "The White House today issued a statement about preparations for Navy Day."

Synecdoche, very similar to metonymy, means giving the part for the whole, or vice versa. Thus, we say a rancher owns one hundred *head* of cattle, when we mean one hundred *cattle*. We report a chess match in which three Columbia players defeat three Princeton men, as "Columbia defeats Princeton," as though the *colleges* had really played against each other.

Both synecdoche and metonymy are useful in providing short cuts and vivid expressions. Newsmen, particularly, welcome them. Common newspaper terms like *pigskin* (a football), *Number Ten Downing Street* (British politics, specifically, the Prime Minister), *redcap* (railroad porter), and *scandal sheet* (sensational newspaper) are examples of synecdoche or metonymy.

ACTIVITY 7. Studying Synecdoche and Metonymy

Change each of the following figurative expressions into a straight literal statement meaning approximately the same thing. Which do you prefer? Why?

EXAMPLE: *Walker's bat brings Dodgers victory.*
Literal: Walker's hitting brings Dodgers victory.

1. I prefer O. Henry to Tarkington.
2. Give us this day our daily bread.
3. Little Eddie is at last learning his ABC's.
4. The Red Sox defeated the Blue Jackets.
5. America has always fought for democracy.
6. In Frost's poem the hired hand dies at the end.
7. "A cup of Java, please," muttered the weary driver.
8. Don't bring these gray hairs with sorrow to the grave.
9. The Kremlin issued that statement yesterday.
10. Louis Napoleon suppressed the republic and restored the throne.
11. The Crescent and the Cross clashed during the Crusades.
12. The kettle is boiling.

13. Though both the bench and the pulpit called, he turned to lecturing.

14. He spoke five different tongues.

15. The pen is mightier than the sword.

## PERSONIFICATION

"The chair kicked me," cried little Betty to her mother.

"Now, Betty, why do you say such things. You know the chair can't kick you. The chair isn't a *person!*"

But Betty insisted that she had fallen because the chair had exerted a malicious influence and kicked her. Many of us agree with Betty. We feel certain that when a drawer sticks it does so intentionally. We feel that a living antagonist is tugging on the other side, preventing us from having our way. We may lose our temper. As children we hit the drawer in anger, hurting ourselves in the process. As adults we merely become angrier.

The tendency to assign human qualities to things or ideas is called personification. We think of the sun as *he*, our automobile as *she*. One book title, *The Stars Look Down*, is nonsense if we take it literally. Stars cannot *look*. We are in this instance giving a human attribute to stars. We say, "Justice rules with an iron hand." *Justice* is not a person, but to express ourselves better we give the idea human qualities.

The threat to world peace dramatized by personifications

ACTIVITY 8.  Analyzing Personification

Each of the following sentences contains at least one example of personification. Point it out and tell what human qualities are being assigned to an idea or thing.

1. War stalked over the land and left nothing but destruction and devastation.
2. The fiery proclamation called the revolutionists to arms.
3. Though the goal lines beckoned twice, Princeton couldn't score.
4. Love is blind.
5. "When Duty whispers low, 'Thou must,' the youth replies, 'I can.' "
6. The tree lifted leafy arms to the sky.
7. The country expressed its gratitude to our late President.
8. He brought with him the music for "When a Gipsy Makes His Violin Cry."
9. The rain-soaked sky scowled at the bedraggled athletes.
10. The door groaned protestingly as he opened it.

ACTIVITY 9.  Reviewing Figurative Language

Some of the following statements are literal; others are figurative. The figurative expressions may include metaphor or any other types described in this chapter. Read each carefully and be ready to answer the following questions for each:

*a.* Is the statement literal or figurative?
*b.* If figurative, how would you say the same thing literally?

1. Walt Whitman lived in Huntington, Long Island.
2. I'd like to thank you from the bottom of my heart.
3. Our city is the biggest little city in the state.
4. Frank Sinatra made a mountain of gold out of his label, "The Voice."
5. In our state the corn grows so fast you have to plant the seed and then run for fear of being struck by the growing blade.
6. New York City's population is seven million.
7. Only by the jagged lines in his face did he reveal the tumult of his emotions.
8. Keats chose as his epitaph, "Here lies one whose name was writ in water."

9. I was deeply moved by today's sermon.

10. In a right triangle the side opposite the right angle is the hypotenuse.

11. "The night has a thousand eyes; the day but one."

12. An old song suggested, "Let a smile be your umbrella on a rainy, rainy day."

13. He opened the book to page 139 and read aloud.

14. The sun never sets on the British flag.

15. When the *Enterprise* was released from active naval service, the men hated to bid her farewell.

16. Fear froze the very marrow of my bones.

17. Stockholm heard the news of the Nobel Prize awards before Oslo.

18. "England expects every man to do his duty," declared Nelson.

19. He took over the reins of government from his predecessor.

20. Most internal combustion engines use gas or oil as fuel.

21. I don't find it too difficult to make a passing grade in history.

22. The batter rifled a triple into deep left field.

23. He preferred forget-me-nots to all other blossoms.

24. He sprang from his chair like a jack rabbit and bounded after the intruder.

25. "Scorn not the sonnet; with this key Shakespeare unlocked his heart," wrote Wordsworth.

# 12

# Idioms, Phrases, Allusions

*When former Vice-President Wallace used the expression*
Monday morning quarterbacks *in a talk, the correspondent for
a foreign agency scratched his head and groaned, "How am I
going to translate it?" An American football enthusiast explained
that the expression refers to those who can give plenty of advice
after an event has happened, just as fans can tell on Monday how
the football game should have been run on the preceding Saturday.
But the correspondent still had a problem in translating the expression into his own language.*

## WHAT IS AN IDIOM?

*Monday morning quarterback* is an example of an idiomatic
expression, peculiar to our language. Some idioms, like the one
just quoted, are rather special and known only to those in a
particular sport or profession. Others, like *to turn the tables*,
are known to almost everyone who speaks the English language.
Although every language has its own idioms (or peculiar expressions), English seems to be blessed with an unusually large
number.

*Definition:* An idiom is a phrase in which the meaning of the
whole expression is different from the total meanings of the
words of which it is composed.

Let's analyze an idiom. "When the speaker had finished, all
agreed that he had *hit the nail on the head*." A foreigner or
visitor to our shores may know English very well, but he
scratches his head at that expression. "What nail? Whose

**Let's go Dutch!**

head?" he rightly asks. Native Americans know immediately that the expression has nothing to do with either *nail* or *head*. They know that the expression means that the speaker had expressed himself exactly and truthfully. They know that the meaning of the whole expression, *hit the nail on the head*, is different from the sum of the meanings of the individual words *hit*, *nail*, *head*. Often American idioms differ from those of England. Thus, while Americans get *on* or *off* a train, Englishmen get *into* or *out of* one.

### ACTIVITY 1.  Completing Idioms

How well do you know your idioms? Try filling in the blanks in each of the following. What does the idiomatic expression mean?

1. Little ——— have big ears.
2. He was as ——— as a doornail.
3. The love of money is the root of all ———.
4. He had his back to the ———.
5. He was a ——— of all trades.
6. When he printed that editorial, he stirred up a ——— nest.
7. "Oh," replied Tom, "that's a horse of another ———."
8. He has to be handled with ——— gloves.
9. He frowned. "That's a hard ——— to crack."
10. When he learned the truth, he dropped the scheme like a hot ———.

ACTIVITY 2. Analyzing Idiomatic Expressions

Complete each of the following.

1. *Crocodile tears* are  (*a*) animal  (*b*) sincere  (*c*) false  (*d*) unhappy

2. The *Kilkenny Cats* were noted for their  (*a*) long fur  (*b*) beautiful calls  (*c*) fighting  (*d*) friendliness to dogs

3. *The fat is in the fire* means about the same as  (*a*) The die is cast.  (*b*) It's an ill wind.  (*c*) That's food for thought.  (*d*) It's a stitch in time.

4. You would probably get a *pig in a poke* at  (*a*) a museum  (*b*) a farmyard  (*c*) an auction  (*d*) a zoo

5. One who *keeps his shoulder to the wheel* is  (*a*) a beggar  (*b*) a peddler  (*c*) a lazy worker  (*d*) an industrious person

6. To *cry wolf* is to  (*a*) announce an enemy  (*b*) give a false alarm  (*c*) ask for supper  (*d*) ask for a wage increase

7. A *dark horse* is  (*a*) black  (*b*) friendly  (*c*) unexpected  (*d*) swift

8. When the Indians *buried the hatchet*, they  (*a*) stopped fighting  (*b*) renewed the fight  (*c*) retreated  (*d*) killed an enemy

9. To *throw up the sponge* is to  (*a*) become ill  (*b*) give up the fight  (*c*) shout  (*d*) win a victory

10. Those who would like to *pick a bone* with you are usually  (*a*) hungry  (*b*) angry  (*c*) deceitful  (*d*) fierce

## METAPHORS IN IDIOMS

Many idioms are metaphorical in origin and cause difficulty to those who take them literally. *To paint the town red* doesn't mean exactly what it says. *To fly off the handle* doesn't mean completely falling to pieces. *To make a mountain out of a molehill* doesn't call for great constructive genius. Consider each one *literally*, though, and realize the difficulties experienced by those to whom the expressions are unfamiliar.

### Activity 3. Analyzing Metaphors in Idioms

In each of the common idioms or proverbs below point out the metaphor. Tell whether you consider each appropriate.

1. He held the reader under his thumb.
2. You're barking up the wrong tree if you think Tom's the one.
3. To cast pearls before swine is adapted from the Bible.
4. He took the lion's share.
5. He wasn't upset, for he had an ace up his sleeve.
6. One swallow does not make a summer.
7. A drowning man will catch at a straw.
8. His enterprise went on the rocks.
9. A tree is known by its fruit.
10. He tried hard, but he just couldn't get to first base.

## ALLUSIONS

Sometimes we cannot get the full meaning of an expression unless we know its history. Every girl is flattered when she is called a Venus, because she knows that Venus was the goddess of beauty in Roman mythology. When she is called a Diana, though, she isn't sure. Should she be flattered? Whenever you see an unusual reference to a god, a goddess, a hero, or a character in a play, check it in a good dictionary. You'll find a wealth of interesting information at the same time.

### Activity 4. Checking Allusions

In Brewer's *Readers' Handbook*, Crowell's *Handbook*, or a good dictionary, check the answers that you are not sure of.

1. Bert hoarded his money selfishly, never getting any enjoyment out of it. His friends called him a *Shylock*. What did they mean?

2. Little Bill had difficulty in taking home a ten-pound bag of potatoes for his mother. A friend called him a *Hercules*. Was he joking?

3. Recently a movie columnist referred to a star as an *Adonis*. Was she flattering him?

4. Mr. Martin bought a new home. A year later he called it a *Pandora's Box*. Had he been happy in it?

5. A masquerade presenting old *Father Neptune* is arranged for those who cross the equator for the first time. Is he appropriate for the ceremonies?

6. Al was very handsome, but his friends called him a *Narcissus*. Why?

7. A woman sprinter was recently called an *Atalanta*. Why?

8. During World War II a horrible, bearded man called *Mars* was frequently depicted in cartoons. Why did he carry a sword?

9. "Watch out for *Cupid!*" one friend called out to another on parting. What did he mean?

10. After the judge made his decision, his friends called him a *Solomon*. Should he have been flattered?

## ACTIVITY 5. Studying Idioms

In the following paragraph ten animals are mentioned, but in every case the meaning is idiomatic. Find each reference and explain.

"Kill the fatted calf," he cried out. "Tom's home! I have forgiven him. Though he's foxy and a wolf in sheep's clothing, I'll not play the dog in the manger. He's as hungry as a bear. Come on; let's beard the lion in his den and speak to him. He won't make a catspaw out of me this time and sell me another white elephant like this house. After he's eaten, I'll make him eat crow; but now, let's lionize him."

## ACTIVITY 6. Studying Groups of Idioms

In each of the following groups of idiomatic phrases one word is used in all four sentences. By telling the meaning of each expression, show how the meaning of the key word varies.

1. *a.* Drowning men catch at *straws*.
   *b.* He put up a *straw man* to knock down.
   *c.* "That," said Jabez Stone, "is the *straw* that breaks the camel's back."
   *d.* The newspaper took a *straw* vote.

2. *a.* "First *catch* your hare, and then cook it," declared the wise old farmer.
   *b.* "Billy's gonna *catch* it," yodeled the little girl mockingly.

    *c.* You can't *catch* me napping that easily.
    *d.* The speaker tried to *catch* the doorman's eye.

3. *a.* Reach for the *moon!*
    *b.* We have good weather once in a blue *moon.*
    *c.* He considered the yarn pure *moonshine.*
    *d.* His father glowered at him. "Stop *mooning*. Get to work."

4. *a.* The race ended in a *dead* heat.
    *b.* It was sent to the *dead*-letter office.
    *c.* "I've been buying oats for a *dead* horse," he complained.
    *d.* They had the intruder *dead* to rights.

5. *a.* They lived from *hand* to mouth.
    *b.* After the atomic bomb's appearance, America had the upper *hand.*
    *c.* Little Billy had to wear his brother's "*hand*-me-downs."
    *d.* The fire was soon out of *hand.*

6. *a.* "*Hold* your tongue!" snapped Vera.
    *b.* In any argument Ted was able to *hold* his own.
    *c.* He can't *hold* a candle to Marie for accuracy in typing.
    *d.* The Ten Commandments still *hold* good.

7. *a.* The new officer *fell* down on the job.
    *b.* The preparations for the party *fell* through.
    *c.* Tom *fell* for the trick.
    *d.* Lucifer *fell* from grace.

8. *a.* *Turn* down that idea, Bert; it's no good.
    *b.* He resolved on New Year's to *turn* over a new leaf.
    *c.* The car *turned* turtle.
    *d.* He succeeds in whatever he *turns* his hand to.

9. *a.* The soldier saved his life by *playing* possum.
    *b.* When he saw he was *playing* second fiddle, he left.
    *c.* Play hard, but *play* fair!
    *d.* The diplomat *played* both ends against the middle.

10. *a.* The mayor *put* across the deal.
    *b.* The retort *put* the saucy child in her place.
    *c.* Edison *put* his shoulder to the wheel and succeeded.
    *d.* The drama critic *put* in his appearance after the second act.

# 13

# Levels of Usage

*You wouldn't wear a tuxedo or evening dress on a picnic, nor would you wear dungarees or sports dress to a formal dance. There's a time and place for everything — including words. Just as there is clothing suitable for different occasions, so there are ways of speaking suitable for different occasions.*

## LITERARY ENGLISH

At the top of the language-ladder are words and phrases we use in careful writing and formal speaking. *Confront, compliance,* and *relegate,* for example, are words often used in editorials, but seldom in conversation. Sometimes we use one word for writing and a much less formal synonym for conversation. Thus we might *write,* "Frank overtook Mr. Miller"; but we'd probably *say,* "Frank caught up with Mr. Miller." While literary English is desirable for most writing, it may sound stilted and artificial in conversation.

## COLLOQUIAL ENGLISH

The language of conversation disregards many of the restrictions imposed upon literary English. Because it is spontaneous and unprepared, it uses certain expressions that are barred to formal English. Good colloquial English is grammatically correct but informal. *Catch on* for *understand, helter-skelter* for *in confusion,* and *fix* for *repair* are typical colloquialisms. Contractions like *can't, won't, I'll, they're,* and *might've* are common in conversation. In the dictionary, *colloq.* is the usual label for colloquial words.

Of course, there are different levels of colloquial English, just as there are levels of formal English. The everyday conversation of an English professor might differ radically from that of a bank clerk; yet both might be colloquial and correct. A person with two-value judgments (see pages 280–285) thinks that English that is not literary English is poor English. Good colloquial English is not inferior English; it is merely spoken rather than written.

Some kinds of writing adopt the colloquial style. Friendly letters, which imitate conversation, are likely to be colloquial in tone. Business letters, on the other hand, usually adopt a more formal manner. You may have noticed that this book has used, in part, the colloquial style for greater informality and conversational tone.

ACTIVITY 1.  Distinguishing between Colloquial
and Literary English

Which of the following sentences would probably be used in conversation? Which seem too formal for ordinary conversation? Label each sentence *colloquial* or *literary*.

1. I'd like to come over, but I have another date.
2. We had a pretty good time at the party.
3. Sir Galahad exemplified chivalry at its finest.
4. As the match was about to start, Winters backed down.
5. *Mathematics and the Imagination* elucidates many mathematical concepts for the layman.
6. You're coming? That's fine!
7. The elaborate symbolism of Spenser is incomprehensible to many readers.
8. I'm nearly through with the book.
9. The arbor vitae is a popular species of evergreen, perhaps because of its sturdy adaptability to many climates.
10. Thanks a lot for your congratulations.

ACTIVITY 2.  Changing Colloquial English into Literary English

The following statements are colloquial. Change each into standard literary English.

EXAMPLE: *I knew I couldn't do it, but I took a shot at it anyway*. We might express the same idea in literary English thus: Even though I knew I would fail, I tried.

1. Do you think you could run the Senior Hop if we all helped?
2. Don't worry me; that's your lookout.
3. You'll find the book where I left it, in back of the desk.
4. Keep jollying Bert, so that he doesn't spoil the party.
5. I can't make it; count me out.
6. Don't bother with Watson; he's a crank.
7. They unfairly got the jump on us, but we've since caught up to them.
8. Don't jump on me; I couldn't help it!
9. Keep an eye out for a good used buggy.
10. Drop in and see us some time at our summer place.

## SLANG

If someone came to you and said, "Twenty-three," you'd probably ask, "What's that?" Your fathers and mothers, though, might remember vaguely that some years ago *twenty-three* meant *go away*. Since then slang expressions like *skidoo*, *beat it*, and *do a fade-out* each had a brief period of popularity, replacing *twenty-three*. It would be impossible to list the current equivalent, for it would probably be out of date by the time this

Levels of usage

book appeared. There you have one of the greatest objections to the too-frequent use of slang: it seldom endures. Like women's fashions, slang goes out of date quickly. For a brief period everybody uses a word; then it is forgotten.

On the language-ladder, slang is below colloquial English. Some words, like some people, rise in the social scale. Such essential words as *fun*, *stingy*, and *clever* started life as slang. They filled a need and became "respectable." The vast majority of slang words die out, though, leaving no trace. Such former favorites as *applesauce* or *cat's pajamas* are scarcely comprehensible to the present younger generation. One danger in acquiring a slang vocabulary is that the words you use will soon be cast aside for others.

## OTHER OBJECTIONS TO SLANG

Not only are slang words soon obsolete, but they are often harmful to those who use them. First of all, constant use of slang encourages mental fuzziness. Certain all-inclusive words like *swell* and *grim* express every emotion possible. A dance, a new car, a sunset, a new dress, a motion picture, a clever remark, a swimming party — all these (at the time this book is being written) are awarded one adjective: *swell* or *terrific* or *super*. Exactness of expression is impossible when all events are described by one adjective.

Secondly, slang is often too narrow, known to a few. Sports, the theater, skating, and the army all have their own slang. The slang connected with "*jitterbugging*" is a closed book to most older people. Communication between different groups is often impossible in slang.

## "STIX NIX HIX PIX!"

This famous headline, quoted from *Variety*, is an example of how slang can almost completely obscure meanings. A clever trick with words, it needs translating: "Rural theatergoers disapprove pictures dealing with country life." Of course, it's brief, dynamic, memorable, but the translation is still necessary.

## ACTIVITY 3. Criticizing Slang

Why is the following an example of bad communication? Change each slang expression into acceptable literary English.

"Have you seen Ingrid Bergman's new picture? It's terrific."

"Yes, and wasn't Gregory Peck terrific, too? They were a swell couple."

"They certainly were swell. I thought the rest of the cast was terrific, too. Didn't you?"

"Yes, it certainly was a swell picture."

## A GOOD WORD FOR SLANG

Slang is not entirely to be despised, however. Many words of slang origin, like *highbrow* and *troubleshooter*, fill a need. A colorful slang word, used wisely and infrequently, can add zest to your vocabulary. An overdose of slang will ruin it. What words that we call slang today do you think will be accepted as colloquial tomorrow? Why?

## SLANG AND FIGURATIVE LANGUAGE

In at least one respect both slang and poetry have something in common. Both rely largely upon figurative language. An exciting book might be called a *hair-raiser*. A sightseer is a *rubberneck*. To talk too much is *to shoot one's mouth off*. Consider each of these literally, and then realize how clever the inventions are.

## ACTIVITY 4. Analyzing Slang

Each of the following colorful slang expressions has seemed useful enough to be retained over a period of years. Explain what each means. When might you use each of these? When would you avoid their use?

1. baby kisser
2. back-seat driver
3. soap opera
4. butterfingered
5. cold shoulder
6. dime a dozen
7. passing the buck
8. pussyfoot
9. sob sister
10. sourpuss

## CLIPPED WORDS

American slang has a tendency to shorten words. Thus *taxicab* becomes *cab*, *omnibus* becomes *bus*, and *zoological park* becomes *zoo*. (See pages 107–108 for other examples.) Newspaper headlines, with their strict space limitations, have probably hastened the process.

## SHOPTALK

All trades and professions have names for objects unknown to most of us. Some of the words, like the scientist's *retort* and *calorimeter*, are standard English. Others are slang, like *baby tripe* (short tripod) in motion pictures, and *bloop* (static) in radio. The popularity of army slang during the war added expressions like *goldbrick* and *shoot the breeze*, if only temporarily. *GI*, for American soldier, seems likely to remain. Many of these slang expressions perform a valuable job — but not for general communication.

## VULGARISMS

At the very bottom of the language-ladder are vulgarisms, words and expressions which are never acceptable, either in speech or writing. *I ain't; he don't; we done;* and *shouldn't ought* are vulgarisms that mark the user as uncultured, illiterate. Slang has a part to play in the progress of language. Vulgarisms have not.

## DIALECT WORDS

Words that are used principally in one part of America or Great Britain, only, are called dialect words or provincialisms. *Reckon* in the American West, *dinna* in Scotland, and *it makes nothing to me* in Pennsylvania Dutch country are typical provincialisms. Many words that began life as dialect words have become acceptable literary English. All of the following words came to us from Scotch and Irish dialects: *fad, grouch, galore, croon, glamour, outcome, greed, heckle, uncanny, queer, gremlin, shoddy, trolley,* and *sprint.*

ACTIVITY 5. Classifying Levels of Usage

Label each of the following sentences *colloquial, slang,* or *vulgarism.* Change each to correct literary English.

1. Snap out of it, Ted; you're dreaming.
2. That bird is strictly a pain in the neck to me.
3. This here ain't the first time I failed.
4. When he has the blues, he feels flatter than a pancake.
5. Look us up in the telephone book when you're in town.
6. The two patched things up after the quarrel, and were able to look others in the eye once again.
7. Them fellows was setting there in our seats.
8. That calamity howler has been a crepehanger for years.
9. All the other workers covered up for him when he was out with the grippe.
10. The twirler was game, but the old pitching arm went dead.

# 14

# Jargon and Gobbledygook

*A young lady, just home from school, was giving directions to a group of women.*

*"Take an egg," she said, "and make a perforation in the base and a corresponding one in the apex. Then apply the lips to one aperture, and, by forcibly inhaling the breath, entirely discharge the shell of its contents."*

*An old grandmother who was listening exclaimed: "It beats all how folks do things nowadays. When I was a girl, they made a hole in each end and sucked!"*

Some writers and speakers, like this young lady whom Jespersen tells us about in his book *The English Language*, persist in using many high-sounding words where a few simple ones are called for. One word for this particular kind of bad English is *jargon;* perhaps a more descriptive name is *gobbledygook*. The latter term was coined by Maury Maverick in imitation of turkeys, which strut and parade importantly, and utter nothing but indistinct *gobbles*.

ACTIVITY 1. Recognizing Jargon

In each of the following pairs one sentence is jargon. Point out the faulty sentence and tell why you consider it jargon. Indicate the words that help to increase the size of the sentence without adding to the message.

1. In order to facilitate an increase in the available, ready-at-hand supply of washing machines, capacity production will be resumed at the earliest possible moment consonant with the present plans of the company.

**Gobbledygook**

Full production of washing machines will be resumed as soon as possible.

2. Those who are able to see this magnificent cinematic achievement will experience one of the most exciting hours in the field of entertainment that anyone could possibly enjoy.

See this motion picture for an exciting hour's entertainment.

3. Lights must be off before the store is closed.

Illumination is required to be extinguished before these premises are closed to business.

4. Leave by the rear door of the bus.

It is essential that all passengers leave this bus by the rear exit door.

5. The patrons of this theater will find at all times a complete selection of those recent motion pictures which are most popular and which the patrons themselves are most desirous of seeing.

This theater will feature recent, popular motion pictures.

## THE INGREDIENTS OF JARGON

Look again at the anecdote that begins this chapter. Compare the girl's directions with those of the old grandmother. What faults in the former's language can you find? Let's draw up some simple rules based upon our analysis.

1. *Avoid wordiness.* Cut out all deadwood. Avoid roundabout expressions. The girl uses approximately four times as many words

to give the same message as the grandmother. She gains nothing by additional words like *entirely, of its contents*. Cut your own sentences to the bone.

2. *Don't use big words merely for effect.* To describe a simple operation use simple words. *Perforation, aperture*, and *discharge* are used here unnecessarily.

We might add three other rules based upon observation of other jargon.

3. *Avoid vague, "fuzzy" abstract nouns.* Words like *case, condition, state, factor, character*, and *type* often befuddle rather than inform. (See pages 214–215.)

4. *Use the passive voice sparingly.* "It will be remembered by all of you that victory was awarded to John." Lifeless, isn't it? How much better it would be to say, "You will remember that John won."

5. *Avoid "counter words."* Words like *swell, grand*, and *fine* have been exchanged over the language counter so often that they have been worn thin. Their meanings have become so general that exact expression with them becomes impossible. (See pages 29–30.)

## Activity 2. Correcting Jargon

By referring to the rules listed above, prove that each of the following sentences contains jargon. Rewrite each sentence, eliminating faulty expressions.

EXAMPLE: *The growing and tending of various kinds of herbaceous plants in the average greenhouse is at the same time an exacting task and a pleasant avocation.*

This sentence is jargon because it is roundabout, uses big words unnecessarily, and includes much deadwood. It can be improved by rephrasing to: *Greenhouse gardening is hard but pleasant work.*

1. It must be admitted that, in a large measure, faithful adherents of the sport of hockey are numerically superior to those who have selected lacrosse as their favorite game.

2. In view of the present financial structure of the club to which all of us have given our allegiance, it is felt that all of us should carefully consider our every expenditure before proceeding to expend club moneys.

3. Sufficient financial inducements have not yet been offered to the baseball player or he might have reconsidered his negative decision not to attend the preliminary training sessions of the team at their quarters in the South.

4. In the light of unforeseen difficulties which have arisen to complicate the present picture, it is believed that our school will have to forego its present plans for expanding the athletic fields.

5. The utilization of those factors which make for success in one's chosen profession should not be forgotten in any analysis of a man's record in reaching his goal.

### ACTIVITY 3. Recognizing Proverbs in Jargon

Can you recognize the familiar proverbs concealed in each of the following? Prove that each sentence is jargon. Why is the original proverb preferable?

1. It is wise to gaze circumspectly about one before one gathers oneself for a step into the unknown.

2. Shedding tears over the occurrence of an event already in the past is to be deplored.

3. It is never the part of wisdom to assume that you already possess that which you have not yet won, or to anticipate the successful completion of a mission before that mission has been brought to a satisfactory conclusion.

4. A person who befriends one in a time of great need is certainly one who can truly be called a friend.

5. Prudence and foresight, the anticipation of difficulties before they materialize, can cut to at least one ninth the problems that do occur.

### ACTIVITY 4. Analyzing a Wordy Paragraph

In the following paragraph point out all violations of the rules listed above.

The proverbial oracles of our parsimonious ancestors have informed us that the fatal waste of fortune is by small expenses, by the profusion of sums too little singly to alarm our caution, and which we never suffer ourselves to consider together. Of the same kind is the prodigality of life; he that hopes to look back hereafter with

**Brevity gets to the point quickly!**

satisfaction upon past years must learn to know the present value of single minutes, and endeavour to let no particle of time fall useless to the ground. (*Samuel Johnson*)

### ACTIVITY 5. Comparing Paragraphs

The following paragraph is another version of the paragraph in Activity 4. Which do you prefer? Why? How would *you* express the same ideas?

"Take care of the pennies," says the thrifty old proverb, "and the pounds will take care of themselves." In like manner we might say, "Take care of the minutes, and the years will take care of themselves."

## WHY JARGON IS USED

No one wants to write or speak poorly. Yet many people do. Why? Ignorance accounts for many blunders; still, many of the worst blunders are made by reasonably intelligent persons. Indeed, jargon may arise from too much education poorly absorbed. Some of the faults which cause people to write jargon are these:

*Snobbishness.* Sometimes people think that high-sounding English is good English, that big words impress others. Many radio comedians poke fun at this tendency by exaggerating it.

*Ignorance.* Jargon often attempts to cover up confusion in the mind of the user. The speaker hopes that his own befuddlement will not be apparent to others. He camouflages ignorance by using jargon. An idea that is clear to its owner can usually be made clear to others. Muddled speech usually indicates muddled thinking.

*Laziness.* The short, crisp, pointed English sentence is more difficult to construct than the long, hazy one. Lazy speakers actually find jargon easier to use than forceful English.

What is a good program of action? Attack jargon when you meet it. Don't allow vague statements to go unchallenged. Avoid jargon in your own speaking and writing. Be concise, accurate. Use big words only when they add a fine shade of meaning to your speaking and writing. (See pages 111–116.)

## JOURNALESE

Too often newspaper writers, who have to turn in daily copy, begin to use jargon. A *fire* becomes a *disastrous conflagration*. A *prize fight* emerges as a *pugilistic contest*. A *third baseman* becomes the *occupant of the hot corner*. Instead of saying, "A great crowd came to see the show," some newsmen say, "A vast congregation of people assembled to witness the tremendous spectacle." Newspaper jargon is called "journalese." It may arise from laziness, an effort to be different, or pure exhibitionism. Whatever its origin, it is a serious fault. In your own newspaper watch for simple things made difficult.

### ACTIVITY 6. Analyzing Journalese

One member of each of the following pairs is journalese. Point out which is newspaper jargon and explain why you consider it faulty.

1. *a.* The annual pigskin classic was held during the Turkey Day celebration.
   *b.* The annual football game was held on Thanksgiving.

2. *a.* The judge confirmed the assumption that he had agreed to the trial.

   *b.* The judge admitted that he had agreed to the trial.

3. *a.* The pitcher substituted successfully in left field.

   *b.* The hurler patrolled the outer gardens with dexterity and gusto.

4. *a.* They object to the process of eliminating women from toiling in certain factories.

   *b.* They object to the exclusion of women from certain factories.

5. *a.* Mr. Larsen, well known golf enthusiast, has indicated his distaste for participation in the coming tournament.

   *b.* Mr. Larsen, well known golfer, will not take part in the coming tournament.

ACTIVITY 7.  Finding Examples of Jargon and Journalese

From your own reading of the newspaper find examples of jargon and journalese. Be ready to "translate" each into good English.

## MEANINGLESS EXPRESSIONS

"As every schoolboy knows, the nebula in Andromeda is of the planetary type and is nearly a million light years away."

How many times have you seen the phrase, *as every schoolboy knows*, and said to yourself, "*I* don't know it"? If all schoolboys knew as much as writers give them credit for, they'd scarcely need further education. Like many other meaningless phrases, *as every schoolboy knows* is deeply embedded in the language; yet it is jargon. It really says nothing; it is merely an unnecessary addition to a sentence. Letters are favorite resting places of useless expressions. Reread carefully the next letter you write. Avoid useless expressions like *wish you were here* or *thought I'd drop you a line*.

ACTIVITY 8.  Striking Out Meaningless Expressions

In each of the following sentences at least one phrase can be eliminated without injuring the meaning of the passage. Point out the unnecessary expressions and explain why you think they should be omitted.

1. It would seem that Julia is unable to come to the club today.
2. With reference to the matter I must say that our firm will ship the refrigerators on the first of April.
3. You will no doubt recall that our team was invited to play in the new stadium on Thanksgiving.
4. Marilyn, it will be noted, was not eager to attend the dance.
5. I wish to state that your order has not yet been filled.

## FASHIONS IN WORDS

Just as slang words have temporary popularity, so more learned words come and go after brief but hectic careers. Professional men and women sometimes succumb to the temptation of using these "fad words." Not long ago public speakers were overworking words like *evaluating*, *dynamic*, *correlation*, *channelize*, and *optimum*. *To study a problem* was transformed into *to get an over-all picture*. After President Truman used the word *know-how*, writers and speakers hastily adopted it. Using words like those listed is not faulty; overworking them, using them to describe all kinds of situations must be condemned. Do you have favorite words that you overwork?

### ACTIVITY 9. Reviewing Jargon

Some of the following sentences contain examples of jargon. Others are straightforward English. Can you distinguish between them? Point out examples of jargon and rewrite each faulty sentence.

1. During the continuance of the present drive for members, it is required that all present members contribute the names of at least three persons who they feel might be interested in becoming members of our club.
2. The fact that housing accommodations are in short supply has made it necessary for the government authorities to plan temporary shelters for those who are unable to find rooms suitable for the needs of their families.

3. Note that the phrase, "Life, liberty and the pursuit of happiness," does not guarantee happiness; it merely emphasizes that every man has the right to seek it.

4. For the comfort of passengers it is essential that train doors be kept closed on days when the weather is cold or inclement.

5. Many of our commonest weeds have come to us, by ships, from lands as far away as China and Peru.

6. The Basque language is strangely unlike other European tongues, even though the Basque country is neatly sandwiched between France and Spain.

7. There would seem to be a direct relationship between the amount of fertilizer added to a soil used for gardening and the yield of that soil in vegetables.

8. An insurance policy is a wager made that you will die shortly; if you win, you lose!

9. The excellent radiation qualities of the color black recommend that it be applied to cover all radiating surfaces, inasmuch as this procedure would be economical of heat.

10. With full realization of the implications of our actions, it is our considered opinion that we should, as a group, support the plan of our esteemed colleague, whose enthusiastic endorsement of the procedure bodes well for its success.

## DISCUSSION QUESTIONS

1. In what sense is it true to say that words are magical in themselves? Provide examples from your own experience to justify the statement.

2. What is a symbol? Can words be considered symbols? Prove.

3. How does figurative language differ from literal language? What does figurative language add to communication? When might we prefer literal language?

4. "Metaphor is not merely a pretty poetic device. It is the very backbone of language." Do you agree with this statement? By referring to expressions you have read or heard recently, seek to prove or disprove the statement.

5. In many ways written language is inadequate and incomplete for communication. Prove, by mentioning ways in which spoken language is more nearly adequate.

6. We often hear the expression: "He kept within the letter of the law, but not the spirit." Discuss connotation and denotation to prove that denotation is the "letter of the law," while connotation is "the spirit." How might it be possible for someone to be "slandered legally."

7. Why do word-tricksters prefer general words to specific ones, highly connotative words to slightly connotative ones?

8. Do you believe that it is wise to suspend judgment until all the facts are in? Prove. What should you do when you find it impossible to get all the facts?

9. In what way do persons who make only two-value judgments narrow their own lives?

10. How does a fact differ from an inference? Why are inferences often unsound?

11. Define subjective and objective writing. Which do you prefer to read? Why?

12. Advertisers are often called master word-tricksters. Do you agree? Introduce specific examples to prove your point.

13. How do idioms place barriers in the way of those learning a new language? How do idioms help those who know the language?

14. How does context determine word meaning?

15. What obligations should newspapers assume in relation to the use of words? How can newspapers give completely false pictures without actually saying anything untrue?

16. What is meant by "levels of usage"? Upon what occasions might colloquial English be preferable to literary English?

17. Define jargon. In what way is jargon a barrier to communication?

18. How is communication influenced by self-interest and point of view?

19. Why is it essential to examine the attitude of the writer or speaker toward us when reading or listening?

20. Do words rule our lives? Prove your contention.

21. Why may the verb *to be* be called the most dangerous word in the language?

# INDEX

# INDEX

Abbreviations, 42–43, 146
Abstract words, 215–218
Accent, 42
Advertising, 182, 186–190, 265–266, 274–276
African, 96, 101
Allusions, 322–323
American Indian, 101
Analogies, 139–140
Anglo-Saxon, 53–64, 65, 85, 96, 122–123
Antonyms, 42, 131, 133–140
  pitfalls in, 135
Arabic, 101
Art, 160–161
Artificiality, 112–113
Attitude, 231
Authority, 238–239

Band wagon device, 224–225, 238
Barnum, P. T., 185
Bible, 55–56, 151–152
Biographical information, 46
Brooke, Rupert, 37
Broun, Heywood, 192
Buck, Pearl S., 56
Bureau of Standards, 3

Capitalization, 42
Celtic, 56
Changing word meanings, 102–107
Charms, 203–204
Circular definitions, 218–219
Clichés, 29–31
  headline, 31
Colloquial language, 42, 325–326
Color words, 34
Compounds, 60–61, 89
Concrete words, 23–24
Connotation
  in advertising, 265–266, 274–276
  and denotation, 242–254
  and emotions, 250
  pleasant, 271–279
  and the right word, 251–252
  unpleasant, 255–266
Context, 164–171, 232–241

part of speech determined by, 234–235
  in place, 236
  quoting out of, 239–241
  and the speaker, 237
  in time, 236
Coué, Emile, 204
Counter words, 29
Cross references, 42
Curiosity, 9, 185

Definitions, 40–42, 45–46, 47, 168–169
Degeneration, word, 104
De Kruif, Paul, 154
De la Mare, Walter, 247
Denotation. See Connotation
Derivations, word. See Etymology
Dialect words, 330–331
Dictionary, 39–52
  abridged, 39–47
  game, 47
  unabridged, 47–52
*Dictionary of Synonyms* (Webster's), 119, 130–132
*Dictionary of Synonyms and Antonyms, A* (Devlin), 130
*Dictionary of Word Origins*, 81
Directive language, 223–224
Directness, 23
Doublets, 72
Dutch, 65, 101

Economy, 10, 11, 27
Editorials, 216
Elevation, word, 102–103
Emotional words, 55, 222–225, 247, 250–251, 255–258, 265–266, 271–275
English language, history of, 56–57, 68–69, 71, 87–88, 96
*English Synonyms* (Crabb), 130
*English Synonyms* (Fernald), 130
Etymology
  Anglo-Saxon, 53–57, 59–64
  in the dictionary, 42, 44–45, 47
  folk, 106–107
  Greek, 85–95

Etymology (*cont.*)
    and interesting word origins, 81–82
    Latin, 65–81, 82–84
    miscellaneous, 96–101
    Scandinavian, 57–58
Euphemisms, 276–279
Exactness, 27
Exchange, word, 96, 101

Families of words, 72–74
Fictional words, 202–203
*Fifty-first Dragon, The,* 192
Figurative language, 308–318
    and hyperbole, 310–312
    and irony, 313–314
    and metaphor, 298–307
    and metonymy and synecdoche, 314–316
    and personification, 316–317
    and simile, 309–310
    and slang, 329
    and understatement, 312–313
Folk etymology, 106–107
Foreign words and phrases, 141–147
Formulas, words as, 208–210
French, 101, 133–134
Funk, Wilfred, 4
Funk and Wagnalls, 39, 40, 47, 49, 130

Game
    dictionary, 47
    word, 90
General science, 158–160
General words, 212–214
Generalization in words, 105–106
Generalizations, 219–220. *See also* Stereotypes
Geographical information, 42, 46
German, 65, 101
Gestures, 229–230
Glossary, 157
"Gobbledygook." *See* Jargon
Greek, 85–95, 96, 152–153
*Gulliver's Travels,* 231

*Hamlet,* 53, 227
Hebrew, 100
Henry, Patrick, 54
History, 162
Hitler, Adolf, 223, 250

Holmes, Oliver Wendell, 53
Human Engineering Laboratory, 4
Hyperbole, 310–312
Hyphenation, 42

Idioms, 320–324
*Idylls of the King,* 281
Incantations, 204–206, 210
Indefinite words, 214–216
Inferences
    distinguished from facts, 290–291
    many, from one fact, 291–293
    selecting the best, 293–295
Intention, 231–232
Irony, 313–314
Italian, 101
*Ivanhoe,* 70

*Jane Eyre,* 145
Japanese, 101
Jargon, 332–340
Journalese, 337–338
Judgments
    many-value, 281–285
    point of view influencing, 296–297
    two-value, 280–285

Keller, Helen, 32
Key, pronunciation, 43

Labels, 187–188, 199–201, 256–257
Latin, 65–84, 96, 122–123, 152–153
Learned words, 110–115
Lewis, Norman, 4
*Listeners, The,* 247
Literary English, 325–326
Literature, words from, 155–156

*Macbeth,* 181
Maverick, Maury, 332
Metaphor, 298–307
    animal, 301–302
    body, 302–303
    concealed, 300–301
    in folk names, 304–305
    in idioms, 321–322
    mixed, 306–307
    in picturesque phrases, 307
    from sports and vocations, 303–304

from verbs of action, 299–300
in word derivation, 305–306
Metonymy, 314–316
*Microbe Hunters*, 154
*Moby Dick*, 55
Motion pictures, stereotypes in, 269–270
Mottoes, 207–208, 210
Music, 161
Mythology, 153–154

Newspaper, 7
journalese in, 337–338
slanting in, 257–259, 261–262, 264–265, 274
New words, 108–109
*New York Herald Tribune*, 164
*New York Times*, 7, 13, 164, 199
Norman invasion, 69, 70, 71
Notebook, vocabulary, 12–14, 28, 112, 157, 172
Number prefixes, 75–76, 92

Objective writing, 286–290
O'Connor, Johnson, 4
*Old Ironsides*, 53

Parts of speech, 42, 234–235
Persian, 96, 101
Personification, 316–317
*Picturesque Word Origins*, 81
Plurals, 42
Point of view, 296–297
Popular words, 110–115, 246–248
Prefixes, 61
Anglo-Saxon, 61–64
Greek, 91–92
Latin, 74–76
Principal parts, 59
Pronunciation, 42, 43, 44, 47, 143–144
Proper names, words from, 99–100, 148–156
Proverbs, 207–208

*Roget's Thesaurus*, 130
Roosevelt, Theodore, 51
Roots, 61
Anglo-Saxon, 61, 63, 64
Greek, 88–91, 92–95
Latin, 76–80

Sales psychology, 182–189
Scandinavian, 54, 57–58, 65, 154
School vocabulary, 157–163
Scott, Sir Walter, 70
Sense impressions, 32–38
Shakespeare, William, 71, 181, 183
Shipley, Joseph, 81
Shoptalk, 330
Shortening words, 107–108, 330
Sight, 33–35
color words, 34
Simile, 309–310
Slang, 327–329
Slanting, 257–265, 274–275
through omission, 262–265
Slogans, 206–207, 210
Smell, 38
Sound, 34–35
Spanish, 101
Specialization, word, 105
Specific words, 212–213
Spelling, 42
Stereotypes, 268–270. *See also* Generalizations
Subjective writing, 286–289
Suffixes, 61
Anglo-Saxon, 61–64
Latin, 82–84
Suggestive words, 182–188. *See also* Connotation
Sumner, Charles, 109
Superlatives, 28–29
Superstition and words, 181, 192–193, 203–204
Swift, Jonathan, 231
Symbols, words as, 190–211, 212, 229
Synecdoche, 314–316
Synonyms, 42, 111, 118–133, 138–140
with different connotations, 242–244
in groups, 126–129, 132–133
pitfalls in, 124

Taste, 35–36
*Thorndike-Century Senior Dictionary*, 40
*Three Days to See*, 32
*Through the Looking Glass*, 194
*To the Daisy*, 247
Tone, 226–229

Touch, 37
Transfer, 272–273

Understatement, 312–313
Unusual expressions, 51–52
Usage, levels of, 325–331
    colloquial English, 325–326
    dialectal, 330–331
    literary English, 325–326
    and shoptalk, 330
    and slang, 327–329
    and vulgarisms, 330

Variety, 23
Verb, 24–27
    phrases, 25–27, 51
    strong, 59
Vigorous language, 23–31
Vocabulary
    newspaper, 7
    notebook, 12–14, 28, 112, 158, 172

recognitional, 14–15, 110
    size of, 4
    use, 14–15, 110
Vulgarisms, 330

Webster, 39, 40–43, 47–49, 119, 129, 130–132
Wordsworth, William, 247
Writing
    avoiding artificiality in, 112–113
    avoiding indefiniteness in, 214–215
    avoiding jargon in, 333–335
    colorful language in, 24
    concreteness in, 23, 24
    directness in, 23
    exactness in, 27
    obstacles to good, 28–31
    use of sense words in, 32–38
    use of verbs in, 24–27
    variety in, 23